Marcello Caroti

Garibaldi

the first fascist

The roots of Fascism in the Italian Risorgimento

Milano, June 2015

Youcanprint *Self - Publishing*

Title | Garibaldi the first fascist
Author | Marcello Caroti
Cover image | © Georgios Kollidas - Fotolia.com
ISBN | 978-88-91198-15-0

Youcanprint *Self-Publishing*
Via Roma, 73 - 73039 Tricase (LE) - Italy
www.youcanprint.it
info@youcanprint.it
Facebook: facebook.com/youcanprint.it
Twitter: twitter.com/youcanprintit

*To those who
Cultivate Understanding*

Table of Contents

Introduction

This essay does not want to be another biography of Garibaldi; we do not think it is possible to add anything new.

We want to propose a series of reflections on the person of Garibaldi, his thoughts, his life, his writings to define his position with respect to the two ideologies that have shaped the history of Europe and of Italy in the past two centuries: Nationalism and Socialism.

We decided to produce this essay because it seems to us that to date the contribution that Garibaldi gave to the birth to this new country has not been properly explained. The purpose of our work is the search of the roots of fascism in the Italian Risorgimento with particular regard to the person of Garibaldi.

Since Garibaldi died, in 1882, many people tried to grab his legacy and have claimed to be the most faithful interpreters of his thought. Socialists, Fascists, the Resistance, the Communists, they all tried to grab his name and image. Moreover we have to consider that together with Leonardo, Colombo and Mussolini, he is one of the most famous Italians in the world; in Italy he is certainly the most popular among the Founding Fathers. But, to what political movement did Garibaldi belong?

To answer this question we have to understand who he really was. If we draw his biography in this book it is because you cannot understand him without examining the entire evolution of his personality in the political and ideological context of the society in which he lived. To do this we must first do a proper and thorough de-mythologizing of this icon of the Italian Risorgimento. Normally it is not easy to demythologize a character that in 150 years of history and political propaganda has accumulated such a stratification of legends that made him become a kind of super hero but in our case a simple and basic research is sufficient provided it is done with an open mind and without bias. We used sources that have been available to the public for years because, surprisingly, it is not necessary to make new discoveries but rather to properly use the sources we already have.

We consider this work of ours as a completion and a continuation of the work of Denis Mack Smith. If the reader will have the impression that we have been somewhat sympathetic to the Bourbon or to the people of the south he must know that this was not our purpose, we did not do it intentionally. We felt it was necessary to clarify the relationship between Garibaldi and the Mafia because much has been written about it, but in a way that we consider very inaccurate and sometimes very imaginative. We had to analyze the Bourbon regime and the society of the Kingdom of the Two Sicilies to briefly describe the genesis of the Mafia.

We have quoted as many sources as possible to let the reader hear our characters and participate to their emotions: the quotes are part of our essay together with our text. In this way the reader can understand the characters we are dealing with not only rationally but also emotionally.

First of all we quoted Garibaldi. He fortunately left us a considerable amount of literary production and, moreover, his actions and his speeches were recorded by a crowd of friends and/or enemies who, in turn, left us their testimony. His *Memorie* are a very useful source for understanding the man; it strikes us his sincerity in telling objectionable episodes of his life, episodes that others would have not even mentioned. As we will not make his biography, the reader is required an elementary knowledge of the Risorgimento and the life of Garibaldi.

Welcome to History.

The years of his training

The *Memorie* of Garibaldi are the most important source for those who wish to understand the man and the motivations that guided him in his patriotic activity. They were written on several occasions, reviewed, abandoned and rewritten.

He wrote the preface in 1872 when he was 65 years old. Already in the preface there are a few things that strike the reader.

A violent anti-clericalism: "*The priest is the personification of the lie. The liar is a thief. The thief is a murderer: and I could find to the priest a number of infamous corollaries. .... The priest! Ah! This is the real scourge of God! In Italy he maintains a coward government in the most degrading humiliation, and restores himself in the corruption and the miseries of the people!*"[1]. A violent anti-clericalism in words, up to the point of ridicule, will remain a constant of his thought. As a boy he had two priests as tutors who left a deep antipathy toward the priests and the Church in general. Besides, his mother, a devout Catholic, wanted to send him to seminary, a detestable thing for a boy extremely lively and fascinated by the adventure.

A deep bitterness: "*I will be accused of pessimism; but ... having believed for most of my life in the human improvement, I am saddened to see so many evils and so much corruption in this would be civil century*". A moralistic-educational attitude is normal in the literature of Romanticism.

This pessimism led him to declare: "*Republican, but more and more convinced of the necessity of an honest and temporary dictatorship at the head of those nations, such as France, Spain and Italy that are the victims of the most pernicious Byzantinism*". This too will be a constant of his thought and action. Whenever he takes power he will appoint himself dictator, still remaining always a staunch Democrat.

A remarkable inconsistency!

---

[1] Giuseppe Garibaldi, *Memorie* (Milano: Rizzoli, 1982), henceforth we will put in italics the quotes taken from this book without quoting the source, we will put the source in the notes only for the quotes taken from other books

He was certainly not a fanatic ideologue: "*Tolerant, and not exclusivist, not capable of imposing by force my republicanism, for example to the English people, if they are happy with the government of Queen Victoria, let them be happy*". This elasticity or pragmatism will be instrumental in his moving over to the side of the monarchy because it was indispensable for the unification of Italy. Always the same pragmatism led him to reject totally the Marxist ideology.

What leaves the reader amazed is the closing to the preface: "*Lover of peace, law, justice – we are forced however to conclude with the axiom of an American general: 'La guerra es la vertadera vida del hombre!'* (War is the real life of man)". In the same sentence where he declares his love to peace he cannot hold himself from declaring his love to war. In fact, to war he will devote his entire life. This inconsistency could be interpreted as a case of senile dementia, but it is not. This is him; it is his way of thinking that will shape his thoughts and his actions, in fact, his entire life.

In his *Memorie* he almost always talks about war, a little about himself, very little about politics and never about socialism.

In describing his youth he says nothing about how and why he became an Italian patriot, it takes it for granted. "*A passionate lover of my country, since my early years, and intolerant of her servitude, I longed ardently to initiate myself into the mysteries of her resurgence. So I was looking everywhere for books, writings, that dealt about the Italian freedom, and for individuals consecrated to it*".

The lightning strike comes during a trip to Taganrog where he meets a young man from Liguria "*... that first gave me some news of the progress of our affairs. Sure Columbus did not feel so much satisfaction to discover America, as I felt to find someone who was looking after the redemption of the motherland. I plunged body and soul in that element that I felt to be mine for so long: and in Genoa, February 5, 1834, I went out of the door of the Lanterna at 7 pm, disguised as a peasant, and proscribed*". This is it. There is no analysis of the reasons that convinced him of the goodness of the cause to which he will devote his entire life.

In this regard, we should note the words "*redemption of the motherland*", "*mysteries of her resurgence*", "*consecrated people*". These terms imply a religious faith.

Now we must add that the war we are talking about was a bit different from those that were waged in Europe: "*After the fighting, both the rebels and the Imperials often dispersed, returning for some time to their families. Another consequence of this situation was that, for the lack of secure bases in which to guard them, frequently the prisoners were slaughtered*"[6].

Having left the sea behind, the war moves on land. "*Among the many adventures of my stormy life I have not failed to have a good time; ... I marched on horseback alongside the woman of my heart, worthy of universal admiration, and throwing myself into a career, that even more than the one on the sea, had immense attractions for me ... My Anita was my treasure, no less fervent than me for the sacred cause of the people and for an adventurous life*".

This faith "*for the sacred cause of the people and for an adventurous life*" will be put to the test again during a retreat: "*That descent was arduous for the difficulties of the road and the bitter hostility of the inhabitants of the district, bitter enemies of the Republicans. Something strange, yet very true: the peasant class, which more than any other, should love a free Republican government, hates it and fights it!*". Now he clearly recognizes that the farmers are fighting <u>against</u> the republic and, just think, he finds it strange. And yet he does not realize that he is on the wrong side!

By the way, by whom the Republican troops were made up? "*Our infantry, composed entirely of black men, less the officers, was also excellent; and the desire to fight general ... The brave freedmen, proud of their stateliness were becoming more firm; and a real forest of lances resembled that incomparable body, composed of slaves, freed by the republic, and chosen from the best trainers in the province, all blacks except the senior officers*". We must assume that the war was going badly for the republic if the only fighters it could count on were the slaves of the landlords.

And in spite of this, war still fascinates him. One day, the imperial and the Republican army are facing each other ready to fight: "*A more beautiful day and a more magnificent sight I have never had. Placed at the center of our infantry, in the highest site, down there at my feet, in a*

---

[6] Alfonso Scirocco, *Garibaldi* (Bari: Laterza, 2001) pag.68

few minutes, shall be decided the fate of the greater part of the American continent: Brazil! Decided the fate of a people! These bodies, so compact, so prosperous, so brilliant, in a short time will be loose, broken, horribly mixed and breathing the lust of destruction! Soon the blood, the broken limbs, the bodies of so many superb youths will sully these beautiful and virgin fields". We must recognize that the writer Garibaldi is giving us a wonderful example of a decadent prose. War as a sculptor of history! However, what to think of this man? What to think of this morbid fascination for death, blood and corpses? What to think of his *"sacred cause of the people"*? An insane pretext to satisfy <u>his own</u> lust for destruction.

For the republic the war was going badly: "*The star of the republic was waning; and luck turned against our leader ... Meanwhile, the situation of the republican army worsened. Every day there were more emergencies and it was more difficult to meet them. In this situation, the Imperialists made proposals for a settlement, which, even if they were advantageous considering the circumstances in which the Republicans were, they were not accepted and were haughtily rejected by the most generous part of the army. That refusal, however, increased the discontent of those who were more moderate and tired*".

The republicans must withdraw through a chain of mountains in the rainy season: "*There were horrible scenes! Many women, as it is the custom in those countries, accompanied the army and they did not fail to be useful, they were driving the packs of horses, something they performed on horseback and they were very experienced in this exercise. With the women there were of course children of all ages. Few children of the more tender age came out of the forest! A few were picked up by the riders, since few horses were saved; and many mothers, also, were dead or dying of hunger, hardship and cold*". He, Anita and his son Menotti barely manage to save themselves: "*In the most arduous part of the road and when fording the streams, I carried my dear son of three months in a scarf around my neck, thereby giving him some warmth with my breast and my breath*". At this point war is no longer fun. After six years of unnecessary killings and destructions Garibaldi was tired. He takes leave from president Goncalves that lets him go. So ends his Brazilian adventure, with a disastrous defeat.

In vain you will look in his writings for any reflection on the tragedy which he participated. No feeling of guilt and no resentment.

The Guerra Grande

It was 1841; he goes to Montevideo, Uruguay. He is 34 years old, has a wife, a son and soon finds himself in misery. However, he carried with him a huge capital in terms of image and relationships. Even if he had been defeated, his courage, his ability to command and his dedication to the cause (right or wrong that it was) gave him a stature far superior to the other European adventurers who, like leeches, rushed on the bleeding ulcers of South America to offer their arm to the highest bidder.

More importantly, England and Freemasonry had decided that he was their man. In his *Memorie* there is no reference to this partnership, the thing is kept secret because they are those who will obtain to Garibaldi his main achievements. He has an obsessive attention for his image and does not want to give the impression of being a puppet in the hands of a foreign country and a secret society: it would be disastrous for his myth. It is in this period that he wears long hairs to cover one of his ears. It seems that it was cut off to him for stealing cattle. Now he has adopted a kind of uniform that he will wear all of his life, a very original clothing for a European: a poncho.

He finds work: "*Two occupations, trivial indeed, I assumed in the meantime, but they served to buy food, and they were those of broker merchant; and some lessons in mathematics ...*". The boredom again of a bourgeois employment.

But South America cannot be boring for long.

Two years before the Guerra Grande had broken out: a Uruguayan civil war, stirred by Argentina, which later will cause a civil war in Argentina too. Hence: "*The Eastern Republic* (Uruguay) *offered me soon an occupation appropriate to my character*"[7]. They offer him to com-

---

[7] Francesco Carrano, *I Cacciatori delle Alpi comandati dal generale Giuseppe Garibaldi* (Torino, Unione Tipografica Editrice, 1860) pag. 84.

mand a small naval squadron for an expedition to the aid of an Argentine province that had rebelled. So, without a reflection, without a motivation he passes from one adventure to another. What matters is to live according to his own vocation: to wage war.

The Guerra Grande

In those years, the Uruguayan political scene is dominated by two parties, the Blanco and the Colorado. The first defends the interests of the big farmers and the second of the entrepreneurial middle class of the town. Argentina is dominated by the dictator Rosas which is allied to the Blanco party. In 1838 France, for reasons related to its imperialist policies, attacks Argentina that is helped by the Uruguayan blancos who were in the government under the leadership of Manuel Oribe. Thus, in the October of '38, France provokes a coup in Uruguay bringing to the government the Colorado Rivera. Oribe wants revenge and, aided by the Argentina of Rosas, attacks Uruguay to oust Rivera. The Colorados are defeated and Montevideo is under siege by the partisans of Oribe allied with the Argentina of Rosas. England and France enter the war with their fleets but they have no land troops to repel Oribe and the Argentines. Thus began the long siege of Montevideo which will last nine years because the allied fleets allow the city to receive all the help that is necessary to resist. In 1850 the allies, tired, withdraw their fleets and the city should capitulate, but in '51 Rosas is overthrown by Urquiza, the governor of an Argentinian province his rival, and therefore Oribe is defeated. Brazil too comes into play alongside the Colorados and Rosas goes into exile in 1852. Thus ends the siege of Montevideo. The Colorados remain in power in Uruguay ceding part of its territory to Brazil. Until 1870 the country is at peace, then the rivalry between the two parties explodes again into another civil war.

He had just closed the Brazilian chapter by obtaining an amnesty from the Empire thanks to the intercession of a friend. This was necessary because the Empire was pressuring Uruguay to hand over the rebels who had taken refuge there. Now that he is no longer a wanted man he can open another chapter of his life.

This chapter opens badly because Uruguay is commanded "*by the imbecile*" Vidal, the minister of war, and "*to complete the work of destruction, I was destined to an expedition, the result of which could not be other than the destruction of the woods I commanded*". And so it went. Maybe this is why there is, in his *Memorie*, nothing comparable to the joy and enthusiasm with which he began the adventure of Rio Grande. There is rather a certain sadness.

The brutality of this war is appalling. He is with this small squadron on the Paraná river in the middle of enemy territory and he has no expert to drive him along the river. Torture is necessary: "*as a result of many investigations I realized one of them had some knowledge of the river, but kept mum for fear. My saber overcame very soon these difficulties: and we got an expert*".

They arrive at a small Argentine village and: "*there were some merchant vessels. We needed both transports and experts. A nocturnal expedition with our row boats got us one thing and the other ... We were obliged to use force: our delicate position required it*". It is a sad enterprise made of lootings, abductions, tortures and killings.

Still he continues, undeterred, to play the role of "the liberator" for the South American and European public opinion. When he managed to get into the Paraná River he sent a message to the Uruguayan government: "*At ten on the twenty-sixth I forced the pass of Martin Garcia. Our crews have proven to understand that we are fighting for the Cause of Humanity*"[8]. By whom his crews were made up? With an amazing candor in his *Memorie* he tells us that his men were always the same: "*In the crews commanded by me there were people of all nationalities. The strangers were mostly mariners, and almost all deserters from ships of war. And I must confess these were the least mischievous. About the Americans, all of them had been expelled from the army for various misdeeds but mostly for murder*".

So, these thugs, redeemed by his leadership, would have decided to fight for "*the Cause of Humanity*"!

To understand his charm consider that, at that time, all European progressives believed it and ... they still do.

---

[8] Montanelli-Nozza, *Garibaldi* (Milano, Rizzoli Editore, 1962) pag.132

His ships are attacked by a far superior Argentine naval force and after a strenuous combat they must be abandoned. He sets them on fire with some Argentine prisoners on board (probably the kidnapped experts) and then he starts a march overland to reach the Uruguayan forces, but a couple of his men are injured and he has them strangled not leave them alive in the hands the Argentines.

They stop for a couple of months in Santa Lucia where Garibaldi has an affair with Lucia Esteche; a girl, Margarita, was born from this relationship who will never see her father.

In the meantime the Uruguayan army is destroyed by the Argentines and 150 of 850 Uruguayan prisoners agree to pass to the Argentines, the other 700 are slaughtered. Garibaldi flees to Montevideo which is besieged and here the Italian Legion is formed. A small fleet is entrusted to Garibaldi: "*Since I was in charge of the flotilla, which was also organizing, I proposed for the head of the legion, a certain Angelo Mancini, of infamous memory, and he was accepted by the government*". Shortly afterwards Mancini passes to the enemy with thirty officers and soldiers, upon a generous payment. The Uruguayan forces are led by General Paz, an Argentine opponent of its regime, who had decided to go and fight for the Uruguayan colorados. Soon after he is forced to flee by the jealousies of the Uruguayans.

When Argentina is about to win, England and France enter the war because they do not want Argentina to take possession of all of the Mar de la Plata. The British Minister in Uruguay takes contact with Garibaldi: "*When I was working as a diplomat in Montevideo with special assignments, I have been for two years in constant contact with this remarkable man. As commander in chief of the navy of Montevideo, he had been placed by the government under the orders of the British and French admirals ... In order to render efficient the flotilla it was necessary to supply Garibaldi with weapons, ammunition and shipboard equipment, or the means to procure all that. Encouraged by the reputation that even then Garibaldi enjoyed, not only as a military man, but for the quality of honor and integrity, I decided to take all agreements with him personally. Of course at the beginning ... a certain wary caution advised me to check his accounts in various ways, and to ascertain indirectly that the supplies were administered properly. The results of my investigation could not have been more satisfying, each test resolved itself in his favor, and the subsequent experience showed the excellence of his judgment and the prudence of his advice. Garibaldi used to come to me generally in the evening, always wrapped up in his poncho or cape, which he did not abandon for the duration of the conversation. It was a strange habit. Later I came to know the reason for him to always come after nightfall: the fact was that he did not have the means to buy a lamp for his private use, and therefore he used the light of day, until he could, to write his orders , maps, etc. He came to me at finished work. Moreover he always kept wearing his poncho to hide the sorry state of his clothes ... while Garibaldi was in conditions of almost poverty, Rosas* (the Argentine dictator) *made him the most pressing advances ... offering a gift of $30,000 gold ... However these overtures did not attempt Garibaldi in any way".*

"Garibaldi has an exceptional quality of the maximum utility, he can command and act at the same time ... I could cite many examples of the audacity of this brave commander, as well as his skill and prudence. The extreme modesty of his ways, quiet and somewhat reserved strike those who see him for the first time ... Naturally courteous, human and kind, he knows how to keep his men disciplined and to obtain obedience. Nobody has ever known him to have caught any of the many opportunities of personal gain ... Not only that, he also always strictly forbade his men looting and other forms of misconduct"[9].

Who writes is William Gore Ouseley, writer and painter as well as diplomat by profession (his paintings still today command good prices). William Gore is describing an ascetic of war, a man totally out of the ordinary. It is striking that a consumed British diplomat manifests so much admiration for Garibaldi; it is clear that he is fascinated by him.

We must ask ourselves again if Garibaldi was really like this.

We think that this description was substantially true.

As we have already noted, Garibaldi lived his life with the dedication of an ascetic. That thing that we called "inconsistency" is the result of his asceticism. Once he decided to support a cause nothing could make him change his opinion: that cause was "the good and the right one" and his dedication could only be total because he was fighting for the "good"

---

[9] Denis Mack Smith, *Garibaldi*, (Milano: Laterza, 1956) pag.204, from *Garibaldi in South America: a new Document*

and the opponent was the "evil". No crime, no disaster could make him think. In other words, his obtuseness was invincible. This total dedication made him a "pure soul" and purity has an irresistible charm. Those who are fascinated love him, the few that remain detached admire him, and those who have suffered from his work of "redemption" hate him.

Let us read the testimony of Bartolomeo Mitre, an Argentine opponent of Rosas, who had gone to fight for Uruguay: *"I was twenty two years old at that time, and Garibaldi's personality exercised a special fascination on my imagination that attracted me irresistibly, for the enterprises I was told about him and for a kind of moral mystery that shrouded him. ... Under a modest and peaceful appearance he hid a burning genie and a mind crowded with grandiose dreams. While speaking about these, his language was passionate and colorful, revealing a well educated man, provided more with feelings than with ideas. His word, although spoken with moderation, was imperative and dogmatic. The impression that I received was of a mind and a heart not well balanced, of a soul aflame with a holy fire, dedicated to greatness and sacrifice. I was persuaded that he was a real hero in flesh and bones, with a sublime ideal, with theories of liberty that were exaggerated and not well assimilated, possessing nonetheless the elements to perform great deeds"*[10].

On the other hand let us see how Rivera, the president of Uruguay, was assessed: *"Rivera was more human than his rivals ... However against him were his notorious bad faith, his lack of probity in appropriating the public money, the unscrupulous means he always used to maintain an illegitimate influence on public affairs"*[11].

It is impossible to understand the myth of Garibaldi if you do not place it in the context of the world in which he lived. In that world everyone betrayed everyone, everybody was for sale, and when they fought they did it for personal gain. Where corruption did not arrive, factionalism reached. Your own person was always more important than the cause and contentiousness and envy exceeded the grotesque.

With funding from the British Garibaldi puts together a small fleet, a small thing compared to that of Argentina but enough to take to the sea.

---

[10] Alfonso Scirocco, *Garibaldi*, (Bari: Laterza, 2001) pag.127

[11] Denis Mack Smith, *Garibaldi*, (Milano: Laterza, 1956) pag.27

When the Argentine fleet moves to conquer an island in front of Montevideo, Garibaldi advances to counter it. It is a foolish move, the forces are too unequal, but Garibaldi does not retreat. When it seems he should succumb here comes a British warship that blocks the way to the Argentines handing Garibaldi an outstanding victory. With its small fleet Garibaldi returns to do the pirate, with terrible results.

He captures a United States schooner causing a diplomatic incident. He captures a Brazilian ship, despite having signed an agreement with Brazil not to attack this country anymore; he was forced to indemnify Brazil. He comes up against a Brazilian merchant provoking the protest of the other foreigners who were helping Uruguay; he is placed under arrest. To be released he must sign a statement where he recognizes his mistake and undertakes not to repeat it. In vain: the Italian Legion captures a few Brazilians and Brazil sends its fleet in front of Montevideo; the Uruguayan government obliges Garibaldi to release the prisoners.

In any case Uruguay cannot do without him and the Italian Legion. The war was getting worse for Uruguay. President Rivera had put together another army; he clashed with the Argentines at India Muerta and suffered another disastrous defeat. On 2.000 prisoners, 800 Uruguayans are slaughtered by the Argentines and others tortured and burned alive. It should not surprise you if in that war it was a common practice to kill your own injured if you could not carry them away, Garibaldi himself tells us to have done this with some of his men: "*It is painful to confess, a seriously wounded, was killed not to leave him to be slain by the cruel enemy*"[12].

Rivera goes into exile, for now. Montevideo is under siege again and now the government must rely on Garibaldi to defend the city. England and France are trying to broker a peace but Rosas refuses; the Allies therefore decided to teach a lesson to Argentina to force it to an armistice and they organize an expedition with their combined fleets on the Paraná river. They ask to have Garibaldi and his small fleet with them. Think about it, a modest merchant marine captain, sentenced to death in his own country that participates in an expedition together with the fleets of the first two world powers and with the post of commander of the Uruguayan fleet, what a career! It is not difficult to understand the rea-

---

[12] Giuseppe Garibaldi, *Clelia,* (Roma: Bariletti Editori, 1990) pag.250

son for their choice; he was the only one they could trust and who was up to the assignment. In his memoirs he writes: "*In the plans of operations, combined between the government of the republic and the admirals of the two allied nations, there was an expedition for Uruguay: and I was put in charge of it*". This is it, he could also have bragged a bit about this but he is a modest person because the cause must always prevail over personal interests. This is a very important element of the charm of his character and it will be instrumental in the development of his myth.

Back in Montevideo he resumes to do the pirate with some success since France and England have seized the Argentine fleet, but at this point everybody is tired. France and England change ambassadors and insist on peace talks. The Uruguayans are divided between hard-liners and pacifists. Garibaldi and his Legion take the side of the extremists, they do not want to lose their jobs and they fear that the new government will not keep its promises of rewards with land and cattle at the end of the war. The Uruguayan pacifists are indignant of this meddling in their affairs by the gringos (Italians) and demand that they be expelled. Garibaldi, embittered by such ingratitude, resigns and so he ends his Uruguayan adventure.

Thus he sums up his thoughts when he writes to a friend in Turin: "*We continue to live here in war, but now it is a lackluster war, slow, lifeless and without glory ... The discord, fomented by the ambition and selfishness of a few aspirants, precipitated us in an immense disaster and offered, helpless, entire populations and generous, to the extermination of a relentless winner!*"[13] Also this war is no more fun.

It was the summer of 1847; he is 40 years old, married with three children and does not have a penny. Anita does the laundress to get by. Her jealousy has reached the exasperation; she said that she kept two loaded pistols: one for his mistress and one for herself! At that time he does not see other wars on the horizon and this is the only thing he wants to do. He participated at two wars, the first lost and the second is still going on but he has been chased. In both wars he has held important positions and has always been at the center of the action but his dedication to

---

[13] Alfonso Scirocco, *Garibaldi*, (Bari: Laterza, 2001) pag.121

the cause left him empty handed and now he finds himself in misery in a foreign country than does not want him anymore. It is a **widespread opinion** in Montevideo that the Italian legionnaires have helped prolong the war and their excesses have earned hatred toward all Italians.

At this point of his life he might be called a loser and today he would be remembered as a footnote on a page of the history of South America. But he has built up a remarkable reputation, he has good experience of war made up of guerrilla warfare and piracy, he has learned to command and to kill. Under his leadership, the Italian Legion fought well, it did not win but resisted and gave an important contribution to the defense of Montevideo even if in the end it made itself hated for its systematic violence and theft against civilians. France and England know him and appreciate his services; moreover, in Montevideo he joined the Freemasons in a lodge dependent on the Grand Orient of France with the rank of Apprentice.

Now we need to step back and see how it was born in Europe the myth of Garibaldi.

The industrial revolution had given birth to a middle class educated and curious about things far away and exotic. Particularly in England, France, Germany and Northern Italy it was greatly increased the circulation of newspapers and other periodicals which were chasing sensations to satisfy the inexhaustible hunger of their readers for exciting news. South America provided an exceptional mine of this news. Progressive Europe took sides with passion in the adventures of all those who fought for "freedom". As we have seen, in the Rio Grande the Italian exiles were publishing *O Povo*; a few copies reached Europe and provided the raw material for sensational news. The adventures of Garibaldi were followed avidly because of his image that we have already described. In Montevideo the Italians publish *The Italian Legionnaire* and also here Garibaldi is celebrated with words from a soap opera: *"With Garibaldi you win or you die with honor!"*. Or: *"Garibaldi drives away from himself with one shake, as you do with the flies, the leads of the enemy"*[14].

---

[14] Francesco Carrano, *I Cacciatori delle Alpi comandati dal generale Giuseppe Garibaldi* (Torino, Unione Tipografico Editrice, 1860) pag. 88,89.

The adventure which most fascinates the European public opinion is the siege of Montevideo. The correspondences from Uruguay are accompanied by illustrations with portraits of the characters, landscapes, fortifications and uniforms of the fighters. The character Garibaldi has a leading part for the good or the evil. Depending on the political orientation of the writer, he is "*the Genoese bandit*" or "*the beau-ideal of a leader of irregular troops*". The opposing political camps clash on his name and his image. For the Catholic conservatives he was the antichrist, "*thief on land and pirate at sea, the terror and the abomination of the good*", while Lord Howden declares in the House of Lords that "*he alone was uninterested in a crowd of people, who did not seek but their personal aggrandizement ... a man of great courage and high military genius*"[15].

Very important for the myth of Garibaldi will be the French novelist Alexandre Dumas. Fascinated by the epic siege of Montevideo he writes *Montevideo ou une nouvelle Troie*, where the protagonists are described as Homeric characters from the Trojan War and Garibaldi is the most prominent: "*Physically Garibaldi is a man of 38 years old, of medium height, proportionate limbs, with blond hair and blue eyes, nose, forehead and chin Greek that is as close as you can to the true model of beauty ... He moves gracefully; his voice, of a sweetness without limits, recalls a song ... but just utter before him the words 'independence' and 'Italy' and there he is, waking up like a volcano, throwing flames and erupting lava. ... When it is the time of the action he grabs the first sword at hand, throws the sheath and rails against the enemy ... journalists, who have treated Garibaldi as a soldier of fortune, write to Montevideo ... and learn that in this republic of which you, Republican, are sponsoring the abandonment, no man has been estimated so universally*"[16]. A little exaggerated and even a little false but such is the myth.

The Italian patriots are desperately searching for a hero. In 1843 Gioberti publishes *On the moral and civil primacy of the Italians*, a clear testimony of the sense of inferiority of the Italians in comparison with the other nations. Mazzini is interested in this follower of his and prints in French a defense of Garibaldi and his legionaries on a brochure to be distributed in France where news have been disclosed not flattering for

---

[15] Alfonso Scirocco, *Garibaldi*, (Bari: Laterza, 2001) pag.129

[16] Denis Mack Smith, *Garibaldi*, (Milano: Laterza, 1956) pag.201,203

This sadness is also reflected in the description of a young niece of his financial backer. In fact he and Rossetti frequented his house: "*He was young blond and strong. He differed from most of his countrymen for the expression of a deep intelligence and a pensive attitude. Often, during an animated discussion, we found him immersed in his daydreams or in an indifferent air. His eyes were those of a saint, he had the sweet expression of a perfect goodness. In those moments he was in intimacy only with the children and played with them as if they were his peers*"[2]. The myth of the "blond hero" had just begun.

The Revolução Farroupilha

In 1841 Dom Pedro II is crowned emperor of Brazil, but he is only 15 years old and the thing generates a widespread discontent throughout the Empire. The province of Rio Grande do Sul was in conflict with the Empire for economic problems. The main activity of the province was the "charque", a salted and smoked meat, that suffered from the competition from the Argentine and Uruguayan productions that had no import duties and had no taxes in their countries, while the charque from Rio Grande was taxed by the Empire. Taking advantage of the weakness of the central power and the discontent in the province, Bento Gonzalves occupies the city of Porto Alegre in September 1835, declaring the republic and the secession from the Empire. The following year he is captured by the Imperial army along with his secretary, Luigi Zambeccari, a noble Bolognese who had fled from Italy following the riots of 1821. Despite being in prison, in 1837 Zambeccari comes in contact with Rossetti and Garibaldi getting them to join the "Revolução Farroupilha", the Revolution of the Rags, as privateers. Later, Zambeccari was pardoned and returned to Italy where he became a follower of Garibaldi until his death in 1862. Goncalves managed to escape and to take back the leadership of the revolt until his final defeat in 1845. The peace ends with an amnesty for all rebels and an import duty of 25% on the Argentine and Uruguayan charque.

Brazil will pay dearly for the hospitality granted to the blond hero.

At that time Europe was providing South America with a small but steady flow of immigrants, some for economic reasons, and others for political problems. Some of these settle down, but many others do not fit

---

[2] Max Gallo, *Garibaldi,* (Milano, Rusconi Libri, 1982) pag.88

Nationalism, the faith in the motherland, had penetrated the society of Northern Italy brought by Jacobinism and the Napoleonic armies. Many young Italians would flare up at the thought that Italy (however you want to define her) was divided and controlled by foreign powers. The sense of inferiority that this entailed was pushing many to risk their lives to put together some sort of motherland that could rival the others (France, Spain, England, etc.). They did not intend to be left behind and be excluded from this European contest, whatever the cost.

Garibaldi gives us no reasoning for this patriotism because he did not have any. Faith is blind, it has no reasons, and it does not need any. To it you must give yourself totally, without asking and (above all) without asking yourself anything. Eighty years after these events 650,000 Italians will give their life to "redeem" Trento, Trieste and surroundings where half the people could not even speak Italian. Then, on that day of February 1834, no inhabitant of the peninsula could have even imagined where this faith would have brought them.

Sentenced to death, he sails to South America where he will remain 12 years. Those will be the years of his personal formation, military and political. He arrives in Rio de Janeiro at the end of 1835.

The Revolução Farroupilha

Garibaldi was already famous in the community of Italian exiles who had found refuge in Rio. His death sentence, that followed the failed uprising of Mazzini, had already made him a hero in a community where there were many who had to leave their country for troubles with the law as a result of subversive activities.

One of these Italians, who had made a fortune, gives him some money to arm a small boat with which to trade between the cities of the Brazilian coast. It will be a miserable affair. Trade and finance were not his forte. As he himself wrote: "*After a few months in an idle life, here we are, Rossetti and I, engulfed in this trade; but to trade, Rossetti and I were not good*". It is evident, through these words, the boredom of a bourgeois occupation, which was particularly odious to him who had dedicated himself to the redemption of the Motherland.

reach from door to roof and are upright—thus giving a more spacious interior. These doors are "fitted with sliding glasses in the top part after the manner of an ordinary brougham door." A *brougham hansom* was introduced in 1887. "This afforded sitting-room inside for three or four; it was entered at the back, and when the door was shut, a seat across it was so arranged that there was no possibility of the door opening till the occupants' weight was off the seat. The driver's seat was in front, on the roof of the vehicle." A *four-wheeled hansom* was also seen in London some twenty-five years ago. Here the driver's seat was behind the carriage on a level with the roof.

"Everybody knows," remarks Sir Walter Gilbey, "that the hansom, by reason of its steadiness, is an exceedingly comfortable conveyance; there is no vehicle that runs more easily, particularly when the load is truly balanced." But in spite of such improvements as rubber tyres and patent windows, the hansom seems doomed.

Shillibeer's huge omnibuses were succeeded by smaller vehicles of similar construction. For some years no passengers were carried upon the roof except one or two beside the driver. Then in 1849 an "outside seat down the centre of the roof was added," to reach which you had to climb an iron ladder. This continued until 1890, when the much more convenient "garden-seats" were substituted, and a curved flight of steps took the place of the rather dangerous ladder. Private omnibuses were first constructed about 1867. They contained a rumble at the back for the footman, but this was speedily dispensed with. As built to-day, they are of various sizes.

One other carriage may be mentioned, and then I am done. This is the *Irish car*. Here, as in the larger *bian*, the seats are arranged back to back and sideways. "The wheels are very low and are concealed as far as the axle-boxes, or farther, by the panel of the footboard, which panel is hinged to the end of the *tray*, either side of which forms the seat, to allow of its being turned up when not in use." Occasionally there is a well between the seats for small packages. In private cars of this kind there is a small seat in front for the driver, but this is rarely to be found in the public vehicles. The width of the *Irish car* is enormous, and occasionally leads the neophyte into trouble. Outside Ireland, I believe, the car is not seen.

"Walking in the pleasant environs of Paris," wrote Mr. H. C. Marillier some seventeen years ago, in an article entitled *The Automobile: A Forecast*, "or even further afield, upon the broad *routes nationales* of Charente and La Beauce, it is no uncommon thing to meet on a summer's day a little open vehicle flitting along without apparent means of motion, upon noiseless rubber-shod wheels, or panting forth a gentle warning from a square-shaped box in front. Two, and sometimes three, persons are seated in it, one of whom drives by means of a handle. To stop or to start again requires the turn of a screw or the push of a pedal. Such, in its most accomplished and most graceful form, is the *automobile*. To see it pass at racing speed—some of these little machines can spurt at twenty miles an hour—takes one's breath away at first. The apparition is uncanny."

In another passage he speaks of these horseless carriages as playing "a prominent part as the natural successors of the hansom cab and the omnibus," and draws what must then have been a fanciful picture of a city upon whose roads there would be seen almost as many horseless as horse-driven vehicles. To-day we know what has happened since these words were written. The hansom is a rarity, except during a strike of petrol-car drivers. The omnibus is a speedy machine with a powerful engine. The growler persists, but only for the benefit of those with much luggage or for those afraid of the internal combustion engine, that extraordinary discovery which has revolutionised locomotion even more than did steam eighty years ago. With such facts as these it would be easy to prophesy a total extinction of horse-driven vehicles except for purely ornamental purposes. Yet I believe that there may be a reaction in favour of a more leisurely means of locomotion. As yet it is impossible to be truly dignified in even the most gorgeously appointed motor-car. "Carriage people" no longer form a class, and the old coach-building firms which have not followed the times and shown one or other make of automobile in their rooms are few in number. Mr. Marillier, moreover, in the article just quoted, speaks of "that ideal future when life shall consist of sitting in a chair and pressing buttons"; but the horse is not yet extinct, and although it is not probable that any horse-carriages of an entirely new type will be constructed, I imagine that the older forms will persist, at any rate, for the next century or two. Indeed, to my mind, there must always be the man who will prefer the reins to the driving wheel. And who can blame him for the choice?

INDEX

Symbols

A

C

E

H

M

X

Y

him. In fact, in Montevideo there was also a French Legion and, of course, this was generating controversy and rivalry between the two nationalities. In 1846 in Florence a subscription is launched to present a sword of honor to Garibaldi; after a few months it is ready and Garibaldi sends a letter of gratitude. He will be given it upon his arrival in Italy.

This was the situation of Garibaldi in Montevideo and of his myth in Europe when something starts to move in Italy and his life takes an unexpected turn that will project him to become the hero we know today.

Italia

In 1846 Pius IX becomes Pope and launches progressive initiatives without realizing their implications. All Italian sovereigns follow him, they grant constitutions and debate about a federation with an Italian customs union; the same thing that was happening in Germany. The Austrian Empire drags its feet, and a '48 explodes. The city of Milan rises and the king of Sardinia, Carlo Alberto, with a clever move of profiteering comes forward to protect the revolution. He adopts the tricolor (the Italian flag) and attacks the Austrian Empire to grab Lombardy.[17]

Garibaldi in Montevideo arouses immediately. His heart had always remained on his native land; the South American wars were only a surrogate of his mission to redeem the Motherland. He writes to Pius IX and to the Grand Duke of Tuscany to offer them his services. He would have given his life for his homeland; surely he could sacrifice his republicanism or his anti-clericalism. He also wrote to Mazzini and to all those who could get him a place in the struggle for the redemption.

Nobody answers and so he decides to collect in Montevideo the money for the return trip to Italy. Actually he leaves without a goal and without knowing what will happen to him. In the Kingdom of Sardinia there is still a death sentence waiting for him. You understand clearly that he was tired of living in exile and in a country that did not want him anymore. He writes to Medici who had been sent ahead: "*You will keep this above all that our purpose is to bring us home not to upset the current trend of things, and the governments which agree to it, but to unite us to the good and, in agreement with them, go forward to the best of our country, and we would prefer to launch ourselves where a road were open to fight against the German, against which must be addressed resolutely the ire of all*"[18]. Simply stated, he wanted a place in any way, in the great drama of the Risorgimento.

---

[17] A hundred years before these facts the Prince of Piedmont annexed the kingdom of Sardinia thus obtaining the title of king and his dominions were called the kingdom of Sardinia even though Piedmont was by far the most important region. In this book kingdom of Sardinia and Piedmont are used as synonymous.

[18] Alfonso Scirocco, *Garibaldi*, (Bari: Laterza, 2001) pag.140

He lands in Nice where he can see his mother and Anita who had been sent forward. Here he learns that the city of Milan had recently liberated itself from the Empire and Carlo Alberto (the king of Sardinia) had found the courage to declare war on the Empire. Hence: "*... but they were fighting on the Mincio, and idleness was a crime for us when our brothers were fighting against the foreigners*". He decides to go to Carlo Alberto, who had reached the Mincio river, to offer him his sword.

He passes by Genoa and here a series of disappointments begin that will accompany him throughout his adventure of Risorgimento: "*The people of Genoa received us palpitating with joy and affection; the authorities with the coldness of an insecure conscience; and initiated that series of grimaces and procrastinations which accompanied us in our country, wherever you could find the negotiators assigned to the middle ground ideas, dragged to free government more by the fear of the people than by the faith and by the disposition of their soul in favor of the human improvement*".

The reception of the people of Genoa was certainly enthusiastic since, shortly after, he was elected Member of Parliament in Turin with 18 votes, without having applied his candidacy. At that time only 1% of the population had the right to vote; it was therefore easy to be deceived about the actual size of your popularity.

He gathers a few volunteers from Liguria which, added to the 63 legionaries who had followed him from Montevideo, led the consistency of his troops to 150 elements. This is how he meets the king, with his death sentence still in force: "*I saw him; I knew his distrust in receiving me; and deplored, in the hesitation and the uncertainty of the man, the badly entrusted fate of our poor country*".

The king refuses his help and advises him to go to Venice or Milan where, perhaps, he would be accepted. Thus writes the King to his Minister of War: "*I hasten to inform you of having granted today an audience to the famous General Garibaldi, who came from America and arrived in Genoa, where he left sixty of his disciples, that he offered me together with his person. The background of these people, and especially of this self-styled general, his famous republican proclamation, make it totally impossible to accept them in the army, and especially to appoint Garibaldi general; if it were a matter of maritime war we could use him as a leader of pirates, but, otherwise, it would be a dishonor to the army.*

I think he will come to Turin ... The best would be for him to go else-where, and to encourage them to this, him and his brave, you could probably give them a subsidy, provided they go away"[19].

At this point he goes wandering around searching for a job.

Even in Milan they try to turn him away but, eventually, they offer him the rank of brigadier general with the task of organizing a corps of volunteers. There are no resources so they are equipped with uniforms left behind by the Austrians in the city. He realizes that he is not wanted, *"... and I breathed jubilant, the day when we left the capital of Lombardy, directed toward Bergamo, with a bunch of naked people and poorly armed, in need to be organized again, a destiny inadequate to my character, and to my poor knowledge of military theories"*. He knows he is a leader and a driver, discipline and organization bore him, but he will always find someone else to whom to delegate these tasks.

At Monza he hears the news of the defeat of the Piedmontese, afterwards of the flight of the King from Milan, disguised as a monk. At that point the city and Garibaldi were alone in front of the imperial army: *"Armistice, capitulation, escape, were news that hit us like lightning, one after the other; and with them, the fear and demoralization among the people, in my ranks and everywhere. Some cowards, who unfortunately can be found among my people, they abandoned their guns on the very square in Monza, and began to flee in all directions"*. He withdraws to Como to *"make war of bands, if nothing else could be done"*; he has no intention to stop fighting.

Along the way they are joined by Mazzini who had a band of his own, but he is going to Switzerland where he is safe from the Austrians and from where he can reach England. *"In Milan I had made the mistake, that Mazzini never forgave me, to suggest him that it was not right to hold a number of young people with the promise to proclaim the republic eventually, while the army and the volunteers were fighting the Austrians"*. In Milan he met Mazzini and it was quite a fight. Garibaldi did not want Mazzini to insist on the idea of a republic since they were fighting alongside the King of Sardinia. However, Mazzini was an unyielding ideologue while Garibaldi wanted to liberate Italy in any way and he realized that only with the Savoy monarchy they had a chance.

---

[19] Gilberto Oneto, *L'Iperitaliano*, (Rimini: Il Cerchio, 2006), pag.49

The rift between the two will be total and Mazzini will be excluded from the project of the Risorgimento.

Now he is alone with just a few men: "*We wandered around those mountains for a few days, collecting the weapons of our defectors, loading them on seized carts that were marching with our column ... and we looked rather like a caravan of Bedouins, than people who were willing to fight for their land*".

When he knows the terms of the armistice signed by the king of Sardinia he explodes and publishes a proclamation where he declares that he will continue the war alone and accusing Carlo Alberto of cowardice: "*If the King of Sardinia has a crown, which he conserves by force of blame and cowardice, I and my colleagues do not want to maintain our lives in infamy*"[20]. It is a delirium, at first the king orders him to leave Lombardy and then that he be arrested, but he does not give in. He will show the world of what stuff the Italians are made!

Now we must read another testimony, it is the *Official Journal of the Kingdom of Sardinia*, nr.21 of August 17th, 1848: "*The general Garibaldi who retired at Castelletto Ticino with 1,300 men, moved suddenly from there on the morning of the 14th taking hostage with him the two brothers Minella and a certain Barberis, since those where voiced to be supporters of Austria, he went to Arona where he seized all the boats that were anchored there, those who came from the opposite Lombard shore, and two steamers, and imposed the city a contribution of 100 liras, 20 bags of rice, three of oats, and 1,285 rations of bread since he was leaving, apparently, to continue the hostilities against Austria, leaving behind serious apprehensions for his return. Upon leaving he also freed, following the insistent requests of a few people, the engineer Barberis, but took with him the two above mentioned Minella and such a Guenzi that he had arrested in Arona, in spite of the intervention of the lawyer Brofferio that was there. It is said that, having landed in Luino on the Lombard side, he shot, against all laws of humanity, the three above mentioned hostages, and afterward he beat a body of three or four hundred Austrians. Therefore, the civic administration of Arona appeals to the government to be protected from such a violence, moreover the government of the King, in order to make the populations safe, to main-*

---

[20] Alfonso Scirocco, *Garibaldi*, (Bari: Laterza, 2001) pag.144

*tain the discipline so severely injured, and finally not to become an ac-
complice of such a breach of the covenants of the armistice, was forced
to make provisions so that the column of Garibaldi could not return to
Piedmont*"[21].

From Luino he goes to Varese where he obtains a list of wealthy citizens and asks them 80,000 francs. They refuse to pay, he has them arrested, then he picks up a peasant and <u>shoots him</u>. The rich pay, in South
America this was normal. He had decided to make war on Austria and he
could not do it without money. After all, he is putting his own life at risk
while he is just asking money to them, damn!

Thus he remembers those days in his *Memorie*: "*It was also moving
the sight of our march, along the west coast of the magnificent lake ...
We could see our beautiful women, protruding from the balconies of
their houses, with those most graceful faces, so lively as if they wanted
to fly to reach those braves who did not despair of taking back their
hearths from the mighty oppressor. We answered to the cheers of our beloved countrymen and we were certainly proud of their acclaim and of
our resolve*". It seems he really believed this.

In the meantime the Austrians have taken Milan, now they can dedicate themselves to him and try to squeeze him in a vise.

These are difficult times but he moves constantly, and always manages to escape from his pursuers: "*It was necessary to move oneself, and to
change our position almost every night to deceive the enemy who, for the
misfortune of Italy, especially in those days, had always a mass of traitors willing to spy for them, while for us, even with fists of gold, it was
difficult to know exactly about the enemy. Here I made the first experiences of the little affection of the people of the countryside for the national cause. Both because they are creature and meal of the priests and
because they are generally the enemies of their masters ...*".

For a couple of weeks he plays hide and seek with the Austrians then
decides to leave the field; a few dozen faithful men are with him and the
vise is tightening more and more. Garibaldi disguises himself as a peasant and flees to Switzerland; 30 men only were still with him.

Thus ends his participation to the first war of independence, it was
August 1848. Through France he returns to Nice where he remains a few

---

[21] Gilberto Oneto, *L'Iperitaliano* (Rimini: Il Cerchio, 2006), pag.50

days, undisturbed by the police. This is surprising because he was still a man sentenced to death, had publicly insulted the king, had disobeyed, had executed a few citizens of Piedmont and Lombardy, had continued the hostilities in disregard of the terms of the armistice, had plundered and robbed and therefore there was enough for another death sentence. Instead, nothing, the Piedmont government does not react and leaves him free in his mother's house to heal a bad malaria fever. Italians!

At this point we must stop and have a series of considerations on these last events.

As we have seen, the myth of Garibaldi was initiated by the European press that had created a character partially true because it had totally removed the element of criminal folly of his bloody wars in South America. This phenomenon concerns only the bourgeoisie and nobility because only a minority of the population was literate and, in any case, those who had to work hard for a living had no interest in the heroes of South America. Not only that, the Napoleonic Wars had requested a monstrous contribution in terms of human lives and destruction that had been borne primarily by the lower classes and these did not want anything to do any longer with Jacobins, patriots, or otherwise. In other words Romanticism, with adjoining nationalism, concerned only the higher classes who had the time and the money to read: the masters. The people, the commoners, hated Garibaldi and his "liberators".

This to Garibaldi was irrelevant anyway because only 1% of the people had the right to vote and they were the masters who gave him their money (and their children) to make war. As he himself wrote, he was perfectly aware "*of the little affection of the people of the countryside for the national cause*". The reason for this, according to him, is that "*they are* (the peasants) *creature and meal of the priests, and because they are generally the enemies of their masters*" that sided with him. This is why when he tries to extort 80.000 francs to the wealthy citizens of Varese, he does not shoot one of them, that he had arrested, but he does shoot a peasant who had nothing to do with them. The rich eventually pay, thanks to their goodness.

These issues will repeat themselves throughout his adventure of the Risorgimento. He is so disconnected from reality that all along his memoirs he tells us of cheering crowds that give him the illusion of being loved by the people. A phenomenon not too different from the crowds that deluded Mussolini on the real size of his popularity. He is deceived who wants to be fooled.

Another stimulus for reflection comes to us by the welcome he receives upon his arrival in Genoa. "*The people of Genoa received us, palpitating with joy and affection*" it is the 1% who will elect him to Parliament whereas "*the authorities with the coldness of an insecure conscience*". These are the leaders of the city and of course they did not feel comfortable in receiving one condemned to death and they did not share the asceticism and dedication of Garibaldi for the "holy cause". For them having to flee in case of defeat, abandoning family and work, is a prospect that is faced with some hesitancy. You can perceive in his memoirs his contempt for these "*negotiators assigned to the middle ground ideas*" who said they were patriots but did not want to take chances. This contempt will be transferred to his disciples who will face his (Garibaldi's) adventures with a motto that still is not official but will become so: "Who cares!".

We should also note that when he is elected he will never attend to this Parliament. This will be typical of Garibaldi that, while declaring himself a republican and a democrat, will have a total disregard for parliamentary life; a lack of interest that will be transformed over time into dislike and contempt. He was a man of action and had an instinctive distrust of politicians who fight with words and are necessarily compelled to compromise.

The king Carlo Alberto hits the mark when he calls his men, his disciples, as if they were a religious sect. An aristocrat from an old family like him **cannot but** despise a South American bandit that appears before him with impunity, despite being a condemned man. The same is repeated in Milan and elsewhere. There is a clear cleavage between his "people" and the ruling class (military or civilian) that necessarily distrusts him and his methods, which obviously they cannot share, but which they must tolerate given the precarious circumstances in which they were. They tolerate his delirium when he declares war alone to the Empire and insults the king who has surrendered. They tolerate his Nazis methods that are in fact accepted by the authorities, first of all the Piedmont government. This will continue to repeat itself because, as we shall see, Garibaldi used easily the firing squad, very easily. As if this were not enough, in those days the authorities of Piedmont put his son, Menotti, in a college in Racconigi at the taxpayer's expenses!

This tolerance by the authorities, is it a phenomenon of opportunism because they think they can use him later or is it a symptom of their awe in front of the High Priest of the Motherland? Or of their awe for his popularity? In fact at this point we need to note that his popularity is skyrocketing. And this is precisely because of his delirium that drives him to fight alone against the Empire when the others have given up. In one fell swoop this solitary man defies the Empire and the Kingdom of Sardinia and ... gets away with it!

Here he is quiet and serene at home with mama, programming other adventures. What a giant!

"He had by now imposed on the general opinion as a personality of great importance, to some extent above the law, a man whose sincere devotion, whose real and capable courage, and even his ostentation undoubtedly shone between the deceptions and betrayals of the time. His proclamations, you may like to call them lapidary or insipid, hit the mark and did not sound entirely false. 'Do not ask victory but to God and to your iron; do not place your hope into void idols, but in justice; trust in yourselves only. He who wants to win, wins"[22].

Who writes this is undoubtedly a very serious historian but it seems to us that he is missing the implications of these delusional statements. We must point out that they are a tragic advance of the *The Triumph of the Will*. Moreover, we must go deeper into this analysis and we have to point out that when he was issuing these proclamations, <u>he had always lost!</u>

As soon as he recovers from malaria, he looks around to see where he can go to continue the fight. His analysis of the situation is quite simple: *"Finally the whole of Italy, full of enthusiasm and elements of action, capable not just to resist but also to attack the enemy on his own ground, was reduced to despair and to inertia, for the stupidity and perfidy of her rulers: king, doctors, and priests"*.

At that time Venice and Palermo were in revolt and resisting, therefore: Palermo. He rents a French steamer *"and with 72 of the old and*

---

²² Denis Mack Smith, *Garibaldi,* (Milano: Laterza, 1956) pag.35,36

new companions" he embarks towards Palermo. He calls at Livorno, but here "*the enthusiasm of the people*" convinced him to move to Florence. Here he is not wanted (indeed!): "*In Florence, magnificent hospitality from the people but indifference and hunger from the government; and I was obliged to commit some friends to feed my people*". In fact, the Prime Minister of the Grand Duchy writes: "*They are like a flood of grasshoppers. We should consider them like a plague of Egypt and let us employ all means so that they soon pass and contaminate as few places as possible*"[23].

At this point he starts spinning around central Italy as a loose cannon. As he tells us, nobody tried to stop him, but nobody wanted him. From Florence he moves to Bologna, then through the Romagna, Marche, Umbria, Tuscany and Lazio, without reliable supplies, in winter, with hunger and cold, his partisans followed him and increased in number. "*We were in November. It was worth indeed to come from South America to fight the snows of the Apennines Mountains. The Italian governments ... they had not been able to give a coat to my poor and brave companions. It was pitiful to see these young people, in that rigorous season, in the mountains, dressed most of canvas, some of rags and lacking the necessary food ...*". In Ravenna: "*The municipality of Ravenna, from which we were fed, made me feel that it would be better such a load be divided with other cities, and therefore to change residence alternately*".

When in December the Pope flees from Rome and the Roman Republic is declared, Garibaldi goes to Rome and finally finds a "job": to participate with his partisans to the defense of the republic. However even here they are not wanted (again!): "*At the same time I received orders to march ... to the port of Fermo in order to defend that point, that nobody threatened, and that proved to me not ceased the mistrust of the new rulers, and their will to keep us away from Rome*".

Why nobody wants him and his disciples who now he calls the Italian Legion?

So he explains it to us: "*According to the necromancers* (the priests), *we were people capable of every kind of violence, on the properties, on the families, dissolute without a shadow of discipline and therefore our*

---

[23] Montanelli-Nozza, *Garibaldi* (Milano, Rizzoli Editore, 1962) pag.194

approach was feared like that of wolves or murderers. This feeling, however, always changed at the sight of the beautiful educated youth who accompanied me, almost all people from the cities and educated, because, you know well that among the volunteer corps, that I had the honor to command in Italy, the class of the peasants was always missing, thanks to the care of the reverend ministers of lies. Almost all my soldiers belonged to distinct families from various Italian provinces".

What a difference from the gangs of thugs he commanded in South America.

Is it possible that the people were afraid of his men just for the gossip of the priests? At this point we must ask ourselves: who were these legionaries? "*At that time his legionaries were a mixture of idealists, aiming at a united Italy, and of trouble makers. A few were from his Liguria, and there was almost nobody from Piedmont or from the South. A company consisted of boys between twelve and fifteen. Probably most were people who, for political reasons or otherwise, had to lead a vagabond life, with nothing to lose and everything to gain from violence*"[24].

Further evidence comes from an English lady, Jessie White Mario: "*They looked like a band of savages or Indians. Garibaldi was in front, ... Next followed the officers with red shirt, lasso and leather whip. And finally the troops dressed in all shapes but with big guns and daggers at the belt, from which hung regularly turkeys and chickens. At every halt ... the legionaries rampaged around to pillage with the lasso. They returned with calves, pigs, chickens, which were quartered and roasted over a wood fire. Then Garibaldi returned and they all lined up. No one asked where they were going. Obedience was ready, the discipline perfect*"[25].

How can we reconcile these testimonies?

The revolutions of '48 had upset most of the European societies. The bourgeoisie had descended on the streets and had built the barricades, but towards the end of the year the conservative dynasties were returning in control and thousands of burghers suddenly found themselves on the wrong side. Someone was executed, someone ended up in jail, many emigrated and many others fled to the countryside in search of a temporary

---

[24] Denis Mack Smith, *Garibaldi*, (Milano: Laterza, 1956) pag.36,37

[25] Gilberto Oneto, *L'Iperitaliano* (Rimini: Il Cerchio, 2006), pag.54

arrangement in the hope that things would have adjusted or maybe who knows. They were people who had nothing to lose, apart from their lives, and Garibaldi offered them a company where they could associate with people like them and carry on waiting for a better solution. Where else could they go? For him they were ideal because they were educated people who had endured great sacrifices and would have fought with the courage of despair. And so they did.

"In Italy in '48 about 350 bands of volunteers were active, formed mostly by burghers, able to support themselves, at least in part, at their own expense, or helped by substantial offers from rich patriots"[26]. The Legion of Garibaldi was one of these, and clearly the most important. He was a magnet, in his wanderings through the Apennines Mountains he gathered elements of these bands and his ranks kept growing, in spite of the desperate situation in which he was. This is because he knew how to keep them united and disciplined but, most of all, because he gave them an ideal that would have transformed them from a gang of desperadoes, just a step from the gallows, into an army of "patriots". The most gifted, who follow him to the end, will become general in the Italian Army or deputies in Parliament.

In Rome, however, they do not want them (again!) and order him to encamp in Rieti, but no more than 500 elements, because the paltry budget of the Republic could not maintain more. When the French landed in Civitavecchia they were called to the defense of Rome: they were more than 1,200 men.

To understand these events we have to say right away that the Roman Republic was Roman only in name. The leaders, inspirers, promoters, beginning with Mazzini and Garibaldi, were almost all from northern Italy. Only after a while they decided to appoint a Roman, Rosselli, commander in chief of the army; Garibaldi considered him an incompetent, but he was a Roman. Who were the defenders of the Republic?

When the Pope had fled, a part of the papal army remained in Rome and declared they wanted to fight for the Republic, an ambiguous situation to say the least. The core of the forces was made up of volunteers who rained on Rome from North and Central Italy as soon as they learned of the new republic; there were also many foreigners. The Gari-

---

[26] Alfonso Scirocco, *Garibaldi*, (Bari: Laterza, 2001) pag.147

baldians were the most consistent part because they fought well. There were few Romans, the Republican government decided right away not to introduce the compulsory conscription because it was strongly opposed by the Roman people. The appeals to arms by the Triumvirate were ignored; in the list of the fallen of 1849 in the ossuary of the Janiculum, only one in ten is Roman. In those days, the Romans took advantage of the absence of law enforcement to engage in looting of churches and convents, vengeance and violence. All this for the Patriots was absolutely irrelevant; they wanted their Italian homeland that was unthinkable without Rome as the capital. Therefore, whether the Romans liked it or not, they too were to become Italians.

The Roman Republic was a romantic and reckless enterprise that had no chance of success. The patriots thought that a Roman republic would push all peoples of the peninsula to rebel against the oppressors and join them to make Italy. Yet they knew perfectly well that this was impossible because the people (the real one) hated them. The romantic and patriotic bourgeoisie was a minority and too weak to achieve such a feat. But then, why did they do it?

While the volunteers were trying to contain the French troops, the intellectuals in the Constituent Assembly drew up a republican constitution which will be approved on the day the French entered the city, the last day in the life of the republic. Garibaldi was also elected to this Assembly but his work was war, he did not have much to say about constitutions. To read his memoirs, it seems that they spent most of their time squabbling, which is understandable considering that their situation was desperate. As for his person, on this occasion the same phenomenon is repeated that we already noticed; even if he was defeated, the reputation of Garibaldi flies across Europe where the progressives hold their breath while watching this unequal struggle and pine for the fate of the patriots. His fame grew dramatically to become an icon.

The Garibaldians fight right up to the last; evidently it is better to die as patriots with the arms in hand than of hunger and cold in the Apennines. Instead: "*In the bodies of the line, that is the old papal soldiers, some were well behaved at first; but now, seeing that everything was going bad, they showed that inert aspect and acted grudgingly, that precedes the mistrust or the betrayal: something they manifested jesuitical-*

ly, according to the school of the priests, by resisting the services they were ordered".

When the end comes, the consul of the United States offers him to escape on an American ship but Garibaldi has other plans: "*I said to him to thank the generous representative of the great republic; but I was willing to leave Rome with those who wanted to follow me and try again the fate of my country that I did not believe desperate*", and he decides to flee from Rome to continue the war as a guerrilla in the Apennines or who knows where; Garibaldi never surrendered, this is why he is a legend.

He had proposed to Mazzini: "*... to leave Rome to march with all available forces, materials and means that were not few, to the strong positions of the Apennines. And I do not know why it was not done! ... The representatives of the people, for the most part young and energetic patriots, beloved in their departments, could be sent there, to arouse the patriotism of the people, and so try again our luck*". The problem was that the "*patriotic people*" did not exist and "*the strong positions of the Apennines*" suggests the Valtellina project of Mussolini. He thought that, even if defeated: "*... perhaps we could leave Rome adorned of the honor of being the last to fall, i.e.: after Venice and Hungary*". This is the cult of the Supreme Sacrifice.

This flight from Rome towards nothingness is madness, Venice and Hungary still resisted but not for long, and all the rest of Italy was pacified and was readjusting to the old conservative governments.

It is July 2, 1849 when he leaves Rome chased by the French. Three or four thousands men are with him including a few papal soldiers who evidently were too compromised. There is also his wife Anita who arrived in Rome a few days before. She is pregnant with her fourth child and despite the opposition from Garibaldi she is determined to follow him. She cuts her hair, she dresses as a man and jumps on horseback. It seems that this is due to the jealousy which devours her; she does not want to leave him alone.

So he begins this disastrous march. His disconnection from reality increases continuously: "*So far things were not so bad ... and if the spirit of the generality: the people and soldiers, had not been so depressed, I could have done a beautiful war for a long time*". The war was beautiful only for him and for his disciples. For the people of the countryside that he ran through, it was a drama to which they had to try to survive. This reality imposes itself by matter of fact because these Italians who yearned to be liberated by him did not exist: *"I soon became aware that there was no desire to continue in the glorious and magnificent enterprise that fate handed in front of us ... not only I was not able to gather one man, but every night as if they needed to cover their shameful act with its darkness, those that followed me from Rome deserted ... by reason of the frequent desertions, many weapons remained abandoned, which were loaded on mules, but the overwhelming number of these and the difficulties of transportation forced us to leave them together with the ammunition at the discretion of those inhabitants that we considered the best"*. This situation it is aggravated by the fact that: *"I could not get a guide in Italy, while the Austrians had aplenty! This thanks to the Italians who go to Mass and to confession to that beautiful black stuff that are called cockroaches!"*.

The hardest blow is given to him by his loyal colonel, Ignazio Bueno, who had followed him from South America; he runs away with the cash and surrenders himself to the Austrians that let him return to America free and wealthy.

To understand to what extent his personal charm could hold together a band of patriots, idealists, students, unemployed and criminals, we read the diary of one of his officers **the garibaldian lieutenant** Gustav von Hoffstetter, a Swiss from Zurich: *"The words of the General have worked wonders. The soldiers fear him as much as they love him. They know very well that Garibaldi is capable of having them shot without even bothering to take the cigar off his mouth. The general knows only two punishments: a reprimand and death ... During the defense of Rome I had many opportunities to admire the firmness of Garibaldi in directing a battle and the speed and accuracy with which he captured the details ... and for these things he was a master unrivaled worldwide. His energy was boundless ... I have never seen a single case of disobedience, or even a simple negligence in performing his orders"*.

"A soldier had been caught stealing a chicken to a woman of this poor village, and he was executed today. When the shots rang out, Garibaldi stood up and said to the astonished soldiers who were not aware of the incident: 'This is how I punish thieves! Are we fighting for the free-

*dom or we are just robbers? Are we here to protect the people or to op-
press them?'. The troops shouted: 'Long live Garibaldi', and I am sure
he screamed louder who had just eaten a stolen chicken*"[27].

No army could shoot a man for stealing a chicken without risking a
mutiny. Garibaldi could do it.[28]

We want to add an episode that can be considered funny: "*Two prisoners of our cavalry, who went exploring, they were captured by the
peasants of the bishop of Chiusi, by a bishop, you understood well; and,
if I remember correctly, Chiusi still has a bishop today (1872). I claimed
those prisoners of mine, whom I certainly believed to be in danger under
the talon of the descendants of Torquemada, and they were denied to me.
Therefore I marched, in retaliation, all the friars of a convent at the
head of the column, threatening to shoot them, but the archbishop,
tough, made me know that there was a lot of cloth in Italy to make friars,
and would not give me back the prisoners. I also thought this: he wanted
the massacre of those soldiers of his, in order to pass them to the peons
as holy martyrs. Then I freed the friars*". It sounds like a story taken
from Don Camillo.

This senseless enterprise is coming to an end anyway, lieutenant
Hoffstetter tells us that "*Every day our number diminished and our mo-
rale was weakening; even the officers deserted ... the column had already disintegrated before Garibaldi formally discharged his soldiers*".

In late July, he is closely followed by the Austrians and his men are
exhausted. He takes refuge in San Marino and releases his small army
that was reduced to a thousand men. The best thing was to disperse in
the countryside and hope to escape from the enemy. However he still
does not give in and decides to continue towards Venice, still under
siege, with 200 of the most faithful (or most desperate). A big problem is
Anita that is seriously ill, besides being pregnant, and cannot face the
hardships of such an adventure. He wants her to stay in San Marino to
seek treatment and to give birth, but she is adamant: "*That heart, manly*

---

[27] Denis Mack Smith, *Garibaldi*, (Milano: Laterza, 1956) pag.211,213

[28] The same episode is also narrated in: Francesco Carrano, *I Cacciatori delle Alpi comandati
dal generale Giuseppe Garibaldi* (Torino, Unione Tipografico Editrice, 1860) pag.145.

and generous, she disdained any of my admonitions on this matter, and she silenced me with the words: - You want to abandon me -"[29].

They leave San Marino at night avoiding the Austrians; the next night they are in Cesenatico and surprise the whole town in its sleep. They arrest the few policemen that were there and open the shops to pick up all the food that would be required to reach Venice. Hence they oblige the fishermen to sail with their bragozzi, but the weather is inclement and they struggle to take to the sea "*with people sleepy and grudgingly, that you had to push with the flat of the saber to make them move and obtain what was necessary*". Who knows how those poor fishermen hated him! Just offshore they are intercepted by the Austrian fleet, most of the bragozzi are directed by the fishermen themselves to the Austrian ships where the Garibaldians must surrender, but Garibaldi is determined not to give up; he obliges the fishermen to run aground on the beach, therefore they flee on foot through the valleys of Comacchio. An extraordinary stroke of luck makes them meet with a local patriot that helps them and accompanies them to avoid the troops that were chasing them, but Anita is exhausted, she can no longer walk and must be transported on a cart. The Austrians are coming and it is clear that they cannot pass unnoticed. They take refuge in a farm where Anita dies, or so it seems. Garibaldi must continue in his escape and Anita is buried, badly. A few days after the body was found, it was taken by the police that performs the autopsy and the report declares: death by strangulation.

Maybe she was not really dead and those who had to bury her strangled her before hastily entrusting her to the sand. Maybe it was the same Garibaldi who strangled her not to leave her alive in the hands of the enemy; in South America this was a normal practice. We are not given to know the truth; in any case thus ends, in the marshes of Comacchio, this Brazilian Creole: a life upset by the blond hero.

Now they are two, he and a certain Leggero, an adventurer from Sardinia who had followed him from Montevideo. He still wants to try to reach Venice but his guide refuses; they will be taken to Tuscany and from there, by sea, to Liguria. It takes about two months and it will be an amazing feat. Through an extensive network of known and trusted people they manage to escape the chasing Austrians, the Papal and the Tus-

---

[29] Alfonso Scirocco, *Garibaldi*, (Bari: Laterza, 2001) pag.172

can troops. Some of these people, who risk their lives for him, are patriots, but the majority are people who help them for that instinctive sense of solidarity that poor people have towards the persecuted. The most decisive is a priest: "*Father Giovanni Verità, since one pursued by the priests for the sake of Italy was passing through these lands, it was his business to protect him, to feed him, and to have him lead, or to take him himself to safety from persecution*". They are brought to the Gulf of Follonica where they are embarked on a sailboat and taken to Liguria, safely in the Kingdom of Sardinia. Upon arriving Garibaldi wrote to father Verità: "*the two bales of silk have reached salvation*".

Although he arrived to safety, he cannot be considered at peace. The Sardinian government was the only government in Italy that had not reneged on the constitution of 1848 but had prohibited from entering the kingdom to all the patriots who had participated to the Roman republic. They might irritate Austria and, even more so, France that had some resentment towards Garibaldi. Now he is not a parliamentarian anymore because there have been new elections, therefore he is arrested to protect him from the enthusiasm of his admirers. General Lamarmora who controls the city of Genoa asks for instructions to the government that answers: "*Send him to America if he is satisfied. He will be given a grant. If he is not satisfied keep him in jail*"[30]. Garibaldi accepts a subsidy for his family and the sum of 300 liras per month for him, with an advance of 1.200 liras. Lamarmora visits him and comments: "*Garibaldi is not a common man, his features, however crude, are very expressive. He speaks little and well, he has a lot of penetration; more and more I am persuaded that he joined the Republican Party to fight, and because his services had been rejected. Nor do I believe he is Republican in principle. It was a serious mistake not to use him. Occurring a new war, he is a man to be employed*"[31]. And so it will be.

He knows he must go away; he asks to see his mother and children and they let him go to Nice. He bids farewell to them: one son is in college at the expense of the Piedmont taxpayer, the other is at a cousin's and her daughter at some friends of them. Afterwards he starts traveling around the Mediterranean always a guest of wealthy admirers, they think of sending him to Uruguay where the Guerra Grande is still going on but

---

[30] Gilberto Oneto, *L'Iperitaliano* (Rimini: Il Cerchio, 2006), pag.66

[31] Alfonso Scirocco, *Garibaldi*, (Bari: Laterza, 2001), pag.185

in the end it was decided for North America. The decision to go to North America was an obvious choice because in Europe and South America nobody wanted him (again!). Some of his friends start a subscription to buy him a ship with which to return to do the sailor and they accompany him to New York where they think they can buy this ship. He arrives in New York in the summer of 1850.

He is 43 years old; he is a widower with three children under the care of the government of Piedmont and of certain friends. From a financial point of view he is not doing badly, a huge improvement compared to his years in South America. He is also so famous that he has no problems finding hospitality in the homes of wealthy admirers; wherever he goes he always finds people more than willing to keep him for long periods of time and, from now on, his admirers from around the world will fill him with gifts. The image of the poor emigrant, in poverty, compelled to humble jobs to survive is a patriotic nonsense. Without any doubt, he could have become if not a rich man, at least well off. But his lack of interest for the money and his chronic inability to manage it will put him sometimes in serious financial difficulties, but it is only because of him. He decided to resume his job as a sailor and to become a captain of merchant ships, a job he does well and can soften his thirst for the adventure, but it will not give him great gains because, as he has already told us: "*to trade, Rossetti and I were not good*".

We cannot at this point not to consider the mystery of his popularity. It is a matter that is difficult to understand because even this adventure of the Roman republic ends in disaster. It is true that he fought well, it is true that his flight from Rome was a masterpiece of guerrilla tactics, it is true that he managed to outwit the papal, the Austrian and the Tuscan troops. But the Roman Republic was destroyed and a large part of those who followed him paid with their lives because the losses among the Garibaldians are very high. Moreover, while in the first war of independence they started in 1.300 and at the end they took refuge in Switzerland in 30, when they joined the defense of Rome they were 1200 and eventually only two of them arrived safe in Liguria! In both cases, the enterprises in which he had launched himself ended in total failure and he had to take a disguise to save himself. What kind of hero is this?

Is it possible that the myth of Garibaldi was just made-up by a bour-geoisie drugged by Romanticism?

In New York, it is a triumph, the Daily Tribune welcomes him as: *"the man of world renown, the hero of Montevideo and the defender of Rome"* The Italian colony sets up a welcoming committee with Italian tricolor ribbons and more, but he refuses these cheers and prefers to play the part of the persecuted emigrant tormented by the nostalgia of his land. He is the guest of a few Italian admirers until they realize that the money collected to buy him a ship is not enough. He abandons this project and departs for a cruise of a couple of weeks in Central America, then starts making odd jobs for Meucci who had started a candle factory, and then ... he gets bored.

An Italian entrepreneur and merchant, passing through New York complains that they left *"to waste away a man who lent so many services and such honor acquired to the Italian name ... he who, the virtues ex-tolled on theaters, puts into practice, he is left to perish into oblivion, in misery; our shame!"*[32]. Hence he takes him to Lima, Peru, where he had some business. The Italian community receives Garibaldi with all the honors and he decides to take the exams for the certification, by the Pe-ruvian authorities, of captain of merchant ships.

In this period he manages to get himself into trouble. In Lima, there was a sizeable French community and, after the affair of the Roman Re-public, there was a bit of animosity between the two communities. One day a Frenchman publishes a letter on the *Correo de Lima* where he de-clares that the Garibaldians were *"junk heroes"*. Garibaldi goes to his home and takes on him with a stick. More French rush in, then other Ital-ians and a fight breaks out. The police intervenes but is rejected; eventu-ally the cavalry must intervene to separate the two communities. The thing ends up in court but, thanks to the intervention of their respective consuls, the affair deflates without any judicial aftermath and Garibaldi can take his good Peruvian license. He gets it in a few days thanks to the help of a Freemason and it is made out to: *"Don Jose Garibaldi, natural de Gènova y ciudadano peruano"*.

With this he can leave for China with a cargo of guano in the service of some Italian ship owners who had done good business in Peru. From

---

[32] Alfonso Scirocco, *Garibaldi*, (Bari: Laterza, 2001) pag. 192

China he returns to Peru with a cargo of "coolies". On arrival the owner wrote to a friend that Garibaldi: "*always brought me the same number of Chinese he took on board and all fat and healthy; because he treated them like men and not like animals*"[33]. The guano trade was very profitable but there was not enough manpower to extract it from the islands of guano therefore the ships that carried it to China, returned with a cargo of Chinese coolies that were a kind of "disposable" manpower because the working conditions were so brutal that they did not survive for long, and therefore for each load of guano that went to China another load of coolies from China was needed. The selection of those unfortunates started along the journey because the captains of the ships made no bones of profiting on the food for their "cargo" and many died during the journey. The fact that Garibaldi delivered his cargo in good health was definitely an exceptional fact that deserved to be mentioned in a letter. Why these Chinese offered themselves for this work? Because in China they had reached the last level of despair and in Peru they had a few remote chances of surviving that job and start a new life. It has been noted that in his *Memorie* Garibaldi carefully specifies all loads he transported during his work as a captain, but he does not mention the load carried on this trip. Evidently he was ashamed to have participated in a trade that was considered uncivilized by the progressive public opinion.

For the same ship owner, he carries a cargo of copper to Boston, from Boston goes to New York to the agent of the ship owner and presents the bill of what was due to him, but there are problems and he is not paid, the deal will be closed after years of negotiations. Offended, he leaves that owner and on behalf of another Italian owner carries a cargo to London, then goes to Newcastle to pick up a load of coal destined to Genoa. His arrival at Newcastle becomes known and a subscription is launched to raise money to give "*to the glorious defender of the Roman republic*" a sword, a telescope and a diploma of honor. In this case it is important to note that 1,047 workers took part in this subscription. As we already know, the country people hated him, not so the industrial proletariat; for them he was a hero. Why is that?

The European proletariat was starting to convert to socialism and therefore it felt an affinity towards those who were fighting for "*the freedom of the oppressed peoples*". The Italian peasants were not social-

---

[33] Angela Pellicciari, *L'altro Risorgimento*, (Ares), pag.229

ist, they did not consider themselves oppressed if not by poverty and, in any case, they had no intention to be freed by Garibaldi. The admirers of Garibaldi were growing and expanding to other social classes outside of the wealthy burghers and the liberal aristocrats. A huge step forward towards his beatification.

In May 1854 he arrives in Genoa. There he was again, in Italy! In those days something was moving in Italy. Vittorio Emanuele II is the new king and Cavour has taken over the reins of the kingdom of Sardinia; he has great ambitions and Garibaldi will have his part because Cavour senses that Garibaldi could give up his republicanism and break away from Mazzini. He lets him know that if he does not cause trouble he can remain in the Kingdom.

Now a series of years begins that we would call happy, but for him these will be gray years, years of preparation for the next war of which he cannot do without. He will remain calm because Mazzini irritates him again with his absurd conspiracies and with his clumsy adventures. A controversy breaks out and Garibaldi writes a letter to the newspapers with which he breaks away from Mazzini: "*Since my arrival in Italy, twice already, I hear my name mingled with revolutionary movements, that I do not approve of, I think it is my duty to manifest it, and prevent our youth, always ready to face the dangers for the redemption of the country, not to let itself be so easily carried away by false insinuations of men, deceived or deceivers, that by pushing it to untimely attempts, ruin, or at least discredit, our cause*".[34] Cavour is happy.

In these years he buys half of the island of Caprera and travels to England where he attends the beautiful world of the rich aristocracy, always courted by the ladies of the high society. He gets engaged with one of them. They buy him a ship to lead an expedition that should free a few patriots imprisoned by the Bourbon in the island of Ponza but, due to his sheer luck, the ship sinks and he has to give up this expedition. If he had done it he would have wrecked the ambitious projects of Cavour who would have expelled him again from the kingdom and excluded him from his projects. His girlfriend does not get discouraged and buys him another ship, this time he decides to have fun and not to cause trouble, but the ship catches fire and sinks. So ends his career as a sailor; he

---

[34] Alfonso Scirocco, *Garibaldi*, (Bari: Laterza, 2001), pag.205

will no longer be a sea captain again and henceforth he will employ his leisure time to make wars and to cultivate Caprera. The engagement does not work because Garibaldi is too "rustic" to fit into the life of the high-society. He gets engaged with the daughter of a German banker, Speranza von Schwartz. She is rich, elegant and beautiful but has already lost a husband to suicide and another to divorce. Also this engagement does not work, but he remains a good friend with both of them and they will always do their best to help him.

While he was busy in these engagements, he asks for a servant to be sent to him from Nice. They send him an 18 year old girl, ugly and illiterate but ... no way, shortly after she is pregnant. A girl will come to life while he is busy in the next war, she is called Anita. Speranza von Schwartz takes the girl with her to try to give her an education that in Caprera she cannot have; his first girlfriend had already taken his son, Ricciotti, to England and put him into a good college. These are good friends indeed! He was bombarded by letters of fans, male and female, mostly wealthy and powerful English ladies. The cream of the England that mattered, was raving for him: *"We do not exaggerate if we say that the cause of the Italian Risorgimento became popular in England especially thanks to the glamorous popularity of Garibaldi, who gained thereby to his country a point not at all official yet of great political importance ... In their eyes he was the romantic successful hero, who treated women as if they were already emancipated and with a gallantry not at all Victorian"*[35].

This sounds as a great way of living to us, but this period of abstinence from war is a torture for him. He wrote to a friend he felt disgusted "*at the likely idea of not being able to handle an iron or a shotgun for the cause of Italy*". Since he decided to be a farmer he wants to do it with diligence and starts writing the Agricultural Notebooks where he keeps accounts of his farm and logs all the experiences that he is making in this new work but still he cannot take himself off from his obsession with Italy and so we can find, in the midst of his accounts of vegetables and livestock, annotations like: *"We must build an Italy first of all. Italy is now composed of the following elements: Piedmont, Republicans, Murattists, Bourbon, Papists, Tuscans and other small elements, these elements are to attach themselves to the strongest or be destroyed; there is*

---

[35] Denis Mack Smith, *Garibaldi,* (Milano: Laterza, 1956) pag.60

no middle ground! The strongest of these Italian elements, I think, is Piedmont, and I suggest joining it. The power, that should lead Italy in the difficult emancipation from foreign rule, must be strictly dictatorial"[36]. He asks Cavour that the king be declared dictator and that he takes the supreme command of the army and the country because, according to him: "*The national will has already chosen the king as our supreme leader*"[37]. Evidently he thought that <u>he</u> was the nation! But Cavour has different ideas.

Garibaldi participates in Genoa to the elections of '57 but is defeated by a conservative; then he is appointed vice president of the National Society, a society that aims to unite all patriots who, beyond their ideological convictions, are loyal to the Italian cause and to the Savoy monarchy. Meanwhile the pieces of the mosaic that Cavour was building were coming in place. He had sent his cousin, the Countess of Castiglione, to Paris to prostitute herself to the Emperor Napoleon III to gain him to the Italian cause, "*the idiot*" takes the bait and also this piece falls into place; now he only has to wait for Austria to attack Piedmont. To make this happen, the king declared in Parliament that he was not insensitive "*to the cry of pain that from many parts of Italy rises to us*" and Garibaldi was appointed major general of a corps of volunteers, the Hunters of the Alps. The enthusiasm of the patriots is sky high and thousands of Lombard volunteers rush to Piedmont to enlist: "*after a few days of my stay in Turin, where I had to serve as a decoy for the Italian volunteers, I perceived right away with whom I was dealing, and what they wanted from me. I was grieving; but what could I do. ... Garibaldi was to peep, to appear, and not appear. The volunteers should know that he was in Turin to gather them, but at the same time, Garibaldi was asked to hide and do not give shade to diplomacy. What a condition!*". In the plans of Cavour Garibaldi was used to attract to Piedmont the volunteers to enlist them in the army and, simultaneously, to provoke the reaction of Austria. Afterwards Garibaldi would be given the scraps of the volunteers, because, as a fighting force, he would not have been of much use. This was also due to the deep resentment that the army of Piedmont had against Garibaldi and his "disciples". In fact: "*a committee of enlistment, established in Turin, chose the stronger and better shaped youth, age 18*

---

[36] Gilberto Oneto, *L'Iperitaliano* (Rimini: Il Cerchio, 2006), pag.78

[37] Denis Mack Smith, *Garibaldi,* (Milano: Laterza, 1956) pag.70

to 26, for the troops of the line. The too young, the too old, or the defective, to the volunteer corps". This will not discourage him: *"Whatever, we were launched to the liberation of our Italy! Dream of a lifetime! ... I, and my young companions, yearned for the time of the battle, as the lover to join the one he idolizes"*.

A few months earlier, he had requested that it be composed a hymn for his volunteers, it will be the *Hymn of Garibaldi*:

"The tombs are opened / the dead arise / our martyrs are all resurrected".

Here we must note that the resurrection of the dead is a fundamental element of the Christian doctrine. The Italian nationalism takes possession of Christian archetypes and assumes features of religious mysticism so extreme as to overcome any other European nationalism in terms of bigotry and obtuseness. This is necessary because, given the Church's opposition to the liberal ideas and to the Risorgimento, they must produce a mysticism strong enough to overcome, in the hearts and minds of the people, the rule so far unchallenged of the Church.

This is why the myth of Garibaldi is crucial; it's because: *"the reputation and the éclat of Garibaldi were an essential ingredient in conquering many ordinary people to the national cause that would otherwise seemed remote and without benefits, if they could have understood it at all. The formation of Italy proved a victory of the intellectuals, the liberal, the middle class ... **There is no doubt that the prestige of Garibaldi among ordinary people helped to hide what was really happening until it was too late to oppose it"*[38].

In these few words lies the basic flaw of the Risorgimento and of the country that will rise from it. A few years after these events the inhabitants of the peninsula will find themselves to be citizens of a state that the majority of them had not asked for and did not want. But by then it will be too late to go back.

This is why Garibaldi is the most popular of the Founding Fathers.

This is why many Italians hate him.

In April 1859 Austria takes the bait and attacks. It's war, alleluia!

---

[38] Denis Mack Smith, *Garibaldi,* (Milano: Laterza, 1956) pag.68

The forces involved are 120,000 French and 60,000 Piedmontese against 170,000 Austrians, while Garibaldi has 3,200 volunteers; an irrelevant force. "*The volunteers were the usual mixture of idealists and charlatans, chivalrous enthusiasts who fought side by side with social outcasts. Many were students; a few were rather looking for excitement, adventure, heroism; the vast majority now truly deserved the name of Garibaldians, the followers of a new and growing cult*"[39].

The left wing of the Allied front is assigned to Garibaldi's Hunters of the Alps, so he will operate in the same area where he operated 10 years earlier, an area that he knows well. He enters Lombardy and issues a proclamation: "*He who is capable of holding a weapon and does not take one is a traitor ... Italy, with her children united together and purged from foreign domination shall reassume the place that the Providence assigned her between the Nations*"[40]. Now, even the Divine Providence is taking an interest to the Italian affairs. The Italians too will win their place in the sun: God wants it! His Hunters fight well, sometimes they win sometimes they lose, in any case nothing decisive or relevant for the outcome of the war. The battle of Solferino will decide its fate. The French came out winners but at a price so high that Napoleon III had a change of heart. Perhaps he realized that he had launched into a war not useful to France just because of his vanity, tickled by the favors of a courtesan. He meets with Emperor Franz Joseph and they conclude an armistice. The Veneto remains to Austria and Emilia, Romagna and Tuscany must return to the old sovereigns.

This is an exceptional feat in the career of Garibaldi: for the first time in his life he took part in a victorious war. Although his contribution was negligible, he is a winner at last! As during the previous war, even during this war Garibaldi must recognize that the people do not side with the Patriots: "*... then, the glorious battles have obviously little interest for those who are indifferent; and the people of the country, at least until now, has always been indifferent to the Italian struggle, when it was not our enemy*".

On the other hand, if the defeats he suffered before have made him popular in the world, now that he has won he becomes a god. The journalists of the world's top papers came to Italy to report on this war, even

---

[39] Denis Mack Smith, *Garibaldi,* (Milano: Laterza, 1956) pag.71
[40] Denis Mack Smith, *Garibaldi,* (Milano: Laterza, 1956) pag.74

from Russia, and Garibaldi is the most fascinating character on stage. Now he is a legend all over the world.

During the war the Patriots have seized power in the Emilia Romagna region and in Tuscany driving out their sovereigns and have set up a Military League to resist the return of those sovereigns; they call Garibaldi who accepts and goes to Bologna. In late July, he had dismissed his troops and had left the active service of general in the Sardinian army to have his hands free. In Bologna he realizes that he has been put in the employ of General Fanti and refuses. Being in Bologna he takes the opportunity to make a detour to Comacchio where he collects the bones of Anita and gets her death certificate that allows him to remarry.

In those days he was contemplating marriage. The servant had just given him a daughter, that he called Anita, and he was thinking that he could have married her and had also asked Speranza von Schwartz, for the umpteenth time, to marry him. She had come to Comacchio along with his son Menotti and a few friends from Nice with his son Ricciotti, that lived in their house, to be all together to the funeral mass that he has asked to celebrate in memory of Anita.[41] Speranza declines the offer but he is in epistolary correspondence with another lover, the Countess Giuseppina Raimondi (in Bologna he has had an affair with a thirty years old widow, Paolina Pepoli, but without consequences). He had met Raimondi three months before, during the war, while he was fighting near Como; she was helping the local patriots and brings him a message. It is love at first sight (again!). She is the daughter of a small noble man from Fino, she is 18 years old while he is 53. The next day he goes as a guest in the house of her father who is a patriot with political ambitions. For four days he dedicates to her with an intense courtship but then he must leave to return to his troops that were fighting somehow without their commander. They remain in contact by letter.

In late November she writes him and he rushes to her home in Fino. *"On the night of the 3rd she, hesitant until then, enters the bedroom of her sweetheart. It's done! A bruised knee of the general delays the marriage that is celebrated on January 24, 1860, in the chapel of the mansion with Teresita as a maid of honor"*[42].

---

[41] This is very strange for an anticlerical like him, but the son of two devout Catholic parents cannot do without it.

[42] Alfonso Scirocco, *Garibaldi*, (Bari: Laterza, 2001), pag.229

It seems that, just out of the chapel, a messenger gave him a letter. He reads it, takes his wife apart and asks for an explanation. She confirmed the allegations: she was pregnant and had an affair with someone else. He jumps on horseback and they will never meet again. It will take him 20 years to obtain the annulment.

There is no mention of these personal matters in his *Memorie*.

In the 6 months after the war he travels continuously and not just for his personal matters, Bologna, Florence, Turin, Genoa, etc. because he wants to take advantage of the victory, to continue the conquest southward and to take definitive possession of Emilia Romagna, Tuscany, Marche and Umbria (in Rome there are still the French troops, and so it is impossible) through popular uprisings (**again!**), hoping to have the support of the government of Piedmont. This government is confused and torn by various currents; Cavour resigned but will return soon. Garibaldi presses like a madman but they tease him and kick him around the place.

"When Garibaldi met Vittorio Emanuele, the king had hinted that he could press forward on his own, as long as he would take responsibility and be ready to be disowned if he had got into trouble"[43]. The king was shamelessly exploiting Garibaldi because at first he warned the foreign diplomats against the Garibaldians who were trying to extend the revolution, and then he offered to put them under his control to block their revolution; obviously taking himself the territories occupied by them. Garibaldi knew that he was being exploited, but he had made Italy: *"the worship and religion of my whole life"*. *"In Florence it was not difficult to understand that I had to deal with the same kind of men when they started talking to me about ... miserable astute! Perhaps I should have renounced everything and go back to private life: but, as I said before, the country was threatened. And then? Was it my custom to ask anything, being it such a beautiful cause! So I accepted the command of the Tuscany division"*. Ricasoli, the dictator of the Grand Duchy, in any case did not dare to dismiss Garibaldi and *"he had good reason to fear that if the government challenged that idol of the crowds it would fall in twenty-four hours"*[44].

---

[43] Denis Mack Smith, *Garibaldi,* (Milano: Laterza, 1956) pag.79

[44] ibidem

He keeps dreaming insurrections: "*in central Italy, in the last months of '59, a hundred thousand young people would have followed me, and with them we would have surely turned in our favour the European diplomacy; or, with just the thirty thousand, then gathered in the Ducati and in Romagna, we could have decided in a fortnight the fate of southern Italy: that is to do, at last, what we did with the Mille a year later*".

In September, in Cremona, he launches a public subscription for the purchase of a million rifles! It is an absurd quantity; he signed for 5,000 lire but paid 1,000 only: he was short on money. Only a few thousands will be purchased and they will be put safely in the depots of the army. In October he is at the head of the troops of the Lega on the border with Marche for an invasion of the Papal States, but the king stops him. In November false news arrive of an uprising in Marche and he orders the troops to attack. The commanders in chief of the Lega order the troops to ignore him!

In December "*it was decided to set up a Society which, under the name of The Armed Nation, would gather all the others. Since then everything went smoothly; and all the individuals belonging to the other societies, who presented themselves to me, adhered to the idea of the merger and they seemed happy*". He wanted to bring together in a single society, *The Armed Nation*, all patriotic initiatives that had arisen in several Italian cities, but at the time of the final decision they could not reach a consensus: "*It was my old idea, and I'm convinced more and more: that to make us Italians to come to an agreement you need beatings and nothing less*".

France did not want more wars and raises its voice: "*The Armed Nation came as a thunderbolt for that miserable diplomacy that wants Italy to be weak ... This should serve to my fellow citizens: they should be aware then, that to pass from being the rabbits, as we have been so far, to being the lions to scare our overbearing neighbors, we need The Armed Nation, that is, two million soldiers; and the priests, honestly occupied to the reclamation of the Pontine Marshes. The king sent for me, and told me that it was necessary to desist from any of these ideas I had designed. ... I do not know when it will be realized this dream of my life, that, with fewer priests, it would make Italy a power of the first order*". This is madness; no European power could afford two million soldiers.

The European diplomacy had applied strong pressures on the government and the king was obliged to stop his personal foreign policy done against his own government and hiding behind Garibaldi.

After his marriage he will have another serious problem when Cavour and Napoleon agree to give Nice and Savoy to France and Emilia Romagna and Tuscany to Piedmont. To give a semblance of legality they will rely on plebiscites. Garibaldi is furious, they are taking away his hometown and he would have become a stranger in his own country. He goes to the Parliament, where he had been elected, and lashes out violently against the government and against the same Parliament. He knew that plebiscites were a fraud because with threats, corruption and police actions you can manipulate any popular vote. Naturally these protests were directed only at the plebiscite of Nice; he had nothing to object to the plebiscites done in Italy. All these plebiscites will give a ridiculous majority for the projects of the two governments and the only thing he could do was to resign from Parliament and ask the Ambassador of the United States to do something to make Nice an independent state. We do not know what the ambassador replied.

The Mille

The enterprise of the Mille (The Thousands) is one of the most incredible and bizarre events of the contemporary history of Europe. It's all crossed by a surreal atmosphere where myth, fantasy and lies are intertwined with history making it difficult to discern reality. In fact the reality described by the reports drawn up by the patriots is so different from that described by the revisionist theories that have flourished in recent times, to embarrass an observer who would want to understand what really happened. The problem is that this whole expedition is amazing and even when the truth is found it is hard to believe it. Strangely, Garibaldi dedicates to this adventure only a tenth of the pages of his *Memorie*. The thing is very strange because this is the only adventure that has him as the main character and the only leader of the army of liberation. This is the adventure that consecrates him a giant in the contemporary history of Europe.

Let us begin by introducing the protagonists.

Garibaldi, is the spearhead of the organization that will lead him to conquer a kingdom, he is famous throughout the world and his name elicits such enthusiasm that thousands of volunteers, from the United States to Hungary to Finland, rush in just by hearing his name. He is one of the forces at play in the Italian arena, only he could gather thousands of volunteers, organize them and throw them against well-trained armies. He is in fact a military and political force you have to deal with. As usual, he has no consideration for the real aspirations of the people; before leaving he told the US ambassador that *"sometimes freedom should be forced on the people for their future well being"*[45]. And this is what he will do.

Vittorio Emanuele II, king of Sardinia, has a good relationshipp with Garibaldi and a very bad one with his Prime Minister, Cavour. He has an insatiable appetite and little regard for the diplomatic niceties. He is determined to push Garibaldi ahead, into the fray, and then to disown him if things had gone wrong. He said that if he had been hanged by the Ne-

---

[45] Denis Mack Smith, *Garibaldi*, (Milano: Laterza,1956) pag. 87

apolitans he would have been very sorry and then would have made him a monument.

Cavour, is the Prime Minister, ambitious, smart and corrupt; thus he is described by the US ambassador: "*One of those temperaments tyrannical and stubborn that nourish a deep contempt for every law that is not their will ... totally unscrupulous in words and deeds ... loves money and while he was taking care of the affairs of his nation he has built a huge private fortune*". Cavour is afraid to go up against the European diplomacy because he knows that the king is making a foreign policy of his own. He is not quite sure that Garibaldi gave up his republican dreams and fears the intervention of France that could jeopardize all that had been conquered so far. He, in any case, has collected two million francs gold for the enterprise and has entrusted them to the National Society. He also sent admiral Persano with two frigates to Sicily with the task of "helping" the expedition. But how could they do it since they were not at war with the Kingdom? In fact they will not be used for military operations, but "diplomatic". They had to get in touch with the Bourbon officers, especially from the navy, to explain that the nascent kingdom of Italy would guarantee them a "post" with the same rank and salary. Admiral Persano was also authorized to "encourage" the undecided with more offers; just for that Cavour had given him a fund of 16 million Euro.[46] The Kingdom of Sardinia will spend for the enterprise an amount between 20 and 30 million Euro.

The Freemasons, they hate the Bourbons because they are the personification of a Catholic-reactionary ideology. The lodge of Genoa, *Ligurian Triumph*, had already funded an expedition by Mazzini, parallel to that of Garibaldi under the command of Rosolino Pilo, that will land in Sicily a month before Garibaldi. The Scottish lodges in England, Canada and the United States have collected, together with the British government, 3 million French francs which were changed in one million Turkish plates (about 15 million Euros) because they are the currency currently accepted in the ports of the Mediterranean. All this money cannot be collected in a few days, evidently it had been decided long before that the expedition would have been done with or without Garibaldi. We do not know how this money has been spent; the revisionists say that Gari-

---

[46] Roberto Martucci, *L'invenzione dell'Italia unita*, (Milano, Sansoni, 1999) pag. 191

baldi used them to bribe the Bourbons and the patriots claim that it is false.

The Mediterranean Fleet, is under the command of admiral Mundy and will follow step by step Garibaldi up to Naples. He has been ordered to "visit" the Sicilian ports to confuse the Bourbon navy. From Marsala to Naples it will always be present to give its help to the conquest.

The British government with Lord Russel, the foreign minister, gives Garibaldi the diplomatic support that is essential to protect the enterprise from "foreign interferences". We cannot understand why England was so determined to take out the Bourbons. It seems clear that she had no interest in giving birth to a united Italy that would have become a Mediterranean power which later she would have to face. England had every interest in keeping the Kingdom of the Two Sicilies independent, a country weak and easily influenced. It is true that the two countries were in sharp contrast for the exploitation of the Sicilian sulfur mines, a strategic product for the production of gunpowder, but in fact the Perfidious Albion had managed to impose her will and a united Italy would have been less malleable. We know that Freemasonry had a massive presence in the British parliament and government. Is it possible that the British Empire acted against its interests just pushed by the ideological hatred of the Masonry? To give you an idea of how deep this hatred was consider that the prime minister Gladstone wrote, after an alleged visit to the Neapolitan prisons, that: "*the Bourbon government is ... the denial of God on earth, the subversion of every moral and social ideal erected into a system of government*" but he had never set foot in a prison in Naples. We should also point out that his family had become rich with the slave trade.

The Americans, with their ships, *Iroquois, Washington, Oregon, Franklin, Charles and Jane Bahl* shuttle between Genoa and Sicily to supply Garibaldi and they prevent the Bourbon fleet to stop them simply by waving the American flag. Colonel Colt gives Garibaldi 100 of his newest and most famous revolvers before his departure. The city of New York contributes with weapons, supplies and money for about $100.000. Garibaldi crosses the Strait on the *Franklin* and when he leaves Naples he embarks on the *Washington*.

Is it possible that this adventure was produced by the Romanticism of the Anglo-Saxon public opinion?

We do not know if there was and who was the great puppeteer who coordinated all these protagonists. Is it possible that all of them were put together driven by the hidden hand of the Masonry? It's impossible not to notice that most of the actors of this drama are Freemasons.

Against this grouping, more or less spontaneous, there is the Kingdom of the Two Sicilies.

It is the oldest state entity of Europe, has 9 million people who are a bit more than a third of the entire peninsula. Has had a disastrous population increase that resulted in serious social tensions but, for unknown reasons, it did not feed a stream of emigration to the Americas as happened to all other European countries. Its cities burst and all foreign travelers cannot fail to note that the misery and grime of its cities put them in a different category from the other Italian cities. The Kingdom is considered by the progressive public opinion a backward and uncivilized country with a literacy rate the lowest in Europe, but a study of 1832 gives a per capita income to the south a little over that of the Ducati in Emilia and lower than the Kingdom of Sardinia of just 28 %.[47] The taxes are the lowest of the peninsula and its finances are in order because it has never had imperialist ambitions. It keeps up with all the technological innovations according to its financial possibilities that, in a not rich country it is the right thing to do. In the industrial, commercial, technological and cultural fields it has conquered almost all records between the countries of the peninsula. Its merchant fleet is the fourth in the world. To its misfortune its entire culture, both popular and aristocratic, is absolutely undemocratic and illiberal. The people are fiercely Catholic and genetically hostile to the Calvinist ethics.

It has 100,000 men in the army and the navy is the most powerful in the Mediterranean, but its armed forces are split. The soldiers, illiterate, are loyal to the king and to the Holy Roman Church, while the officers are primarily interested in their rank. Despite many notable exceptions, they have no intention of risking their lives and no patriotic pride to-

---

[47] Gilberto Oneto, *La strana unità* (Rimini: Il Cerchio, 2010), pag.168. From this study it may be noted that, if we exclude the Lombardo-Veneto, the per capita income of the South is in line with the Italian average. In fact, the per capita income of the Lombardo-Veneto is more than twice this average. Hence it was not true that the South was as poor as it is now believed, it was rather the Lombardo-Veneto to be among the richest regions of Europe.

wards the Kingdom. They are the Achilles heel of the Bourbon regime because the nascent Kingdom of Italy can offer them a much more secure and prestigious position. It was a common practice for the children of wealthy families to buy the rank of officer so **an "offer"** by the Sardinian government finds them interested. The story the Mille is the history of the betrayals of the upper echelons of the Neapolitan armed forces and ministers.

The real problem of the Kingdom is the king himself. Francis II became king just a few months before, he is 23 years old, he is an exquisite gentleman but he is pathologically inept and this, in an absolute monarchy, is a terminal illness. The job appropriate for him would have been to do the sexton in a small country parish. The queen Maria Sofia is the sister of Empress Sissi of Austria, she is 18 years old, is an energetic girl and courageous but not enough to dislodge her husband and take the reins of the Kingdom.

Thanks to a systematic slanderous propaganda, the Kingdom is completely isolated diplomatically. Even a casual observer would have noticed that no European power would have lifted a finger to defend the Bourbons. If there was a right time to get them off, that time was now!

We do not know by whom, how and when the project of the conquest of Sicily (and perhaps of the entire Kingdom) was conceived, we know that in February 1860 Vienna warns Naples that an expedition of Garibaldi against Sicily was in the works. At that moment Garibaldi is haunted by the question of Nice and hates Cavour and his government. In fact Cavour is planning to entrust the adventure to someone else who pulls back and therefore he must rely on Garibaldi which is still very hesitant and with reason. He remembers the two expeditions, tragically failed, of the Bandiera brothers and Pisacane. In both cases, the southern people had activated immediately to stamp out these raids and had helped, with enthusiasm, the Neapolitan army to exterminate the bandits.

Only the patriots, blinded by nationalism, did not know that the southern peoples were fanatically opposed to Jacobinism and related ideologies such as the Italian nationalism. It was clear that the southern peoples were loyal to their monarchy and to the Holy Roman Church.

The exception was western Sicily where the 'Sicilianism', the desire for a Sicilian statehood, more or less independent, had never subsided. This had nothing to do with the Italian patriotism but the systematic riots that broke out in the province gave the impression that there was a movement of people in favor of the new liberal and democratic ideas. Since he is fooled who wants to be fooled, the Patriots had always considered these uprisings as the expression of a common ideal.

As we have repeatedly seen, Garibaldi never stopped dreaming about patriotic revolts but this time he is afraid to get into a trap as happened to Pisacane and he wants to have some feedback that there is really a revolt in Sicily. In early April some riots erupt in Palermo (18 rioters) and surroundings (we do not know their consistency) that are immediately repressed. Crispi, a Sicilian, is in contact with the rebels from Genoa and tells Garibaldi that in Sicily the uprising is spreading. Garibaldi settles in Genoa and decides to go. An organizing committee is established and the enlistment of volunteers is called throughout the Kingdom of Sardinia. A flood of volunteers rushes to Genoa, but in late April a telegram arrives from Malta, encrypted, where they announce that the Sicilian revolt had been crushed. Despite the disappointment of his men, Garibaldi cancels the enterprise and asks for a ship to return to Caprera saying through the tears: "*It would be madness - he exclaimed, wiping a generous tear - Patience! Our time will come again. Italy must and will be*".[48] At this point Crispi says he made a mistake at deciphering the message and gives another reading where they are informed that the rebels have conquered Palermo. Garibaldi takes the bait, we're off! Thus begins the adventure, with a hoax.[49] It is needless to say that on their arrival they will not find any ongoing insurgency.

In early May they meet in the home of the notary Baldioli in Turin (they do not meet in the office because the thing must remain secret): Medici (representing Garibaldi), Rubattino (the owner of the shipping company), a lawyer and a general (representing the Sardinian government) for the sale of two steamers to Garibaldi (*Piemonte* and *Lombardo*), upon payment of 3-4 million Euro, the exclusive for the steam service to Sardinia and other benefits.

---

[48] Giuseppe Bandi, *Da Genova a Capua*, (BUR Milano 1960), pag.20

[49] Alfonso Scirocco, *Garibaldi*, (Bari: Laterza, 2001), pag.239. This episode is confirmed by Bandi.

A forerunner of fascism

Francesco Crispi was born in Sicily in 1818, he goes to Naples to practice as a lawyer but when the '48 bursts out he returns to Palermo to join the insurrection, he is elected to Parliament and becomes member of the interim government of Sicily. With the Bourbon restoration he flees to Turin where he participates in a republican conspiracy by Mazzini and must flee to Malta where he marries Rosalia Montmasson, an Italian patriot. Expelled he goes to Paris where he signs up in the Masons and frequents republican revolutionaries learning to produce bombs. Suspected of having participated to an attack against Napoleon he is expelled from France. Back to London, then Lisbon and in 1859 he secretly enters Sicily to prepare the revolt that should provoke the intervention of Piedmont. When he learns that Garibaldi is organizing the expedition he runs to Genoa and joins the expedition, one of its leaders, with his wife Rosalia that is the only woman among the Mille.

He stands out as a trusted man of Garibaldi that assigns him several posts in his government. In 1861 he is elected to the Parliament of the new Kingdom of Italy in the left but in the following years he turns from rabid Republican to faithful monarchist. In 1873 he impregnates a noble and rich girl whom he marries in 1878 hoping to keep it a secret but it becomes known and he is accused of bigamy. He gets away with it for a formal defect of his previous marriage; the poor Rosalia remains alone and in poverty. In 1887 he becomes Prime Minister and begins an ultra nationalist and imperialist policy approaching the German Chancellor Bismarck of whom he becomes a fanatical admirer and thus the revolutionary bomber becomes a pillar of European imperialism. He is obsessed with the prestige of Italy and under his leadership the country squanders its meager resources to build an army that might live up to his delusions of grandeur while the country is flooded by corruption, mafia and misery. By posing as the leader of a large and powerful country he ended up with the illusion that this was true, provoking a trade war with France to favor the nascent Italian industry. The result was a severe economic crisis that endangers his government for which he relies more and more on authoritarian methods. The situation is particularly desperate in his Sicily where the revolt of the Fasci Siciliani brakes out. He sends in the army and using the martial law crushes the uprising by dint of executions and deportations; the Parliament reacts and he suspends it with a royal decree declaring himself ready to rule without Parliament with the support of the king. Furthermore he dissolves the newborn socialist party. His government wobbles and given that patriotism is the last resort of the scoundrels, he launches Italy into a colonial enterprise without the necessary preparation and sends the army into the fray that is slaughtered at Adua in 1896.

Rightfully Mussolini will define him a "forerunner of fascism".

The *Lombardo* just returned from Naples where they regularly purchased on behalf of the Sardinian Ministry of War, several copies (a few
not to arouse suspicions) of the maps of Sicily and of the Kingdom.

As for the weapons Garibaldi cannot obtain the brand new rifles purchased for the project of a million rifles because the governor of Milan
refuses to deliver them not being the Kingdom of Sardinia officially at
war with the Bourbons, and Garibaldi must settle for a thousand old and
shabby rifles. The money is not lacking, various documents of credit are
changed into gold at the last minute and delivered to Garibaldi at the
time of embarkation, among them there is the million Turkish plates of
gold. The cashier is some Bertani; he remains in Genoa to reach the expedition a few days later with the volunteers that keep coming and could
not be boarded into the two steamers. At the end of the adventure he will
be a rich man. Thus Italy began and so it continued.

On the night of May 5th, the day after their purchase, Nino Bixio pretends to attack the two ships in the port of Genoa with forty Garibaldians
because he has to stage a representation that will convince the European
diplomacy that the whole expedition is done illegally against the will of
the Sardinian government. It's ridiculous because there is a crowd of
people who came to watch the show. The ships are brought in front of
the beach of Quarto to take the Garibaldians on board because you cannot use the port: what would the diplomats think? Garibaldi and his men
must make their way through a crowd of silent and moved people made
of onlookers, mothers and wives that are fearful for those heroes who go
to the conquest of a kingdom virtually unarmed.

In fact they do not have the ammunition that has been entrusted to
"smugglers" (always to give an impression of lawlessness) that should
reach the ships off for delivery, the ships await but the smugglers are not
seen. Garibaldi departs anyway; after all, what are the ammunition for?
That's not all, the ships do not even have enough coal to get to Sicily;
but after all, what is the coal for?

Now we stop to ask ourselves who were these Garibaldians, *"the followers of this new and growing cult"*?

According to the list provided by the Italian Ministry of War they are:
800 from Padania, 78 from Tuscany, 35 foreigners, 71 Sicilians, almost
all from the western part, and other Italians. Lawyers, doctors, pharma-

cists, landowners, artisans, merchants and several fugitives but no farmers nor laborers. Of these 80 will die of which 34 in Calatafimi. All of them will receive a pension in 1865.

To describe in detail this adventure we will use the witnesses written by three of them: Cesare Abba, Ippolito Nievo and Giuseppe Bandi. We will also take more contributions from Charles Stuart Forbes, a romantic English traveler, and Sir Rodney Mundy the English admiral of the Mediterranean fleet.

Cesare Abba is a young Piedmontese 22 years old, enrolled in the Academy of Fine Arts, he is the candid soul of the Garibaldians plagued by a romanticism that cannot but move. During the conquest of Palermo he enters a house and throws out of the window the furniture of a bedroom to make a barricade. In this room there is a young girl who strikes him and, in his diary, he fantasizes to marry her and take her to Piedmont where later they would remember their meeting: "*... she would blush bowing her face on my chest and I, kissing her hair, would bless the memory of that chaste and heroic encounter*". Unfortunately we have no way of knowing what the girl thought of this stranger who was destroying her bedroom. Sicily was for him: "*an island that burns in the sea*". When off Trapani they see the island: "*Sicily! Sicily! It seemed something fluffy down there in the blue of the sea and the sky, but it was the holy island*". His is a religious mission. His sensitive soul of an artist perceives that land with a deep sensuality: "*Under this sky of inebriating ardors; under the ancient shade of these buildings as old as the faith, ... in the middle of the voluptuous flowering of the gardens, ... the voluptuousness that enters through all the senses prostrates the spirit, and asking for God's mercy, the flesh triumphs*". At the end of this adventure his romanticism will be changed, changed a lot.

Giuseppe Bandi, a Tuscan 26 years old, is a patriot and has been in prison. He is a solid person and an enthusiast of the action. Garibaldi wants him as his orderly officer; he will be promoted on the field and ends the enterprise with the rank of major. Always involved in politics, he will die assassinated by an anarchist in 1894. When the volunteers are called he is a lieutenant in the Sardinian army and one day he is sitting in "*the most beautiful café in Alessandria, when the old Gusmaroli came to me saying - the general wants you; come! - ... and without allowing me to go home, he took me right away to the station, and put me on a second class coach*". Thus he joins Garibaldi risking a conviction for desertion.

Abba did not say anything to his parents and, while in Genoa waiting to leave, he meets a friend and gives him a letter for them to be delivered after his departure, then: "... *I ran into Mr. Senator that I knew as a boy*". The senator is stunned to find him among the Garibaldians: "*What? Could it be that the world has turned so much, to be found in such circumstances a young man, coming out from the bottom of an unknown valley, brought up by good friars, son of quiet people, adored by his mother! Then came the threats. He would write, he would ask for help to those from my town who were there; He would face me at the boarding, to hold me ... And I nothing. Last test, almost crying with his hands clasped together, he cried: but what the king of Naples has done to you who do not even know him and you go to make him war? Bandits! Yet one of his sons will come with us*".

While in Quarto, waiting for boarding, he hears some guys talking: "*They are Venetians, young, beautiful and of elegant ways.*
 - 'Do you know that Luzzatto's mother came to find him?'
- 'From Udine?'
- 'Or from Milan, I don't know. She run here and there, from Genoa to Foce, from Foce to Quarto, asking, begging, until she found him.'
- 'And he?'
- 'He pleaded her not to tell him to come back; because he would leave the same, but with the remorse of having disobeyed her.
- 'And his mom?'
- 'She left alone '".

For nothing in the world they would have given up that which they will remember their whole life as their Great Adventure.

Unlike Abba, Bandi is not romantic at all. When in Genoa, waiting to leave, he comes out from the house where he lived with Garibaldi with three friends of his to take a walk, along the way they meet two priests who are talking to each other laughing. The laughter of the priests irritates them and his friends collect from the ground a handful of dung and "... *they were upon the unfortunate and, holding them, they sealed at both the mouth with a powerful slap, which had neither the color nor the smell of the roses*". The priests flee spitting the dung and he is so amused that "*half dead from laughing, I had to cling to a bollard, not to fall into the ground*".

The Garibaldians of Bandi are very different from the Garibaldians of Abba, a lot!

Bandi tells us that two days after the departure, they are at Talamone to fetch the ammunition from an army depot. Garibaldi wears the uniform of a Sardinian general and his charm manages to convince the militaries responsible for the garrison to provide them. There they remain for two days, the Garibaldians come down to land and start harassing the women and stealing causing the reaction of the inhabitants; their officers fail to bring order even under the threat of the sabers and they must request the personal intervention of the general. All Garibaldians are confined in the ships.

After Talamone they go to Santo Stefano to load the coal from a storage of the Sardinian navy but this time Garibaldi is not there and the officer responsible for the depot does not want to oblige; Bixio jumps on him, beats him then they enter the depot and take the coal. It's the Garibaldians' style!

Thus they make route to Sicily, to the conquest of a kingdom of nine million inhabitants. Bandi is on the *Piemonte* with Garibaldi and Abba is on the *Lombardo* with Bixio.

In Palermo, the English community is informed of the departure of Garibaldi and organizes a party on the British ship *Argus* to celebrate the event. Hence the ship leaves towards Marsala.

The conquest of the kingdom

Abba lets us know that the sailing is quiet until off Trapani where they are spotted and chased by two Bourbon ships. They put all the sails to the wind. Then, when they are off Marsala: "*A small wood comes from the land. English flag. Bixio took a sheet, wrote something on it, had a loaf of bread cut and put the sheet in it. Then when the wood passed almost hugging us, he threw the bread that fell into the sea. Then he shouted doing the trumpet with his hands,- Tell Genoa that General Garibaldi landed at Marsala, today at one hour afternoon!- On the small wood was a rising of the hands, a beat of applause, a waving of handkerchiefs, hooray, hooray!*". We must assume that the organization was working well and that the decision to land in Marsala had been taken before leaving.

The port of Marsala was chosen for the landing because the city had for many years a substantial British colony for the production of the Marsala wine, very popular in England. The firms that produce and sell the wine are English and it is plausible that British warships are there to protect the subjects of her majesty. A British ship leaves the port and informs Garibaldi that there are no Bourbon ships in the port, just two British warships. They sail into the port while the bells of Marsala ring noon and the landing begins.

Abba notes that: "*On many houses flags are waving of other nations. Most are English. What does it mean?*". It means that they had been alerted of the arrival of Garibaldi and to protect their homes from the fight that would be unleashed in the city, the foreigners exhibited their flags. No one could have predicted that there would have been no fight. Abba is amazed: "*But we are certain to land, although the two ships are still chasing us. They gained a nice stretch*". In fact entering the port and start landing with two Bourbon warships at your heels is suicide; there was no time to land and then move away to safety. Bandi estimates they are four miles away. Evidently Garibaldi knows that someone will protect the landing; still his is a risky decision and thus begins a series of incredible events that will enter the Mille enterprise into the legend.

The port of Marsala was very large but it was half silted up and the big ships could not pull over to a small dock on the beach, it is therefore necessary to use the boats of the ships to carry all men and materials on the dock: the landing is necessarily very slow. To begin with, the *Lombardo* runs aground on a sandbank in the port and cannot approach the pier as does the *Piemonte*. The boats that ply between the ship and the pier must travel more space and the landing operations are still slower.

Bandi will stay alongside Garibaldi during the whole landing; this is how he relates it to us in his memoires.

The *Piemonte* just started the landing when the Bourbon warships arrive, now they are three, and "*... the two English ships were anchored at* *such a distance from the port and in such a position that they could not prevent the Bourbon cruise any maneuver, nor they gave to see they wanted to mingle in other people's affairs. ... The happy outcome of the landing at Marsala was due to a happy hitch, to the courage of our leader and to the inexplicable decision of the captains of the Neapolitan cruise"*. Bandi realizes that the city is quiet, there has been no rebellion and no one will help them: "*... I turned my eyes to the land, and not seeing any sign of revolution, or any indication of the presence of the famous insurgents, I realized immediately that if God and our hands did not help us, we were done"*. He is afraid of the Bourbon ships that are maneuvering to aim their guns: "*A Neapolitan steamer was very close to Lombardo. Looking through the telescope, I could see the gunners aiming the bow piece, and I saw the officers who looked at us as I was watching them"*. He begs Garibaldi to abandon ship but he replied: "*Let them do, even if they fire they cannot hit us"*. How can he be so sure? They are within easy reach and there is not a breath of wind, how can they miss the shot? The Bourbon ships instead of opening fire drop a boat who heads towards the British ships. When also the Lombardo is downloaded Garibaldi decides to land together with the poor Bandi who is terrified. As soon as the rowboat comes off the ship Garibaldi remembers something and orders to go back, he boards the *Piemonte*, enters the engine room and opens the taps of the scuttling. Then he returns on the rowboat and orders to go to the Lombardo that is very close to the Neapolitan corvette to repeat the same operation, and so <u>they parade on a rowboat in front of the Bourbon cannons</u>. The poor Bandi is amazed: "*We went to the Lombardo which was very close to the Neapolitan corvette, and I thought we were going right into the jaws of the wolf. And I was saying to myself - either this man believes he is bewitched or he wants to die before evening-"*. Garibaldi enters the Lombardo while Bandi is waiting for him on the boat, he returns soon after and finally they land! Now the Garibaldians, together with Garibaldi, are all on the beach, the Bourbon ships are deployed with their guns trained and ... in silence: *"we did not know what to think of their inexplicable silence"*. When the Garibaldians begin to move the Neapolitans begin the shelling but the grenades do not explode and the Garibaldians march towards the town ... singing! The bombing of the Neapolitans will last a long time and no Garibaldian will be hit, the sole victim, a dog. Who knows whom they were firing to?

This is Garibaldi's comment in his *Memorie*: "*The presence of the two British ships of war, influenced somewhat on the determination of the commanders of the enemy's vessels, naturally impatient to fire at us, and this gave us the time to complete our landing. The noble flag of Albion contributed, once again, to save the shedding of human blood; and I, the darling of these lords of the oceans, for the hundredth time I was their protégé*". But what do the British have to do with this?

The commander of the British ships is an old acquaintance of Garibaldi from Montevideo, where he designed the uniforms of the Italian Legion. The commander of the Bourbons is William Acton, born in Castellammare di Stabia from a family of British descent; his grandfather was a Scottish nobleman who had moved to Naples. While the Garibaldians landed the two commanders were discussing what to do and it seems that the English said to Acton that he would have been held responsible for the damage he had caused to the property of British citizens. It seems that these British pressure on Acton convinced him to keep his artillery in that "*inexplicable silence*" that had surprised Bandi.

So, as not to waste a few barrels of Marsala wine, the Mille expedition is not destroyed!

At this point we have to inform the reader that five months after these events, William Acton abandons the Bourbon, enters the Italian navy, takes the command of a warship and with this he participates, the following month, to the siege of Gaeta were the Bourbon king and queen had taken refuge for the last desperate resistance. At the command of this ship he bombards from the sea the king to whom he had sworn allegiance and it seems he did it diligently since many of his crew will be decorated. Thus Acton began a remarkable career, he became admiral, deputy, senator, minister of the navy and moreover he will enjoy the favors of the Countess of Castiglione who at that point was a mature lady but still a good bite.

Perhaps Garibaldi is wrong or he is not sincere in his *Memorie*, perhaps it was not the British flag which blocked the commander Acton. Perhaps these "pressures" of the English are just an excuse. One cannot but be impressed by his audacity when he parades in front of the cannons on a rowboat to go on the Lombardo to sink it, it does not make sense to sink a shelved ship. Evidently he knows that those guns will not shoot and his is just an incredible effrontery.

The Mille enter Marsala where they are greeted "*like dogs in the church*". Garibaldi convenes the city council that was made up of thirty councilors and manages to put together ten of them, the others had fled, but this is not a problem, they are enough for him. He obliges them to declare the end of the Bourbon rule and to appoint him dictator in the name of **Vittorio Emanuele** King of Italy. Later on he will write in his *Memorie* when narrating the meeting he had in Teano with King Vittorio that took place six months later: "*I deposited in the hands of Vittorio Emanuele, the dictatorship that had been conferred to me by the people, proclaiming him king of Italy*". So those 10 councilors of Marsala were acting in the name of all the people of the south, an extravagant way, to say the least, to consider a popular mandate.

Meanwhile Crispi appropriated all the money which was in the municipal coffers. It has been **argued that the** subsequent Italian administration had been guilty of looting the finances of the South, but this is not true. This looting started immediately with Garibaldi.

The most tragic thing is the *Proclamation of Marsala* where Garibaldi announced that some land will be allocated to the peasants who will fight for him. This is a dirty cheat. The lands mentioned in the proclamation are not the baronial lands that were usurped by the barons years before and which are the bulk of the arable land in Sicily. The other lands are already cultivated in common use by farmers or tenants, for a very modest rent, and may not be distributed to anyone. With this proclamation, irresponsible and criminal, Garibaldi unleashes the anger of the Sicilian laborers who, fifty years before, had suffered a monstrous injustice.

The next morning, before heading inland, Garibaldi sends Bandi to the English consul with some letters that must be sent to Malta and to recommend him a few Garibaldians who are sick and cannot walk. The consul assures Bandi that the letters will be sent immediately via one of the two ships that are in the harbor and that he will give to the sick a British passport that will keep them safe from any Bourbon retaliation. Then the consul saddles his horse and starts with the Garibaldians to escort them out of town where he greets them, moved.

So Garibaldi begins the conquest of the island that is garrisoned by 20,000 Bourbon soldiers, where no revolt is in the making. He is sure that at their first victory the people will rise up and, together, they will wipe out the Bourbons.

At this point we have to stop our story to examine the recent history of the island because otherwise it is impossible to understand what is going to happen and the impact it will have in the history of Italy.

Mafia

At the end of the XVIII century Sicily had 142 princes, 788 marquises and 1.500 between dukes and barons; it had more noblemen than any other European country. These nobles had the feudal lordship on 280 villages out of a total of 360.[50] In no other European region feudalism is still so rooted and widespread. With the necessary exceptions, the nobles are arrogant, squanderers, hostile to progress and absentees. They prefer to live in the city to dissipate the rents of their estates while the management of the fief is entrusted to their administrators that subdue the serfs with ferocious methods and have no concern to invest for the promotion of the cultivation of the lands.

The nobles have autonomist pretensions against Naples because they resent the opposition of the Bourbon kings, which was very weak anyhow, to their injustices and abuses against the people. According to the feudal code, much of the administration of justice is in their hands with an outcome that was considered intolerable in the Europe of the Enlightenment. It seems that slavery was still practiced. At the end of the XVIII century the Bourbons are conquered by the ideals of the Enlightenment and send to Sicily a decidedly progressive viceroy: the Marquis Caracciolo.

Caracciolo quickly realizes that Sicily was populated by "*oppressors and oppressed*" and almost all its ills could be traced back to the "*tyranny of the big landowners*". He knows that he must come to terms with the barons because "*two hundred people had swallowed a million and a*

---

[50] For the data and the quotations of this chapter: Denis Mack Smith, *Storia della Sicilia medievale e moderna*, (Editori Laterza, Bari 1973) Volumi II e III.

half". However, the main problem for Caracciolo was to overcome the resistance to change of the same Sicilian people that are incited against the "Neapolitans" that are considered invaders: "*So much the long servitude degrades the soul, that it does not resent the weight of its chains*". In any case he considers his duty to "*remove them from the claws of these wolves, because wolves are the barons of Sicily*". The problem is to force the barons to respect the rules of feudalism with its rights and duties. First of all the last word belongs to the king (i.e. the central power) because it was the king who gave them the investiture, the barons also have the duty to provide for the spiritual and material welfare of their servants who have been entrusted to them by God. Both the king and the bishops have the duty to intervene and recall the feudal lords in default. The serfs, both individually and in community, have many communal rights on the land that make it impossible to improve its productivity but provide a kind of protection from the arbitrariness of the feudal lords. First of all they cannot be dismissed. Feudalism is a lifeless and constrained society where change is impossible and its economy has a disastrous productivity. Since birth everyone already knows what will be his place in the society until death; they cannot progress but have a considerable degree of safety and stability in their lives. It is not a good life, but it is better than the barbaric anarchy of Europe before feudalism.

The problem is that the social, economic, cultural situation of Sicily could be defined as pre-feudal because anyone who has got some power is not willing to accept not even the rules of feudalism. It is a culture genetically predisposed to violence and abuse, where the law is just considered an obstacle to your will and your whim. All those who ruled Sicily have always clashed against the anarchist tendencies of the barons and the people, but the seat of their central power has always been distant. Madrid, Paris, Turin, and Naples they all undertook to enforce the law onto the barons but they always lost because the people, who they were trying to help, considered them as foreign invaders in their island and were always reluctant to collaborate.

The reforms of Caracciolo have a measure of success and the barons realize that if they want to keep their dominance they must obtain some autonomy from Naples. The Sicilian autonomism has always been the tool of the powerful Sicilians to abuse the Sicilian people at their leisure.

All these enlightened initiatives are cut short by the French Revolution that dismantles the feudal structure of society and gives birth to a new society based on private property, equality in front of the law, free enterprise and labor relations based on the consent of the parties and not on the feudal rights and duties. It was a very painful delivery. In America, this society had already developed during the colonial period and materialized, politically, thirty years before with the American Revolution. In Europe, the dismantling of feudalism caused problems more or less dramatic depending on the social and economic situation of each country. In Italy, north of Rome, feudalism had already been dismantled centuries before by the civilization of the municipalities and the private property, particularly of the land, was not new but in the Kingdom of the Two Sicilies everything must be done.

It is essential to highlight that the romantic patriots who ran to Sicily to "liberate" the Sicilians from the Bourbons, they had seen feudalism only in the historic novels, very popular in the literature of romanticism.

At first the barons are hostile to change but they did not take long to figure out that it was convenient to them. If they become owners of the land they have the full availability of it, they no longer have any obligation towards the feudal king but especially towards the serfs. For the peasant people it is a disaster. They have been used for centuries to take for granted the right to make firewood in the forest, but if the property of the woods goes to the baron, they may be obligated to pay; how? It was obvious that they could get water to a source, but if the source becomes the property of the baron they may be obligated to pay; how? Many villages have common land where the people have the right to pasture or to grow something for themselves, but if these lands are to be distributed, will there be land for all? If it is not enough, those who remain without, what can they do?

The dismantling of feudalism is an organizational nightmare that will be a boon for the lawyers and a tragedy for the people. Many of them will lose the world where they had lived for centuries and will face the ordeal of going through the conditions of serf, farm laborer and proletarian, in the desperate attempt to overcome poverty and hunger. Once lost the rigid and oppressive security of the feudal society the single individual is completely abandoned. In northern Europe a mass of dispossessed flees to the cities where they will provide the human fuel to the amazing progress that will give life to our industrial civilization. The last stage, the proletariat, is the end of the journey and it is a dead end. In this cul de sac an ideology ferments and comes to life that (of course) will call for the abolition of private property: Socialism.

In northern Europe this evolution is possible because a systematic reduction in the birth rate begins immediately and also because those societies promote the entrepreneurial initiatives that in few years will create the jobs for the mass of laborers who invade the cities. In the next century these free societies produce a middle class that will eventually absorb the proletariat; but, at that time, no one could have imagined it.

In Sicily this story will take quite a different course.

It is 1812 and King Ferdinand I had to flee to Sicily because the French have conquered the South of Italy and Sicily is protected by the British fleet and army. The barons have de facto control of the island and they "host" the king provided that he renounces his reformist initiatives. The British, at the vanguard of progress, are pressing to abolish feudalism and also the barons agree. Ferdinand knows that he is delivering the sheep to the wolves but "progress" is unstoppable and his power is very limited. The barons become owners of huge estates nipping in the bud any attempt to have something given to the serfs. Entire communities are suddenly dispossessed of their livelihoods and are at the mercy of the masters that now, in the new legal system, can also dismiss them. They are no longer serfs; they are finally free ... to starve!

In the following years, back in Naples, the Bourbon king tries to get some kind of compensation to the peasants for the common rights they have lost but the courts are, in any case, in the hands of the rich and the poor will not receive anything. The landowners even manage to push through the principle that it is up to the peasants the burden of proof; after the damage also the insult. Various land reforms were attempted but were all emptied by the passive and sometimes active resistance of all the Sicilians. The burden of taxation fell disproportionately on the poor because the only tax that could be collected was the tax on flour. The Bourbon king therefore begins a census of the lands to tax the estates, but with threats and corruption the officers could be blocked; it took fifty years to complete it. Now all of Sicily hates the Bourbons and all social classes hate each other.

Just one example: "... *there was the Prince of Villafranca that, when the town of Salaparuta in 1829 accused him of illegal appropriation of the communal forests, burned the forest as a challenge; and although the superintendent condemned him, it took seventy-four years of lawsuits before they could take away from him the land he had ruined*".

It is a strange situation. You must consider that four years after the publication of the research on smallpox by Jenner, Ferdinand I sent an English physician to Sicily to give a demonstration of the effectiveness of the vaccination and, since the Sicilian doctors boycotted him, he had himself shot. Before dying he cut his pigtail to break from a reactionary past. Unfortunately it was all useless! "By *gathering around themselves their employees and their bravos, by taking advantage of the local patriotism, the diffused xenophobia and the widespread aversion to every law and rule, the landowners convinced the people that it was not them, but the hated Bourbons, who prevented any progress and kept Sicily poor*".

Here we should note that the Bourbons were more successful in the continental South where a socio-cultural reality less anarchic than in Sicily, allowed them to achieve significant successes with "*the ordinance which was called the administrative reintegration of the usurped domains to the public good, that is, to the rightful owner of the public good: the people. ... Very great is the amount of the usurped domains that were reintegrated and distributed to the destitute peasants. In only four years, from 1850 to 1854, more than 108,950 bushels of usurped land were restored into communal domains and distributed to the needy farmers*"[51]. This success of the Bourbon land reforms in the South had as a consequence that the landlord class, noblemen, gentry, liberals, etc., became relentlessly hostile to the Bourbons and, on the other hand, consolidated the attachment of the masses to the monarchy.

With an obstinacy that one cannot but admire, Ferdinando II still tries to make the land reforms work in Sicily, but now there is a new enemy that will break down definitively any attempt: the Italian Risorgimento. "*The government tried to continue to implement its policy of reform until the revolution of 1848 put an end to a period of more or less enlightened despotism. This phase of the vilified Bourbon administration constitut-*

---

[51] Carlo Alianello, *La conquista del Sud,* (Milano: Rusconi Editore, 1972), pag. 121

ed the last chance for almost a century in which a government tried to develop a serious and balanced program of agrarian reform".

When the '48 bursts out Sicily is in a state of semi-anarchy. The barons have lost the management of the feudal justice but this does not bother them because they had never loved justice. Since time immemorial they exert their power by means of bands of thugs who lord over the feud in defiance of any law. Now with these gangs they try to gain control, and then the ownership, of all the land on which they can get their hands, usurping the rights of the villages or clashing with their neighbors.

Also the serfs and the villages try to put together other gangs to oppose those of the barons. These gangs are headed by cunning and ruthless individuals that eventually free themselves from the dependence of the landowner or village and take in their hands the control of the gang. Now even the owners can be victims of their abuses. Naturally the landowners have a chance to defend themselves taking other teams of criminals, but for the villages or for the small landowners there is no escape. They must bow their heads and adapt themselves to the abuses.

These ringleaders are not interested in becoming owners of large estates; they understand that the ownership only makes sense if there is an impartial justice that enforces the relative rights. They know they can easily control the courts by intimidation or corruption, so they know that they have the real power. The property can be a weakness because it exposes the owner to extortions; much better to own nothing and control everything. A new kind of power comes to life; it is a hidden power that is exercised behind the scenes by means of corruption, intimidation and murder. These gangs are inspired to feudalism and to the Church. Those who enter the gang go through rituals and oaths. These are initiation rituals that establish a life subjection and a fidelity that only death can break. Of course it is a world where everybody betrays everybody and any oath is made to be broken; the only glue of these structures is the ruthless application of the death penalty. They consider themselves "men of honor" because they risk their lives every day; they would never stoop to work, their "honor" is to exploit the work of the servants who have what they deserve because they are cowards.

It is an ethics taken from the Europe of the barbarian kingdoms that in Sicily was grafted on the disastrous Arab-Byzantine culture by the invasion of the Normans. An ethic that in Sicily had never waned.

Our reader must consider that a thousand years ago this was the ethics that dominated the whole of Europe. The prevailing culture that had emerged during the Dark Ages, after the collapse of the Greek-Roman civilization, considered the depositories of power those authorities who had the power to give death to the body or to the soul. It was fear, or rather the fear of death and torture, the attribute that defined the authority in the hearts and minds of the people, the holder of the power to whom you owe obedience and respect. The rule of law with its culture of legality is still far away; it will take several centuries of evolution to achieve it.

A century later the Americans will call these structures, organized crime, a definition that is technically correct but too reductive. It is impossible to understand the phenomenon if you do not understand its ethical component.[52]

When the '48 bursts out the authority of the Bourbon kings collapses, a disaster from which it will never recover. The gangs jump out and march on Palermo; the Bourbon abandons the island that declares independence. It is an independence that the Sicilian separatists pay by accepting the gangs in the new order. *"Some gang leaders had already become heroes of popular ballads, had been appointed honorary colonels and, to appease their followers, special assignments had been conferred on them, even of public security, in which they had the widest possibility to use their familiarity with the underworld. Scordato and Di Miceli were authorized to execute people at their will"*.

These are the "patriots" that Garibaldi wanted to join before going to defend the Roman Republic.

A Sicilian parliament is established in Palermo where Crispi, La Masa and La Farina are appointed. This parliament declares Sicily independent and refuses any subordination to Naples; also refusing, at the same time, to participate in the unification of Italy: they want to be inde-

---

[52] If the reader thinks that our society has overcome this barbaric ethic, we invite him to watch *The Godfather*

pendent. Obviously it does not work, and when the following year the Bourbon army lands in Sicily the gangs abandon this newborn state and thus this short experience of Sicilian self-government is closed.

But Crispi, La Masa and La Farina have realized that to oust the Bourbons and secure some autonomy to the island they need the help of a foreign power. They flee from the island and Crispi and La Masa join the Garibaldians while La Farina associates himself with Cavour. Officially they are Italian patriots that fight to oust the Bourbons and secure some autonomy for Sicily, but they are in perfect bad faith because it is impossible to suppose that the nascent Kingdom of Italy has any intention to grant any autonomy. In 1848 they had to deal with the gangs and so they know whom to contact when the right time comes to raise the "Sicilian patriots".

<u>These are the Sicilian patriots that join Garibaldi in the Mille expedition.</u>

After 1848 the Bourbons are completely discouraged and even they adapt to compromises with the gangs and waive further attempts at reform. Their authority on the island has so weakened that the police chief accepts the "collaboration" of the gangs: "*Scordato, the illiterate peasant who was head of Bagheria, and Di Miceli of Monreale, were among the ringleaders now employed with the unusual task of tax collectors and coastguards, and they made themselves a fortune*". In addition, thousands of "gentlemen" had taken advantage of the power vacuum caused by the revolution and had arbitrarily "privatized" large tracts of common land of the villages usurping the rights of the inhabitants. These are the new rich who were able to seize upon the opportunity and had a gang on their payroll.

The Bourbons are facing the dilemma of whether to use the force to compel the ruling classes, barons, gentlemen and gangs, to return the land to the people or to find a compromise with them. The compromise with the usurpers would have led to an unstoppable lawlessness with the final loss of the island. The use of force would have required a systematic intervention of the army for a long period of time and with a result to say the least uncertain but definitely with a blood bath. The problem was that the Sicilians always refused the military service and therefore they had been exempted; the army was composed of Neapolitan troops only, provoking charges of being an invasion force. This army would have found itself fighting against everybody and involved in the wars between the gangs. In addition, a prolonged war would have surely attracted the intervention of jackals like Piedmont, Britain or France.

It is impossible to understand the defeatist attitude of Francesco II unless you consider the dramatic situation in which he was. Whatever he could have done, he would have caused a bloodbath and a great injustice and he is king by divine grace and has duties towards his people. The patriots do not have these qualms, for them the blood baths are the "Crucible of Nations" and must be addressed with pride. As for the injustices ... it is the fault of the Bourbons!

In the years before the fall, the Bourbons devote themselves to works of public utility such as seven hundred miles of electric telegraph, several submarine cables, the arrangement of a few ports or the construction of roads and, on top, they complete the census of the lands. Meanwhile the island increasingly eludes their control.

When Garibaldi lands at Marsala, Crispi and La Masa resume their contacts with the gangs that now participate to the "liberation" of the island and enter fully among the forces that have made Italy.

<u>Thus began the collusion between politics and organized crime in Sicily and as a consequence in Italy</u>.

Having joined the Kingdom of Italy, Sicily is in a completely new situation. The Italian government is much more centralized than that of Naples, the tax burden is at least doubled and no compromise is allowed with draft dodgers. The disappointment of losing what little autonomy they had from Naples alienates the population from any sense of loyalty towards the new country that was ruling them with the most reactionary and repressive government of Europe. The countryside is full of draft dodgers who go to swell the ranks of the gangs that begin to collect taxes from those who live in their territories ousting the authority of the state. *"When you consider Sicily as a whole, the number of murders was ten times greater than in Lombardy and Piedmont"*. It is a power that strengthens over the years on a river of blood.

Compared to the Bourbon kingdom the main novelty is that now there are elections to a national parliament and juries in the courts. For the gangs to manipulate the elections or the courts it is a breeze and they already have some pretty good credentials since they participated in the Mille expedition. Now, through the representatives of the people, they can get to Rome, the center of power. Something that under the Bourbons they could not even dream.

"In 1863 a comedy in dialect that described the life in the main prison of Palermo was a huge success: it was called 'The mafiusi of the Vicaria', and this title popularized a word from the slang of the underworld of a suburb of Palermo".

So this phenomenon has found its name: **Mafia.**

Through the elections the mafias can infiltrate all the institutions of the state and get a control of the territory that discourages any business initiative. As we have seen, in northern Europe the mass of laborers produced by the dismantling of feudalism found refuge in the cities working in the factories. In Sicily this is not possible; you cannot develop an industrial and service economy under the heel of the Mafia. The Sicilian businessmen who do not want to compromise will have to emigrate to Northern Italy or abroad.

The Italian governments carry on the policy of secularization of the state *"... dissolving some monasteries and confiscating church property. They will confiscate a tenth of the total area of Sicily ..."* thereby depriving the people of the only form of social assistance existing on the island and consolidating the alienation of the people from this new motherland. *"The worse opposition was the one elicited by the Church. From now on, the hostility towards Italy and the disregard for the law and order, received the ecclesiastical support; the same, sometimes, even the mafia itself"*. Now the control of the territory by the mafia empties and ridicules the power of the State; it is they who collect taxes and administer justice in their own way. Now the power of the Mafia has a certain "moral" consistency that, in a certain way, is accepted and recognized by the people with the blessing of the Holy Roman Church. It will take more than a century for the Church to express a clear and unequivocal condemnation of the Mafia.

In the countryside, thanks to the authority of the mafias, the landowners keep the laborers in a situation of complete subjugation that has no equal not even in the darkest Middle Ages. The only way out: death or America. In America, the mobsters too arrive who have lost in the struggle for power between the gangs. Here they find a society so open and law abiding that blows up this phenomenon to unimaginable levels. The Mafia penetrates American society and makes a further evolution. It discovers other areas to conquer: the unions. It discovers and learns to use another weapons of blackmail and extortion: the strikes. The rest, you know it, is the chronicle of our times.

From Marsala to Volturno

Upon leaving Marsala Garibaldi marches towards Salemi in the direction of Palermo. It looks more like a trip to the countryside than a military operation. For Abba Garibaldi is a God: "*And the General, sat at the foot of an olive tree, eats bread and cheese slicing them with his knife and talking friendly with those around him. I look at him and I have the sense of an ancient greatness*".

These are the first impressions of Abba on Sicily: "*Through a sleepy street, walking before some little houses, where poverty is awakening in the rooms on the ground floor, half open and disgusting, we reached the country at the opposite side. ... Here misery invades and hunger, and at each step you encounter the sad spectacle of begging. It seems that the prevailing spirit in these people is religion rotten by ignorance. In no part of Italy you would find a home as poor as that of a Sicilian*". When they arrive at Salemi: "*Great, populous, filthy, its streets resemble the sewers*".

The opinion of Bixio is even more violent; he wrote to his wife: "*What a country! You might call it a pigpen! This, in short, is a country that we should destroy or at least depopulate and send them to Africa to make them civilized*".

At Salemi Garibaldi assumes solemnly the dictatorship of Sicily in the name of Vittorio Emanuele, the decree is affixed on the streets while the criers read it aloud, then he goes on a balcony to harangue the crowd. Bandi informs us that the Garibaldians are puzzled and worried because they have not seen any riot and there is no ongoing insurgency. He accuses the Sicilian La Masa of having lied when, in Genoa, he had insisted that Sicily was on fire and they had to rush to help the rebels. La Masa replied: "*Wait before speaking; you will see in two or three days that I was not a liar ... The revolt was extinguished ... but you'll see that to turn it on again, a hundred times greater, a match is enough*". Then, at the order of Garibaldi, La Masa leaves toward the interior to recruit the gangs that he knows well. Later on, he will boast that he managed to recruit up to 6,000 "insurgents".

Abba notes the arrival of the first Sicilian insurgents: "*During the night bands of insurgents came, they are armed with shotguns, hunting rifles and strange spades. Many wear sheepskins over the other clothes, all seem resolute people, and they are taken with us*". The next day they keep coming: "*The squads came from all over, on horseback, on foot, in the hundreds, a heck. ... I saw the mountaineers armed to their teeth with some ugly faces, and some eyes that look like like mouths of guns. All these people are led by gentlemen whom they religiously obey*".

Bandi is greeted with cries of "*Long live La Talia*", Sicilian for: long live Italy. But he calls them "*those Bedouins*". You understand that neither he nor Abba are pleased to have these people in their midst. They do not have the faintest idea of whom these insurgents are, but they understand that they are people of ill repute and that they do not care at all for the unification of Italy; they are completely undisciplined and obey only their leaders.

Ippolito Nievo had been instructed by Garibaldi to keep the cash and the accounting of the expedition. In a letter to a cousin, Nievo writes: "*In Marsala squalor and fear; the revolution was put down everywhere, or, rather, had never existed: only some gang of half robbers, known here as squads, they beat, and still do, a few of the inland provinces with much indifference by the government and some kind of fear by the landowners. The next day near Salemi we began to gather some of these squads*"[53]. For Nievo Salemi: "*It is a real Saracen town, actually a dump ... We meet the first friars; we realize that we are in the Middle Ages*".

Here Nievo seems to have sensed something of the situation but he is mistaken when he says that the government (Bourbon) was indifferent; he has yet to see the squads in action. The Bourbon government knows,

---

[53] Ippolito Nievo, *Diario della spedizione dei Mille*, (Ugo Mursia Editore, Milano 2010) pag.58

from long experience, that the squads can unleash a monstrous ferocity which can lead even to cannibalism and they are terrified of it. It is fair to say that "*the revolution had never existed*" if you talk about a revolt of Italian patriots because there had never been a Italian patriotic revolt in Sicily and the government could not certainly be worried of it, but of social revolts there had been so many that he could have not imagined.

Abba is right when he says that "*these people are led by gentlemen whom they religiously obey*", the problem is that those criminals obey only their gentlemen who are the ringleaders and are murderous beasts. It is clear that our heroes do not have the slightest idea of what the situation is in Sicily.

We can assume that Garibaldi was at ease with these people; after all, he was in a situation very similar to that of the Rio Grande where he commanded criminal gangs in the service of landowners. However, he has an absolute need to show to the Anglo-Saxon public opinion that "the Sicilian people" are with him and are rising against the Bourbons. He orders his men to give some of their very few and very precious rifles to the "insurgents". The Garibaldians obey, grudgingly.

They leave Salemi and the next day they clash with the Bourbon army at Calatafimi. The Bourbons are commanded by General Landi who is 68 years old and is sick but they are almost twice as many and much better armed. Inexplicably Landi holds the majority of his troops in the town at three kilometers from the battlefield where the Bourbons are outnumbered: Garibaldi orders to attack relentlessly. Yet at some point it seems that the Garibaldians are going to be surrounded and overwhelmed. Bandi tells us: "*... Sirtori arrived just then and asked the general: 'General what shell we do?', Garibaldi looked around and called out in a trembling voice: 'Italians, here we must die'*" and continues to attack. Bandi realizes that, even if it looks like a suicide, this is the only tactic that you can adopt. He sees that the heights around the battlefield are full of Sicilians waiting to see who will be the loser to jump on him and take him everything. It is clear that a retreat would be the end. Therefore: "*It was necessary to make our way through the enemies, or be ready to die repeating the cry of the Bandiera brothers: He who dies for his country / he lived long indeed*". This is the spirit of the Garibaldians: the Cult of the Supreme Sacrifice. It is through this vocation to martyrdom that they win, in fact the Bourbons retreat and leave the field; they, if they have any cult, it is that of the Virgin Mary who does not want anyone to get killed.

According to Bandi the retreat of the Bourbons was due to the cowardice of their officers because if they had kept fighting they would have eventually won: evidently they fought well. The squads of the "Sicilian insurgents" have vanished or stayed away from the battle so now the Bourbons would have been more than twice as many if Landi had committed all of his troops. Instead he retires and accepts defeat.

According to the Bourbon historian De Sivo, general Landi was bribed with a bill of 14,000 ducats (which will prove to have been falsified) but the sons of the general, who make their careers in the Italian army, they will get a letter of denial from Garibaldi. We do not know if Landi was a corrupt or not; still he behaves as if he were. After nightfall he does not simply withdraw but he flees towards Palermo as if they were a routed army. Why to escape? With this battle, tiny, the fate of the expedition is decided, the whole world sees that Garibaldi wins and the Bourbons flee.

When Landi passes through Partinico on his way to Palermo, the people see that they are defeated and fleeing and attack them. It is a massacre. Three days later, Abba walks through Partinico and sees: *"Dead bodies of soldiers and villagers, horses and dogs dead and ripped open among them. Upon our arrival the bells were ringing, I do not know whether to glory or to fury; the houses were still smoldering; the people rejoiced among the ruins; priests and monks were shouting frantic cheers. Women writhing their arms furiously; and around seven or eight dead, swollen and charred, as many maidens danced wildly in a circle, holding hands and singing".*

For the Kingdom of the Two Sicilies it is the beginning of the end.

Nievo begins to realize in what kind of hell they got themselves: "... *the Neapolitans of Landi assaulted on one side by the squad of Partenico, retire leaving some dead and wounded who are quartered, scorched and fed to the dogs in this town. More similar feats in Borghetto and under Montelepre. ... Marching through Partenico. In this town the dogs are still busy eating the roasted Neapolitans – it is not a sign of civilization ... "[54].*

So Garibaldi comments this episode: *"Wretched view! we found the dead bodies of Bourbon soldiers, on the streets, eaten by the dogs! They were corpses of Italians slaughtered by other Italians that, if grown in the life of free citizens, they would have effectively served the cause of their oppressed country; and instead, as a result of the hatred aroused by their wicked masters, they ended up mangled, torn to pieces by their own brothers, with such an anger that shocks the hyenas".* It is clear that for Garibaldi it is all the fault of the Bourbons; it is their fault if there is so much hatred in Sicily. This mindset will be a constant of the political and social thinking of the Italian patriots who, for <u>150 years,</u> will keep repeating that the issue of the South is a legacy of bygone eras of Bourbon oppression and misrule. Who knows for how many more centuries it will be the fault of the Bourbons.

Now Garibaldi aims at Palermo which is manned by at least 20,000 Bourbon troops while he has 800 Garibaldians and perhaps 2,000 or 3,000 Sicilian insurgents. These insurgents have proven useless in battle, they know how to shoot in the back or to start fires at night but when you are fighting in the open field they disobey and flee. The presence of the squads always gives problems: one night they steal Garibaldi his blankets, then they infuriate Bixio when he surprises them robbing the corpse of a Garibaldian. It is a very difficult relationship. But these are the Sicilians who joined him and, at this time, he cannot do without them: without the participation of the people his conquest would not be legitimate.

Now Garibaldi is on the hills around Palermo and with a brilliant move succeeds in dodging an attempt by the Neapolitan army to corner him, afterwards he sends a small group of his men inward feinting to run away so that several thousand Neapolitan soldiers run after them thinking they had him, while he approaches the city that is still manned by at least 15,000 Bourbon troops while his Garibaldians are less then 800. Despite being in a situation to say the least precarious, the spirit of his men is skyrocketing; they have no doubt that he will lead them to victo-

---

[54] Ippolito Nievo, *Diario della spedizione dei Mille*, (Ugo Mursia Editore, Milano 2010) pag.29

ry. An episode related by Abba shows us the strength of the bond that holds them together: "*He had just finished to comfort those poor soldiers that Captain Cenni, a friend of his, introduced him a young man of the expedition who was carrying a handful of strawberries in a little basket made of leaves: 'General, this hunter of the Alps offers you these straw-berries'. Garibaldi looked at Cenni, looked at the young man, then smiled a little, shook his beautiful head and asked, 'where are you from?' 'Genoan' replied the young man almost trembling. And then the General in Genoese dialect: 'And do you still have your mother?' 'General yes' and the eyes of the young man saw very far, 'What would she say - continued Garibaldi - if she were here and saw me taking your strawber-ries?' meanwhile, he held out his hand and raised two or three of them just to accept, adding: 'go, go, you can enjoy them, they will taste better to you than to me'*"[55].

They pass the Renda pass and come within sight of Palermo; they are camped out waiting to attack when Abba notices a few joung Sicilians from the squads that stand guard to a man who is lying on the ground with his hands and feet tied; something that arouses the curiosity of the Garibaldians: "*The Garibaldians who went to see him, they heard that he was such Santo Mele, who since the outbreak of the revolution had started running the countryside with some rascals, robbing the public coffers and murdering people. He even had set fire to the village of Calamina. He had done everything in the name of his own justice that he seemed to have the right to exercise; indeed he gloried himself. The Si-cilians ... they said that he had to be a "Maffioso"; and they explained to their fellows the nature of a shadowy society which had its ranks throughout the whole island ... I like to recall that the continental ex-cused the island ... and said ... that also the Maffia would have passed. That Santo Mele disappeared the next day. Perhaps the most powerful Maffia had aided him even in our camp*". In this way Northern Italians become aware of this phenomenon and, of course, they think that their revolution would have eliminated also the Maffia, together with the "misrule" of the Bourbons. How wrong they were!

They try to join the band of Rosolino Pilo that had left Genoa a month before but this band was intercepted and destroyed by the Bour-bons.

---

[55] G.C.Abba, *Storia dei Mille*, (Bemporad, Firenze 1928) pag.140

Now, to conquer the city Garibaldi relies on the support of the people of Palermo and of the Anglo-American allies. A couple of American ships have arrived at Palermo and the Mediterranean fleet has about a dozen ships between Sicily and Naples but, most important, in Palermo there was the deputy commander of the fleet, Admiral Bundy, on the *Hannibal*. The bay is full of ships of all nations that do not want to miss the show.

While they are outside the city, before attacking, Garibaldi tells us in his *Memorie* that: "*there were many foreigners in our camp, especially British and Americans, expressing much sympathy for the good cause of Italy. A young American officer withdrew a revolver from his belt and kindly offered it to me as a token of the interest he was taking to us*".

Abba too meets these foreigners: "*This news were given us by some officers of the American and British ships anchored in the port of Palermo. An act of friendship that made us much good. They spoke with the General, then they started walking around the camp. What handshakes, frank and fraternal! ... we loaded them with letters, torn pieces of paper taken here and there and written by pencil; greetings, cries of affection, that they will deliver to our families with the first vessel that will sail from Palermo. ... We know they brought to the General the plan of Palermo, with the signs where are the barricades or the stationing of the Bourbon army*".

In town there is the Hungarian Ferdinand Eber which is officially a correspondent of the Times but in reality is a British agent who regularly informs Garibaldi about the movements of the Bourbons.

With this information Garibaldi attacks at night on a door of the city walls, but sends ahead the Sicilian squads that start shooting in the air and screaming giving the alarm to the Bourbons. Luckily for him the Bourbons are under the command of General Lanza who is 75 years old and is a Freemason. Instead of sending troops to the rescue of those who defend the door he withdraws and closes his troops into three buildings within the city walls and far from each other, thus fragmenting his army and abandoning most of the city. The Garibaldians manage to break through the door, in spite of the fierce resistance of the few remaining Bourbon troops that have been abandoned, alone, at the defence of their post and occupy the emptied neighborhoods.

So Nievo narrates to his cousin the conquest of Palermo: "*What a miracle! - I swear to you, Bice! We saw it and we almost hesitate to believe it! – The Sicilian insurgents fled everywere: inside the walls it looked like a city of the dead; no other revolt, just later on some chiming. And we alone, eight hundred at most, scattered in a space as big as Milan, deployed without order, without direction (how can you order or direct the nothing?) to the conquest of a city against twenty-five thousand men of regular troops*"[56].

The population sees that the Garibaldians win while the Bourbons withdraw and arises. So in a few hours Garibaldi enters Palermo and besieges 20,000 Bourbon troops with 800 Garibaldians and with some support from the population. We realize that it is grotesque, but this is what happened.

Back in 1848 Palermo had arisen and the Sicilian separatists had adapted themelves to cooperate with the squads. For the people of Palermo it is nothing new to see these squads coming after a "liberator".

For a couple of days Lanza makes a few timid attempts at breaking the siege, then he asks admiral Bundy to mediate a truce with Garibaldi. The Admiral agrees. The negotiations are held on board of the *Hannibal* and the commanders of he naval squadrons that are in the bay of Palermo participate to it: French, Sardinian and American. On the 30th the truce is agreed upon. Lanza cannot walk and sends General Letizia to deal with Garibaldi who dresses the uniform of a Sardinian general.

The terms of the truce allow Garibaldi to occupy the building of the Bank of the Two Sicilies. Crispi rushes in and picks up, in gold ducats, a sum estimated at 80 million Euros. Garibaldi leaves to the bank a note as a receipt which, of course, will not be honored. So the people of Palermo who had deposited their money in the bank lose everything.[57] Garibaldi asks for more money to Bertani who is still in Genoa and must reach him with more volunteers; it seems that the moneis are never enough. This truce is providential because Garibaldi is left without ammunition. The Americans give him a little from the ships they have in the bay while the British send from Malta 1,500 rifles with ammunition. Meanwhile thou-

---

[56] Ippolito Nievo, *Diario della spedizione dei Mille*, Ugo Mursia Editore, Milano 2010 pag.61

[57] Gilberto Oneto, *L'Iperitaliano* (Rimini: Il Cerchio, 2006), pag.127. The bank has still this receipt

sands of volunteers from Genoa sail toward Sicily carried by American ships and this time they are very well armed.

While both sides prepare to exploit the break granted by the truce, the Bourbon forces arrive in Palermo who were fooled by a faint made by Garibaldi and had left Palermo chasing inland a small group of Garibaldians. They came back racing, they are furious and attack the defenses of Garibaldi without even contacting general Lanza. They overwhelm the resistance of the insurgents, come into town and arrive a few hundred meters from the Pretorio Palace, the residence of Garibaldi. They have the victory in hand when two Bourbon officers come who warn the commander, colonel Bosco, that there is a truce that just begun and he must stop. Abba is present and sees the scene: "*Over there, down the street, in the midst of those grim faces of strangers, you could see colonel Bosco prowling furiously, like a scorpion in the ring of fire. Oh, if he would have arrived just half an hour before! He would have entered straightaway and come into the Pretorio Palace almost by surprise, with all those people, who had their body full of anger for the march on Corleone, that they had done chasing our shadows. Who knows what a fortune got out of hand to this Sicilian, young, bold and rich of talent?*".

Ferdinando Beneventano del Bosco is the scion of a noble family of Siracusa and is loyal to his king.[58] He cannot be bribed and is the only Bourbon officer who fights valiantly. He is the only one who will give a hard time to Garibaldi, but he alone cannot turn the tide of a disintegrating kingdom, ruled by an idiotic king. It is beautiful the analogy of Abba "*a scorpion in the ring of fire*" with the anger of Bosco who knows he has the victory in hand but must obey the orders and stop, thus remaining he too besieged in Palermo. His is a tragic fate; he will have to drink again at the bitter cup of betrayal and defeat, until its final conclusion. It is also beautiful the tribute that Abba gives to this enemy "*young, bold and rich of talent*", a little recognition to the only Bourbon who fought with courage.

On the 31st Garibaldi receives in the Pretorio palace two Bourbon officers, general Letizia and colonel Buonopane, who want to prolong the truce without a deadline. Garibaldi naturally accepts, this truce seems made purposely for him who desperately needs time to receive the rein-

---

[58] Today the tourists can admire the mansion of the Beneventano family in Siracusa

forcements and the supplies that are on their way. He offers cigars and then, while peeling an orange with a boxcutter, he complains that the Neapolitan soldiers have caused some conflicts; in response Letizia protests that they are doing their best to keep their men disciplined. You can understand that the Neapolitan soldiers feel humiliated by this shameful truce, they despise their officers who led them to this disaster and are eager to take revenge. Garibaldi offers a clove to both of them sticking it on his boxcutter and handing it as they discuss. Letizia talks with his mouth full and it seems a quiet conversation between old friends. Suddenly a noise bursts of rifle fire. The Sicilian squads, as usual, did not obey and had started shooting on their own. Garibaldi is annoyed and orders to stop it immediately. The two Bourbon officers are terrified, fearing for their lives: "*The two officers appeared more dead than alive - Oh God! General - said Letizia - make them cease. Do not give us more heartaches! - ... - Yes General, for goodness sake, it is time that we stop this - said the Buonopane, joining his palms as in prayer*". Garibaldi reassures them: "*you are in the house of a gentleman*". What soldiers!

Letizia takes leave saying he will be in Naples the next day to push through to the king the armistice with which all of Palermo is left to Garibaldi while they withdraw into the castle and under Mount Pellegrino. Garibaldi is now the master of the city. In the harbor there are 50 warships of all nations. There is admiral Persano who goes to work immediately with excellent results.

The Pretorio Palace where Garibaldi resides becomes the goal of a crowd of visitors.

Bandi is amazed by the arrival of a crowd of clergymen. "*It was the Archbishop of Palermo who, accompanied by all the clergy of the city, came to make reverence to the dictator*". He holds back his hatred for the priests and politely lets in this crowd of visitors while the Garibaldians who were there get excited and do not refrain from demonstrating their indignation. Before an incident might occur, Bandi runs to Garibaldi. "*I informed immediately the general, and he came out of his room and moved to meet that little old man, with whom he spoke lovingly ... comforting him as best as he could; then with nice and clear voice and with honest words he harangued all those priests; and when afterwards he took them to the top of the stairs to greet them, they were madly in love with him and they would have sanctified him*". Here we have another example of the charm of our hero. He was well known for his hatred of the Church and yet, in a few words, he managed to win the bishop and the priests; a success that leaves us amazed.

Alexandre Dumas comes with a young slut in tow that could have been his daughter. He came to Palermo with his yacht and stops for lunch. The Garibaldians are very irritated by the fact that, without any respect, the girl sits to the right of the general and the two are eating so immoderately. Garibaldi knows what influence has Dumas on the French public opinion and treats him with the utmost consideration; not for nothing he is a genius of public relations. After lunch the poor Bandi must accompany Dumas to his yacht to take delivery of an aid that Dumas brought from France for his friend Garibaldi. Those are weapons that he would want to jettison for being so old and rusty, but he knows how much Garibaldi cares the friendship of Dumas and, politely, he loads those few things on a cart and takes them away.

The truce foresees the exchange of prisoners and the Garibaldians are brought to the Palace for questioning by Garibaldi. They come all happy to have been freed but Garibaldi does not see it that way. He interrogates them, asking them if they have been injured; they answer to be well. Then Garibaldi asks them why they had been taken prisoners and at this point they do not know what to say. Garibaldi is furious, he tells them that they are cowards and that he has no use for people like them! Bandi is sorry and saddened but basically he agrees with Garibaldi. According to the Garibaldian ethics, they are fighting for the Redemption of the Motherland and this means that a Garibaldian must never give up; only a debilitating wound can justify the surrender. Otherwise, the Cult of the Supreme Sacrifice implies that he fights to the death. This is what Garibaldi has always done and pretends that his men do the same. For him, the Supreme Sacrifice is not a poetic expression taken from the novels, it is a commitment of honor that must be taken up to the extreme consequences.

At the initiative of Bixio a small revolt arises because they have families and they must let them have something: "*The general has some wonderful ideas about the contempt of money ... and we all know he can just make out a penny from a pound*". It is fine with them to fight for the glory, but their families need to eat. The thing was particularly galling if you consider that the Sicilian squads were paid regularly otherwise they would have returned home. With much fear they venture to ask to be paid but Garibaldi answers that he does not need to be paid and this must be good to them too. The poor men are desolate and distressed, what will they get to their loved ones? Two days later they are informed that the general has decided that every Garibaldian will receive the pay in use in the Sardinian army. The atmosphere relaxes.

Bandi takes advantage of the truce to walk around the city, he sees the squads that, under the command of La Masa, are headquartered in a palace in the center of the city complete with sentinels at the entrance. It almost seems that they want to establish themselves as an alternative center of power. He hates those criminals while he loves the boys of Palermo who are guarding the barricades. He knows that they can be trusted.

General Letizia returned from Naples where he had the approval of the king to the truce. Garibaldi receives him and at one point Bandi realizes that he is not wanted, Letizia intends to desert and to pass with them but he does not want to speak in front of others. Bandi leaves the room.

La Farina arrives from Genoa. He works for Cavour and insists to do immediately a plebiscite for the annexation to Piedmont. Cavour is afraid that Garibaldi could take republican initiatives, or worse, that the people of Palermo reconsider their desires for autonomy. Garibaldi and his men are outraged by this lack of trust while the Sicilians are perplexed. They never asked to become Italians and they are afraid that the situation will evolve in an unwanted direction. They fear that their desires for autonomy will end up in the trash. Garibaldi draggs his feet and nothing is done.

A few days pass, the Neapolitans do not do anything and the Garibaldians, without ammunition, have no interest to resume the fight. Then on June the 6th, without a reason, since from Naples no precise orders arrive, general Lanza gives up and leaves the city embarking with all his men and all his weapons. Bixio is commanded to guard the harbor with 400 volunteers while the Bourbons embark. General Von Mechel, a Swiss who remained to fight for the Bourbons and is faithful to his duty, marches past Bixio. Von Mechel is angry for the humiliation and "*arrived before Bixio he exclaimed ... - We will meet again! -. And Bixio replied, raising his finger: - I'll see you in Naples! -. The soldiery responded to that challenge of the brave Genoese with a roar ...*".

When General Lanza embarks he wants all his troops at the port to have the honors due to the Viceroy. Evidently the word "shame" is not in his vocabulary. It is a grotesque scene because the Bourbons are 30 times more numerous than the Garibaldians. A soldier *"breaks ranks and rises up in front of the horse of the general ... - Your Excellency, do you see how many we are? And we are leaving like this? - ... - That man is drunk - says the general addressing his aides and proceeds to the embarkation"*[59].

Three months later, in Naples, Lanza will pay a visit to Garibaldi to congratulate his Freemason brother for his beautiful victory. It will take 13 days to evacuate by sea all the Bourbons with their material.

Garibaldi has won, he landed in the island with 1,000 men badly armed and in less than a month he routed the Bourbon army which oversees the island with at least 20,000 very well armed men. He has raised thousands of Sicilian patriots and with them he conquered the island's capital by popular acclaim. These are the news that the telegraph spreads to the world. In the Anglo-Saxon countries the enthusiasm explodes.

Fundraisings are promoted and the proceeds of theatre performances are offered, Florence Nightingale and Charles Dickens get into the action, the Enfield factories offer a cannon, the dockers of Glasgow and Liverpool offer a shift of their work without pay to supply Garibaldi.

On the New York Times, Marx and Engels praise Garibaldi for the wonderful march from Marsala to Palermo and the conquest of the city is defined as: *"one of the most amazing military exploits of our century"*. Others call him the Washington of Italy and write that: *"there is no similar incident in history, not even among the feats of mythological heroes"*. General Avezzana, who had fought for the Roman republic, rushes in from New York with a group of American volunteers; they will arrive in time to fight on the Volturno.

In France the conservatives are hesitant because they fear that this radical change in the geopolitical situation in the Mediterranean will create problems for France but the popular enthusiasm overwhelms any doubt. Progressive France can no longer hold his joy and cretinism spreads.

---

[59] Gilberto Oneto, *L'Iperitaliano* (Rimini: Il Cerchio, 2006), pag.128

George Sand writes that "*Garibaldi does not resemble anyone and there is a kind of mystery in him that makes us meditate!*". According to her the life of Garibaldi "*... is like a poem: this man becomes, almost alone, the man of miracles. He shakes the thrones, he is the banner of a novel era. The whole of Europe keeps an eye on him and when it wakes up every morning, it wonders where is he, what did he do the day before. He carries in himself the faith of the heroic times, they reappear in the midst of the nineteenth century the wonders of the ancient chivalry*".

Victor Hugo asks himself: "*what is his strength? What makes him win? What does he carry with him? The soul of the people. He goes, he runs, his march is a trail of flames, his handful of men petrifies the regiments, ... he has the Revolution with him; and sometimes, in the chaos of the battle, amid the smoke, between the flashes, like a hero of Homer, you can see the goddess behind him*". The European Catholics are hesitant, they fear for the Papal States, but as a political force they are on the defensive.

Fundraisings are started from Sweden to Portugal and from the United States to Chile. Now it seems that the whole world wants to participate in the killing of the hated Bourbon tyranny; volunteers rush in from Algeria, Turkey, India, Canada and of course the United States and England. Even in ultra-reactionary Russia the news of the conquest of Palermo arouse enthusiasm. Bakunin, who was in exile in Siberia, will later say that the march of the Hero was followed in Irkutsk with trepidation. In Poland, oppressed by the tsarist rule, the image of Garibaldi enters the houses as that of a national hero. "*In Warsaw, in the fall, a woman that sells vegetables calls for the release of his son who was arrested for political reasons, she shouts to the police chief that Garibaldi will come in a week and his son will be freed by him*"[60].

A lady from Palermo asks Abba: "*if I had ever seen the angel that repairs Garibaldi from the gunshots with his wings*". All over the world Garibaldi is an icon, the patron saint of all the dispossessed and the oppressed.

Nobody in the world has the faintest idea of what is really happening in Sicily.

---

[60] Alfonso Scirocco, *Garibaldi*, (Bari: Laterza, 2001), pag.260-264.

Let's go back to Sicily. Now Garibaldi is the master of almost the whole island, the Bourbons are barricaded in forts of Messina, Catania and Siracusa with a strategy that can be described as defeatist. They have 22,000 men on the island and still have a fleet that, at least on paper, is the most powerful of the Mediterranean, but the most daring action that comes to their minds is to hire a Calabrian gunman to assassinate Garibaldi. Their soldiers are loyal and are calling for a revenge; the king should make a strong purge of the senior echelons of the military and go on the attack, and instead he plans assassinations.

In vain the queen tries to spur the king: "*Mount your horse, Francesco. I will come with you. I will ride at your side. Your presence will galvanize the soldiers and those damn pirates will be driven back into the sea*"[61]. It's useless. The forces on the island are entrusted to General Clary who has taken refuge in the fortress of Messina, he has no plans but he is thinking of it. He will do nothing. Probably he is paralyzed by the popular ferment that is shaking the whole island and threatens to provoke a generalized rebellion against the Bourbon government without realizing that this inaction of the Neapolitan army excites more and more the population.

The Garibaldians are reduced to a few hundred fighters, they have very few guns and no ammunition; their situation would be hopeless if the Bourbons had a minimum of courage. The Sicilian volunteers of the squads have proven useless in battle and difficult to control. Here Garibaldi must face a situation that is quite new for him. In South America he had never had any problem to control his gangs of criminals, his charisma always succeeded to keep them in check and make them fight for him, but here in Sicily his charm does not work. The squads have amply demonstrated that they only obey their leaders and do not care for the unification of Italy; Garibaldi for them is nothing more than a puppet. The people of Palermo have proven reliable when it came to chase the Neapolitans, but when they heard about the annexation to Italy they got chilled; also with them the charm of Garibaldi does not work. As for the Bourbons also for Garibaldi they refuse to pay taxes and to serve in the army. In his *Memorie* he has always said that the people of the country-

---

[61] Arrigo Petacco, *La Regina del Sud*, (Milano: Mondadori, 1992) pag.96

side was hostile to him and to his cause, but now he makes no mention of this difficulties with the Sicilians.

On June 13 he dismisses the squads and issues a proclamation in which all Sicilians are called to the arms to complete the liberation of the island. It seems that he wants to replace the squads with an army taken from the people of Sicily. Evidently Garibaldi thinks he will have more success then the Bourbons. He will be disappointed; few are those who come and they steal the weapons and run. He too, like the Bourbons, must give up on having a Sicilian army.

Now there is a problem, Abba notes that: "*These people that made us the feast the night of May 25, when we were few and with little hope, now we can no longer recognize them. But what have we done? They do not say it and you can not guess it. They talk, they smile, they are gay; they talk with us, but, by imperceptible gestures they communicate between them. Can it be that they have many souls? Monk Pantaleo put his finger on the wound, he! These people, they became hostile because of the conscription decreed by the Dictator*". Now the people of Sicily have become hostile: "*Bixio complained that Sicily does not give soldiers, does not pay taxes, and if the applications for jobs were made of canvas they would cover the entire island. He complained also about the spread of contraband and the fact that they were stealing the weapons and the ammunition for resale on the black market*"[62].

For Garibaldi this is not a great loss, now the public opinion, both Northern Italian and Anglosaxon has metabolized the idea that the southern people yearn to be liberated by him and he no longer needs to justify the conquest by a real popular participation. At this point, his charisma is such that they follow the opposite approach: it is the struggle of Garibaldi that justifies the desire for freedom of the people, if Garibaldi has taken the field the people want to be freed by him, obviously!

Garibaldi cannot conquer the island with the few hundred men he has left, but the situation is quickly re-balanced by the commitment of the Anglo-American allies, by the Northern Italian patriotism, by the European Romanticism and ... by corruption.

---

[62] Denis Mack Smith, *Storia della Sicilia medievale e moderna,* (Bari: Editori Laterza, 1973) Vol.III pag.592

While Cavour has already begun its massive recruitment drive among the Bourbons, a *Fund for Garibaldi* is opened in London. Together with other funds, for a total estimated at two billion Euro, they will buy 5 steamers in England and 3 in Marseille in spite of the fact that the thefts perpetrated at the expense of these funds are legendary. The ships fly the American or English flag and start a sea bridge that, in a couple of months, carries to Sicily up to 20,000 Northern Italians that will create an army that Garibaldi will call the Southern Army. Very important is also the contribution of European volunteers, they are thousands, all inflamed by the poems of Byron: at any cost they will have their romantic adventure.

A couple of these vessels are intercepted by the Bourbon navy and taken to Gaeta. The British diplomacy is immediately activated and points out that they are flying the American flag and their passengers are directed to Sardinia. Napoli must surrender and must release ships and passengers that are brought to Genoa and from there re-embarked for Palermo where they will arrive a few days later.

Cavour has opened accounts with banks in London and Naples. Through information received from a Neapolitan diplomat, a traitor, the interventions are focused on the army and navy officers who should have an open mind for the "newness". A huge success is acheived when Persano convinces the commander of the *Veloce*, a Neapolitan corvette armed with modern rifled guns, to go to Palermo and surrender to Garibaldi. Here a problem arises when the sailors refuse to join the betrayal and ask to be set free to return to Naples. In vain Garibaldi tries to convert them to his new motherland, they do not intend to betray the king to whom they have sworn allegiance. Almost all the officers betray and almost all the sailors remain faithful. Garibaldi lets them go and replaces them with Sardinian sailors sent on leave (for the sake of appearances) from the vessels of Persano and with fishermen taken from the harbor of Palermo. The ship is renamed Tuckory, and so now Garibaldi has also a modern warship. *"In a letter to Cavour dated August the 6th Persano communicates that: 'We can say that the General Staffs of this navy is ours, few being the exceptions'"*[63].

---

[63] Gilberto Oneto, *L'Iperitaliano* (Rimini: Il Cerchio, 2006), pag.132

In the few days that he stays in Palermo Garibaldi starts playing the enlightened dictator and launches progressive reforms, including the abolition of the tax on flour, without considering that without taxes no reform would have been possible. As usual he ignores the value of money and systematically robs all institutions that have some: banks and public administrations. He establishes a Committee for the seizure of funds from the tax offices thus leaving the island penniless.

His genius for the public relations pushes him to seek an agreement with the Sicilian Church because he knows how the people are attached to the Catholic faith; his parents were like this. For the feast of Santa Rosalia he participates, in representation of Vittorio Emanuele, at a solemn Mass with red shirt, poncho and a drawn sword. He tires of La Farina, arrests him and puts him on a boat to Genoa thus returning him to the sender, Cavour. La Farina had been sent to Sicily by Cavour to controll him because they knew that Garibaldi wanted to use his conquest as a springboard towards Rome and Venice, something that Cavour cannot allow. In addition he was sending reports to Cavour that denounced the sacking of the finances of the island its state of anarchy and the amateurism of the Garibaldian government. From Genoa they send him Depretis who assumes the title of Pro-Dictator, he takes over the Garibaldian government revealing himself a perfect nullity and so will not give any trouble to Garibaldi who can now resume the conquest of the island.

He divides his forces, that grow each day, in three groups. One across the island in the direction of Catania, another makes a turn towards the south and the third along the north coast towards Messina. This is meant to establish the authority of the new government on the whole island. But how does he know that the Bourbons will not attack these small Garibaldian forces? They still have at least 20,000 soldiers on the island.

Actually many of these troops patrol the eastern part of the island in order to curb the popular ferment excited by the success of Garibaldi. All social conflicts accumulated in the past centuries come, for the thousandth time, to the surface threatening any legality. His irresponsible statements on the transfer of land to the peasants have unleashed violence again. The squads had been driven away from Palermo and when they returned home the anarchy returned to the countryside. *"And when Garibaldi promised to repair this kind of wrongs there was a spontaneous movement to occupy portions of the old estates. Like wolves driven by hunger, wild individuals dressed in goatskin came down from the mountains and any landowner who had not managed to escape ran the risk of being assassinated to the cry of - Long live Italy! - In an extreme case one was burned alive and his liver roasted and eaten*"[64].

Nievo remains in Palermo and it seems he has finally understood the situation: "*The whole revolution is concentrated in the bands of peasants that here are called Squads and are composed mostly of bloody robbers who make war on the government in order to make it to the landowners. So much so that now we must take the role of policemen against our allies of yesterday*". The poor Nievo is ordered to stay in Palermo because he is in charge of the accounting of the Garibaldian expedition in Sicily, an assignment that he does not like at all. After the conquest, when his comrades have all returned home, the Piedmontese government asks him to return to Palermo to bring all documents to Naples to be controlled by the new Piedmontese administrators. However the ship sinks for unknown causes and Nievo, with all the records of the expedition, disappears under the sea. It disappears, along with this writer-patriot, the documentation on the use of the million Turkish plates collected by the Freemasons and donated to Garibaldi. We can not know anything about the charges by the Bourbons to Garibaldi about the corruption of the Neapolitan officers. A tragic accident or the mysterious hand of Freemasonry with some help from the Mafia? Italian mysteries!

Abba is in the column that crosses the center of the island toward Catania and will have to deal with these problems. They are led by Ferdinand Eber, the Hungarian who was a correspondent of the Times in Palermo. Fascinated by the Garibaldian epos, he throws his pen away and joins Garibaldi who appoints him brigadier general. His experiences in this kind of war will not be romantic at all.

Abba meets the first bandits: "*They passed, bold on certain black stallions, burning coals in their eyes, manes that touched their chests. Heads held high barely looking at us, had their guns on a shoulder strap, pistols and daggers at their waists, ribbons on thair hats and on the harness of their mounts. The leader who was riding first was not new*

---

[64] Denis Mack Smith, *Storia della Sicilia medievale e moderna,* (Bari: Editori Laterza, 1973) Vol.III pag.593

to me. ... Who are those seven? I asked a gentleman. ... Patriots young gentleman, have you not seen?". He lies. A Garibaldian runs after them and arrests them, it seems they are the band of Santo Mele. There is a trial: *"And there was no way to find one who would tell the truth! ... 'I a robber? Your Excellency! I fought against the Bourbons, I set fire to the houses of the royalists, I killed policemen and spies, from early April I am serving the revolution, here are my papers! ... However the council did not send him free"*. He is dispatched to Palermo where he will be shot. So Italy began and so it continued.

Nobody wants to talk, no one tells the truth, everybody hold their resentments and hatred explodes suddenly and unpredictably. *"I saw the battalion of Bassini leave in a hurry. At Prizzi, that must be a village not far away, there are people that started to make blood and things, as if nobody were in charge"*.

The more they advance inland the more they are involved in the riots: *"Poor major Bassini, he has been exchanged for the executioner. He will have to go again to a village called Resotano, where some wickeds are shaking the people. ... Those of Bassini are back ... They say they arrived at Resotano around midnight, they found the armed people determined not to let them in. Bassini ... proceeded with due precautions, and was able to get his hands on eleven villains, guilty of a thousand bullying and blood letting. One managed to escape, but a Sicilian like a demon, chased him, reached and killed him"*.

The Northern Italians are increasingly alone: *"Done the math, of the Sicilians who followed us from Palermo to here, a half hundred have already gone, some taking away the weapons. They are peasants who light up like straw and soon get tired. The War Council condemns them to death; we post the judgments as sheets at the corners of buildings, but we let the condemned men leave to their destiny, provided they go far away"*.

It seems incredible but his patriotism is not nicked by all this, he writes: *"After us freedom will come sweeping all this aftermath of the middle ages"*. How is it possible he does not realize that he came in another country with other people of which he knows nothing and does not understand anything? How can he believe he's doing the right thing? How can you be so obtuse, conceited, arrogant? Finally they arrive at Catania that seems a quiet place, but the worst has yet to come.

Bandi is in the column, commanded by Medici, which runs along the north coast to Messina, he is no longer the orderly officer of Garibaldi, he has the rank of major and has his own men.

Now they are very well armed and stop one day to practice the use of the new rifles. At the height of Milazzo they clash with a small Bourbon force. General Clary has sent about 6,000 men under the command of Colonel Bosco to face the Garibaldians. It is not clear why he sent a contingent so small and has not taken advantage of his numerical superiority. Maybe he wanted to get rid of Bosco and take time to calmly consider other career options.

They collide at the height of Milazzo, which is a peninsula that extends into the sea for eight kilometers and on its top there are the city of Milazzo and a strong fortress in the hands of the Bourbons. Bosco wins and stops the advance of the Garibaldians. Bandi is desolate, without the physical presence of Garibaldi they cannot fight, his presence is invoked.

Garibaldi is in Palermo and he knows that he cannot afford not even a small defeat. The squads of the island are watching and if they thought that the Bourbons could regain the upper hand, they would jump on the revolutionaries, who are now the Garibaldians, as they did in the revolution of 1848. Garibaldi rushes in from Palermo on the British ship *City of Aberdeen* with 2,000 volunteers just arrived in the harbor, while thousands more are sent by land at the command of Speeche, an englishman. Just before the battle the *Queen of England* arrives from Liverpool and downloads large quantities of arms and ammunition. The *Tuckory* is off Milazzo assisted at some distance by the warships of admiral Persano that should not intervene in the fighting, he is there to salvage whatever possible if the Bourbons were to overwhelm the Garibaldians.

Garibaldi attacks relentlessly and succeeds in rejecting the Bourbons towards the fortress on the tip of the promontory, but at some point he is in trouble because Bosco fights back with force and he has had too high losses. At that point he runs to the beach, he has a rowboat take him to the *Tuckory* and he maneuvers the ship toward the side of the Bourbon deployment. Bandi sees the *Tuckory* arrive and through his binoculars he sees Garibaldi atop the crow's nest who directs the ship: "*... when a column left the city* (Milazzo) *to renew the assault, the Tukeri started hitting it on its side with her big guns, and forced it to go back, broken and* *routed, within the walls"*. Bosco is trapped in a small space and cannot return the fire of the Tukory; his field artillery can not duel against rifled guns. He asks for help from Clary that in Messina has at least 10,000 men and they are only 25 km away, but Clary does not move. He asks for help to the commander of the fortress who replies that he has a higher rank and does not want to favor him. Bosco knows he is surrounded by traitors and if he has to surrender he wants to hear it from the King. The fighting stops for a few days.

In Naples the confusion is such that we can not lay down the responsibilities, the king has promulgated again the constitution of 1848 and has adopted the Italian flag with the emblem of the Bourbons at the center to compete with the Savoy. Pathetic!

On July 23rd, the Bourbon fleet arrives off the coast of Milazzo and Garibaldi must hide the Tuckory that, alone, can not cope with a fleet. Now the Bourbons could wipe out with their cannons the Garibaldians from the peninsula and instead they send a delegation to Garibaldi to negotiate the surrender! Bosco will have the honor of the arms but will lose his beautiful thoroughbred. The Garibaldians had losses six times higher than the Bourbons but they won! Garibaldi writes: *"The triumph of Milazzo was bought at a very high price. The number of our dead and injured was vastly superior to that of the enemy"*.

Bandi attends the surrender of the fort, he sees the Bourbons leaving to board the French ships that will take them to Naples and *"... the officers salute with their swords, but by their eyes we knew that they would have much rather driven them into our hearts"*. When Bosco comes out shouts, whistles and curses; the Garibaldians must defend him from the crowd. While the Bourbons are in the port of Milazzo waiting for boarding the Garibaldians mingle with them and try to convince them to desert but *"... in the end maybe ten or twelve, on five thousand, these many were those who remained on land joining us"*. What's more, as soon as the ships comes off the pier, some rifle shots depart aimed at them, such is the anger of the Bourbon soldiers for a defeat so shameful and undeserved, they had fought well.

During the pause of the hostilities Garibaldi has the commander of the *Tuckory* arrested and establishes a military tribunal to judge the officer that is charged with insubordination in front of the enemy, under the penalty of death. Garibaldi had ordered him to make a maneuver that would have brought the ship under the guns of the fort of Milazzo and the officer did not do it. Bandi partecipates at this tribunal and you understand he is seriously embarrassed. They start the interrogation and the officer explaines that a cylinder of the machine had broken and he should have executed the maneuver with the sails only staying too long under the fire of the fort and he had judged it too risky. He was trained to take care of his ship and this action would have been judged a suicide. Bandi and the other judges are hesitant, they do not know what to do. They know that Garibaldi wants him dead but they realize that his behavior was reasonable and are unwilling to send him to death. Then one of them offers the solution: they know nothing on how to maneuver a ship and therefore the court should declare itself incompetent. For Bandi it is an ingenious solution, but Garibaldi does not give in; he reconvenes the court with a new president. This president is a Pole who barely speaks Italian and before the hearing he explains to the court that the officer had disobeyed and must be condemned. In so doing he gets the opposite effect. Bandi is irritated to be overtaken by a Pole who speaks a bad Italian and in the end the court issues the same sentence again: the tribunal is incompetent. Garibaldi is furious but accepts the ruling, the officer is sent to Palermo where he is judged by a court composed by officers of the Sardinian navy and is acquitted.

The officer in question is from Veneto, he comes from the Venetian and Austrian navy and did not adhere to the Cult of the Supreme Sacrifice. He was trained to calculate the risks and to take them into account. However this is not the way that Garibaldi fights, his whole life is inspired by the vocation to martyrdom for the motherland and he requires that all Garibaldians behave in the same way. The followers of this cult know that the life of the individual has no value and, if it has any, it is only based on the achievement of the goal of the Redemption of the Motherland. His men must always attack without counting the enemy forces and without paying attention to their own losses. To us today, after two world wars, this way of looking at the human life may seem fanatical and criminal, but this was the faith of Garibaldi and it is by this faith that he wins. In fact he has won and the Bourbons have lost. If they had considered the risks, the adventure of the Mille would have not even begun. Garibaldi knows that if he fails to inculcate this faith in his men he has no hope of victory.

We should note that although he is furious because he had to cede, Garibaldi yields. His tuning with his Garibaldians is wonderful, Garibaldi knows how far he can push, as when in Palermo he relented and gave a salary to his men. Even now he knows that the rope could break and he yields. There will never be any rift between him and his men, his legend will always remain intact and for his disciples he will always be a God.

Bandi agrees with Garibaldi when he has to risk his own life and he has always done so, but he cannot bring himself to send another person to death. Nationalism has not yet penetrated deeply enough into the psyche of the Europeans to give ordinary people the determination to kill another person who has behaved in a manner that is not brave but still reasonable. It is clear that in the mind of Bandi there is still a limit that his sense of humanity refuses to trespass. As we'll see in a few lines, this limit is about to be passed.

They leave Milazzo to go to Messina. Bandi observes the area around Milazzo and realizes the ineptitude of the Bourbon generals when "... *we saw up close the great danger that we had been in and we marveled that, masters of those wonderful places, the Bourbon generals left us alone in the two days we stayed in such a small number in the village of Meri*". They arrive at Messina without a shot being fired, in Naples they had decided a strategic retreat and abandoned the island. They left in the fortress of Messina a small garrison that should not disturb Garibaldi's operations and will not be attacked. Now Garibaldi and his people are on the Strait and must find a way to pass it.

Let's go back to Abba who now has arrived in Catania. Here the contrasts between Sicilians are becoming more dramatic. The whole area west of Etna is devastated by hordes of unfortunates who, excited by the proclamations of Garibaldi on the restitution of the land to the people, have let themselves loose. They are bands of desperate people who have nothing to lose having already lost everything, perhaps even death may have seemed a liberation. They are completely disorganized, they appear out of nowhere and disappear into thin air.

The perfect henchman

Nino Bixio was born in Genoa in 1821, at nine he lost his mother and then he had serious problems with his stepmother. He grows with a violent and quarrelsome temperament for which he is expelled from school at 13 and must embark as cabin boy on a ship bound for America. He remains at sea for three years and when he returns to Genoa his stepmother does not let him into their house. He lives in the street helped by the brothers that pass him food on the sly until he joins as a **volunteer** the navy of the Kingdom of Sardinia. Here he can study to become a good sailor and seven years later his brother manages to pull him out of the Navy. **Nino returns to** Genoa and finds a job as second in command of a merchant ship bound for Brazil but misfortune persecutes him and in Rio the ship is sold to another shipowner who decides to use it in the slave trade. The new owner offers him the command of the ship but he refuses and abandons the ship. He embarks as boatswain on a ship bound for the Far East under the orders of a Quaker with which he has a violent quarrel and must abandon the ship, he falls prisoner of savage tribes and is sold as a slave but the captain reconsiders and rescues him. Somehow he manages to go to Paris to the brother who had already helped him and here his life takes a turn because he meets Mazzini that converts him to the cause of the Italian Nationalism. He participates in the War of Independence and then in the defense of the Roman Republic where he is under the command of Garibaldi. For Garibaldi, Bixio becomes an ideal 'dog of war', always obedient, bloodthirsty and violent to the edge of insanity.

Bandi tells us that in September 1860, while Garibaldi has already entered Naples, he is under the command of Bixio in Calabria and his division must embark in Paola as soon as possible. Bixio is out of his mind at the thought that someone might reach Naples before him and take credit for its conquest. When they arrive at Paola the Medici division is embarking, Bixio intervenes and blocks them by pushing his troops ahead. Blood could flow but Bandi and others manage to convince Medici to let it go. Bixio realizes that not all of his troops can enter the ship and orders that all remain standing and as tight as possible but the captain made it known to Bixio that this is not enough and decides to leave without him. Bixio is furious, he boards the ship and sees that many men are lying on the deck; they are foreigners who have been there for some time and are sleeping tired of the long marches. Bixio grabs a gun and beats these men like a madman: one dies instantly and five others are taken away almost dead. Their companions wake up and jump on Bixio to lynch him but Bandi and others manage to take him away. Once in Naples the incident is reported to Garibaldi that calls for Bandi to know the truth, Bandi confirms. Garibaldi shakes his head: "*Bixio! Oh what a man! What a man!*". A few days later Bixio is again at the head of his troops. He was the perfect henchman.

The town of Bronte is at the center of the storm. "*The news of the revolt in Catania put more firmness in Bronte. Dead were the hopes of the few Bourbonists, took heart the liberals, and in June 29, the Committee sent an address to Garibaldi: "Please receive, the wishes of the people of Bronte that rejoices of your victories and shouts full of joy: Long live a united Italy! Long live Vittorio Emanuele! Long live Garibaldi! Bronte, 29 July 1860. With this address sent to the Dictator, the town officially accepted the new government. The mob, however, not only saw in Garibaldi the liberator from the tyranny of the Bourbons, but also the deliverer from the hardest tyranny, misery; and impatient expected to be taken off the tax on flour, made the division of the municipal land, already ordered by the same Bourbons and by Garibaldi anew with the decree of June 2. The rulers had not taken care of this matter for natural indolence and not to infringe upon the interests of a number of civilians, who had become usurpers of the volcanic lands of the Municipality.*

The Bourbon restoration of 1849, in Bronte as elsewhere, had given rise to abuses and intrigues, and everywhere there was suffering and oppression, everybody were craving for vendettas and reparations"[65].

None of them could have imagined that the future would have been far worse than they had hitherto suffered. Now the people go wild.

This is what Abba tells us: "*In Bronte, division of property, fires, vendettas, orgies to obscure the sun and, on top, long live to Garibaldi. Burning houses with the owners in; people slaughtered in the streets; in the seminaries the youngsters murdered at the foot of the old Rector; one of the horde is there that tears with his teeth the breasts of a killed girl ... Those ferocious men are taken, bound, so many that you have to work hard to choose the most miserable, a hundred ... And the guilty are judged by a council of war. If they go to death, shot in the back with the lawyer Lombardi, an old man of sixty years, head of the infamous horde. Among the executioners of this sentence there were young Garibaldians sweet and kind, doctors, artists in red shirt. What a pain! Bixio watched with eyes full of tears. After Bronte, Randazzo, Castiglione, Regalbuto, Centorbi and other villages they saw him, they felt the hold of his powerful hand, shouted back at him: Beast! But no one dared to move ... If not, here is what he wrote: With us, just a few words; either you stay quiet,*

---

[65] Benedetto Radice, *Memorie storiche di Bronte*, it can be downloaded from: http://www.bronteinsieme.it/2st/mo_601.html

or we, in the name of justice and of our country, we will destroy you as enemies of humanity".

Now let us read the chronicles of Bronte.

When Garibaldi arrives in Sicily, the territories around Bronte are the property of the 'Ducea', ie the heirs of Horatio Nelson who had the Duchy as a gift from the Bourbons for having put them back on the throne after the French invasion. Most of these lands are disputed between the Duchy and the neighboring towns who claim that the land had been illegally occupied and should be returned to the municipalities. The municipality of Bronte was in court for those lands with a trial that had lasted 350 years! We are in Sicily. Lombardo, a lawyer, was at the head of the Communists or Communals and was carrying out the demands of the municipalities in the courts but with poor results.

The arrival of Garibaldi, his irresponsible proclamations, his total ignorance of the socio-economic situation of the island precipitate the situation. On August 2, the city is besieged by people who want to have what Garibaldi has promised: the return of their lands. These are people that come from the surrounding countryside along with criminals who escaped from prison, *"Lombardo harangued the multitude, urging them to be peaceful, promising them that he would work for a peaceful and legal division; but the crowd went away dissatisfied"*.

Between the 3rd and the 4th of August this crowd decides to take justice into its own hands, it goes wild burning 46 homes and killing 16 bourgeois including the notary and the accounting officer of the duchy. On the 5th troops arrive from Catania and despite their poor efficiency the massacres stop, on the 6th the rioters flee. The owners of the Duchy are British and those days they are in England. Through the British consul in Catania they call for an exemplary punishment. In those days Garibaldi is camped on the Strait and has an absolute need for the help of the British fleet to overcome the blockade of the Bourbon fleet. He sends his dog of war, Bixio, with the order to set an example; the Mille cannot afford to be involved in social issues that he does not know and does not have time to understand.

Bixio arrives on the 6th. He orders the troops from Catania to leave and immediately asks for the arrest of Lombardo. The commander of the Sicilian troops understands the situation, he tells Lombardo that he must flee and, before leaving, writes a note to Bixio where he explains that

Bronte was now liberated and: "*I recommend to Your Excellency a people so docile and so good*". After all the residents too had been victims of the unrest, but Bixio must obey and wants his retaliation. Lombardo does not heed the advice to escape and goes to Bixio to explain the situation. Bixio refuses to talk and arrests him immediately; an exceptional Joint Commission of War is established. After a farcical trial, on the 9th, with false accusations, 5 people are condemned to be shot including Lombardo: all innocent. The day after the sentence is executeded by a firing squad made up of Garibaldians.

Abba tells us that the executioners "*were young Garibaldians sweet and kind, doctors, artists in red shirt*"; from his words transpires the shock to have to kill innocents and yet these young men, sweet and kind, have obeyed and have pulled that trigger. That limit of the sense of humanity that Bandi did not want to overcome has been passed and these beautiful young Northern Italians, who departed from Genoa disobeying their moms, have turned themselves into executioners. So ends romanticism.

We should note the Garibaldian logic for which their executions are done "*in the name of justice and of our country*" and are therefore progressive executions while the Bourbon executions (few) were reactionary. Despite the pain he feels for these executions Abba seems to justify them and he seems to be proud of the "*powerful hand*" of Bixio. He does not even show any remorse for the epithet "*Beast*" that innocent civilians threw at him and he seems proud of the result: "*But no one dared to move*". With this story Abba wants to justify in the eyes of the reader the brutality of Bixio exaggerating the barbarity of the rebels; it is very unlikely that Bixio had "*his eyes full of tears*".

Charles Stuart Forbes, was not present, and this is what he was told: "*Garibaldi ... could not have selected a better man for his purpose than Bixio, who, ... arriving with his brigade at the focus of the movement, shot thirty-two of the ringleaders before twelve o'clock .. A story is told very characteristic of Bixio, who is, perhaps, the most uncompromising soldier of this army, and who would shoot his brother on the spot if he thought he was not doing his duty. On arrival at Bronte, the ringleader of the movement was brought in prisoner whilst his own troops were at their breakfast, after a long march. Having satisfied himself of the man's guilt, Bixio said, "Well, I can't disturb my own men now" and drawing his revolver, shot him through the head*"[66]. It must be noted that Forbes, a romantic English traveler, does not hesitate, in his memoirs, to praise the rigor of Bixio and never misses an opportunity to show his contempt for the Bourbons, uncivilized and corrupt.

This episode of Bronte is not a fatality, is not a collateral damage of the conquest.

As we have already seen, Garibaldi always told us that the people of the countryside were hostile to him and to his revolution, while the masters were with him. Now in Sicily Garibaldi stands with those who have always been on his side: the landlords.

*"Garibaldi, matter of fact, never took against the former baronial estates a position as precise as it had been that of the Bourbons; and therefore some landowners, who so far had been neutral or hostile, began to think that working with Garibaldi and Piedmont could be the only hope of restoring order and preserve as much as possible the privileges of the past. **By demonstrating that he was ready to curb one of the most powerful forces of the Sicilian revolution, Garibaldi succeeded so unexpectedly and decisively to associate many conservative members of the aristocracy, the "gentlemen" and the social elites, to the cause of the unification of Italy**"[67].*

The myth of Garibaldi has taught generations of Italians that while Garibaldi loved the people because he was a socialist, the hopes of social renewal were betrayed by the successive governments, reactionary,of the Kingdom of Italy.

This is false because the betrayal of the hopes for a more just society began immediately with Garibaldi. It begins immediately an ultra reactionary and ultra repressive policy that will start Sicily towards the most tragic years of its history.

Now Garibaldi is at a standstill on the Strait and is looking for a way to overcome the barrier of the Bourbon fleet. In those days all European diplomacy is stirred for this unforeseen development of the Italian situation, a development that disrupts the equilibrium of the region.

---

[66] Charles Stuart Forbes, *The campaign of Garibaldi in the Two Sicilies*, (Blackwood and Sons: London 1862), pag.127

[67] Denis Mack Smith, *Storia della Sicilia medievale e moderna,* (Bari: Editori Laterza, 1973) Vol.III pag.593

Bandi is near Garibaldi when an adjutant of King Vittorio arrives with a letter to Garibaldi; he reads it: "*You know that I have not approved your expedition, to which I was absolutely extraneous ...*" and asks him to stop in Sicily and not to pass the Strait. Garibaldi responds to the king that he has the duty to continue because of "*... the embarrassment ... in which I would be today for a passive attitude in the face of the population of the Neapolitan continent, that I had been forced to restrain for a long time, and to whom I promised my immediate support*". Lies, absurd, shameless lies on both sides. With another secret missive king Vittorio encourages him to go ahead and as for the population of Naples that Garibaldi would have had to "restrain": grotesque!

In Genoa, Bertani is still raising funds and volunteers; Garibaldi decides to change strategy and plans to send those troops to conquer Rome with a landing on the coast of Lazio. France intervenes, Napoleon III sends a warship to the Strait to the aid of the Bourbon navy; it seems he is determined to defend the Pope. Cavour sends the men of Bertani to Sicily with a subterfuge, without their knowledge. On their landing there will be a mutiny, but it's done; Garibaldi has to settle for Naples and his hatred for Cavour reaches the paroxysm.

At this point, England intervenes and dislodges the French from the Strait opening to Garibaldi the way to Naples. Thus Garibaldi summarizes these events in his *Memorie*: "*That party* (Cavour)*, based on corruption* (oh Lord!)*, had left nothing untried. At first it had deluded itself to stop us at the Strait and limit our action to Sicily alone. Then it called for aid the magnanimous master* (Napoleon III)*, for which a vessel of the French navy had already appeared at Faro* (on the Strait)*. Here it was determinat the veto of Lord John Russell* (the British Foreign Secretary)*, who in the name of Albion imposed upon the lord of France not to meddle into our affairs*".

On August 19, after sunset, Bandi is on the American ship *Franklin* along with Garibaldi and 1.200 men while Bixio embarks on the *Torino* with 3.000 volunteers. On the *Franklin* there is also Origoni, a friend of Garibaldi who followed him from South America and is now the admiral of Garibaldi's fleet. At 2 am they are on the Calabrian coast and start landing without having met any Bourbon ship. Bixio runs his ship aground, again, but the sea is calm and they can land using the lances of the ship. Garibaldi tries to refloat the *Torino* by means of the *Franklin* but he cannot make it. It is sunrise and he decides to return to Sicily while Bixio hides into the woods. On the way back they are intercepted by two Bourbon ships, the *Fulminante* and the *Aquila*; the *Franklin* is unarmed and must stop. The *Fulminante* had already met the *Franklin* two months before when it seized it and took it to Gaeta from where the *Franklin* had to be released following the pressures of the British diplomacy. This time the Bourbon commander is more prudent and the two Bourbon ships position themselves on both sides of the *Franklin* without firing. "*Suddenly Garibaldi shouted: 'Origoni, raise the American flag'*". From the *Fulminante* they ask: "*'Where do you come from?' ... Origoni, in turn grabbed the megaphone and answered in English 'I do not understand you'*". The *Fulminante* puts a lance to sea that draws near the *Franklin*. "*A voice of on the lance renewed the question: 'Where are you from?'*". Origoni answers something but his voice is covered by the noise of the engine, Garibaldi has given the order to leave and to ignore the Bourbons that at this point let them go. "*Indeed, in that moment it was some sort of miracle that cannon shots did not fly from the sides of the Fulminante; the American flag did that miracle*". While slowly they move away, they see the *Fulminante* heading towards the *Torino* and destroy it with cannon fire, it was the only way they could vent their anger. Garibaldi's comment: "*These are their battles*". What a chutzpah.

When the *Fulminante* and the *Aquila* leave the scene Garibaldi goes back and lands in Calabria. It's done.

The Bourbon navy is now paralyzed and does not oppose any resistance: the officers have all been acquired to the Italian cause. On the ship *Fieramosca* exasperated by the continuous yeldings, the sailors revolt and close the officers in the cargo hold. They sail for Naples and deliver the officers to a military court, but the court agrees with the officers and the sailors are imprisoned.

Bandi sets out along Calabria, according to him the Bourbon army is still 80,000 men strong but the troops in Calabria are falling apart: "*From Reggio on, along Calabria, up to near Cosenza you could only see crowds of Bourbon troops who wandered the countryside deaf to any prayer, to any rebuke and adamant in the intention to want to return to their homes*". Garibaldi cries: "*What a pity! What good soldiers they would be! How beautiful it would be to march with these people up to*

Rome!". Only his sick mind could imagine that the Neapolitan soldiers would have been available to move against the Pope.

For the Bourbon soldiers it's "all go home!" The regime is breaking apart and the troops do not respect the authority of the officers any more. Now it is happening what will happen in Italy 80 years later, on September 8, 1943, when another regime comes apart and each Italian soldier will have to decide, alone, on which side he wants to be. The revenge of the Bourbons.

At Mileto the soldiers hear the general Brigante give another order of retreat: they lynch him. And then, what could they do?

At Soveria, Bandi sees some Bourbon gendarmes sell their horses in the city market. A Garibaldian colonel approaches them and proposes *"... ten crowns apiece if they had agreed to keep their horses and form a handsome cavalry squadron at the service of Garibaldi ... not one of those gendarmes accepted those terms ... One of those gendarmes told me ... we have capitulated and we want to go to our homes. Are we supposed to take charge of your Italy!"*. That soldier could not have been more mistaken than that, he does not know the meaning of "woe to the vanquished!". In the following years it will be the Kingdom of Italy that will take charge of the Bourbon soldiers as agnostics as him.

To understand how the Bourbon soldiers were hostile to the national cause, you need to consider how their situation was desperate. Forbes tells us that while he is racing towards Naples, he comes across these crowds of defeated Bourbons; he knows that they had no money to buy food and yet: *"Their conduct,nevertheless, has been most exemplary; they have neither robbed nor invaded the villages ... I believe that the Italian peasant ... is honest and patient in the extreme; some are gay enough, but the majority never allow us to pass without making the usual "lazzaroni"gesticulation with the forefinger and thumb, which means "dying of hunger". Many are poorly clad and shoeless, and from sleeping in the fever districts, ill and emaciated; ... In all there must be 25,000 of these poor wretches on the road, and many must perish"*[68].

Forbes notes that only in few cases the Neapolitan officers were able to convince their soldiers to desert; he had seen in what situation they

---

[68] Charles Stuart Forbes, *The campaign of Garibaldi in the Two Sicilies*, (Blackwood and Sons: London 1862), pag.212

were yet he does not accept their desertion not even for a good (for him) cause: "*Anyhow, the thing hurt my feelings. You can not respect them*". This is what was left attached to the southern people after the adventure of Garibaldi. The world will not remember the sacrifice of those soldiers who faced death not to betray; it is with this last judgment that the world will remember them: contempt.

The Garibaldian army rushes towards Naples by land and by sea. By now the sea is completely under their control as Garibaldi tells us in his *Memorie*: "*Another circumstance, very favorable to the national cause, was the tacit consent of the Bourbon navy which could have, if entirely hostile, much delayed our progress towards the capital. Indeed our ships were carrying freely the troops of our southern army along the coast of Naples, without obstacles, something that could not have been done with an absolutely contrary navy*".

Garibaldi must hurry because Cavour is trying to precede him with his emissaries to convert as many Neapolitans as possible to his cause and block any ambition of Garibaldi to attack Rome or, worse, to give life to a political entity independent of the Kingdom of Sardinia.

Cavour had written on August 3rd to Persano: "*Do what you can to start the revolt in Naples before the arrival of general Garibaldi, not only to pave his way but also to save us from the diplomacy. If he were to arrive first, without hesitation take the command of all naval forces, getting along with the general but also without his consent if this were necessary*"[69].

Cavour has acquired to the Italian cause the uncle of the king, the minister of the interior Liborio Romano, the adjutant general of the king Nunziante and the minister of war Pianell. With these people Cavour tries to start a revolt or a coup in Naples before the arrival of Garibaldi. He had given instructions to Persano to rely on Liborio and Nunziante: "*I think we can rely on them: on the minister because he is an old unitary liberal; on the general because I have so much in hand to have him hanged if necessary*"[70].

Ships of war of the Sardinian navy are in the port of Naples with two battalions of riflemen while weapons and munitions are prepared to help

---

[69] Giuseppe Bandi, *Da Genova a Capua*, (BUR Milano 1960), pag.400

[70] Gilberto Oneto, *L'Iperitaliano* (Rimini: Il Cerchio, 2006), pag.157

the rebels, but the attempt shipwrecks among the total indifference of the people; the uncle of the king and general Nunziante must take refuge on the Sardinian ships. Only the charisma of Garibaldi can trigger more or less popular riots.

Francesco II has still 50.000 men that, under the command of Bosco, could face Garibaldi in front of Salerno but on September 5 he decides to leave Naples and with a proclamation he explains that he wants to save his capital "*from the ruins of war, to save its inhabitants and their properties, the holy temples, the monuments, the public buildings, the art collections, and all that make up the heritage of its civilization and of its greatness that, since it belongs to the future generations, it is superior to the passions of the past*"[71]. He orders Bosco to withdraw and to go to position the army on the line of the Volturno river, north of the capital. What is the point of all this? Salerno is 70 kilometers from Naples and a battle could not cause any harm to the city. Not only he leaves to Garibaldi his capital without a fight, he leaves also all the finances of the kingdom and even his personal wealth! What is the point to leave everything to Garibaldi to retire and then face him with a weakened and discouraged army at the northern border of the kingdom? Just think that to prove his good will a few months before he had brought back to Naples the sum of 50 million francs gold that his father had deposited in London for the "you never know".

Yet, despite this defeatist and rambling strategy, soldiers and sailors remain faithful and follow him, which indicates an attachment that is difficult to understand. How can you be so loyal to an idiot? Admiral Mundy arrived in Naples with his fleet and this is his opinion on Francesco II: "*It was now known in the city that the king was making preparations for his departure: alas! not to put himself at the head of his faithful soldiery, who had and would still have fought gallantly for his house and dynasty, but to secure the personal safety of himself and his brave young Queen ... What an opportunity lost for the youngest sovereign in Europe to have made himself a name never to have been forgotten in history! The remembrance of the bravery shown by his troops at Melazzo should have made him feel they would not desert the Royal standard when properly led; and an act of daring resolution on his part might have*

---

[71] Alfonso Scirocco, *Garibaldi*, (Bari: Laterza, 2001), pag. 288

checked the tide of invasion and gained him the approbation of the world"[72].

On September 6, the king left Naples on a couple of Spanish ships to take refuge in the fortress of Gaeta with his entire family. The ships pass by the *Hannibal* from where Admiral Mundy was watching the departure: "*He left the palace of his ancestors, and headed for the Mole amidst a vast crowd of the inhabitants, but not a tear was shed, nor was a 'God bless you!' even heard. It was the desolation of indifference. Indeed a melancholy spectacle, which it grieved me to behold*".

Before leaving the king had declared: "*Only their eyes to cry will be left to the Neapolitans, I do not know how the remorse does not kill all those who betrayed me*". The Neapolitan warships remain in the port to be acquired in the Sardinian navy, but most of the crews abandon the ships to follow the king.

Garibaldi runs, he goes by boat to Salerno and from here he takes the train to Naples; he is alone with five other comrades. His nearest troops are two days away, but he is not afraid because before arriving in Salerno he met an emissary of the British government and had sent Alexander Dumas with his yacht to Naples to take contact with the minister of the Interior Liborio Romano, a Freemason brother. In the port of Naples there is Admiral Bundy with the *Hannibal* and other British warships that can take him on board if necessary while for his personal safety he already knows on whom he can rely: on the Camorra!

"Garibaldi was in fact already in contact with Liborio Romano, which is still formally a member of the royal government: it is he who provides him with the contact and the agreement with Salvatore De Crescenzo (called Tore'e Criscienzo), which is the recognized leader of the Camorra and is held in prison. Romano negotiates with De Crescenzo his release and that of all Camorra prisoners in exchange for their "revolutionary" help to Garibaldi, that consists on the elimination "by knife" of the police officers and the takeover of the city"[73].

On the afternoon of September 7, he arrives at the station of Naples. There is a huge crowd waiting for him. The forts of the city are manned by 6.000 Bourbon soldiers but they had orders not to shoot, someone

---

[72] Sir Rodney Mundy. *H.M.S. "Hannibal" at Palermo and Naples*. (London: Murray, 1863), pag.230

[73] Gilberto Oneto, *L'Iperitaliano* (Rimini: Il Cerchio, 2006), pag.158

could get hurt. Besieged by a delirious crowd, Garibaldi gets on a coach prepared by the Camorra: "*The honored society settled his men all the way around to ensure, at the same time, the warmth of the people and their discipline in showing it. In the front row, just in front of the horses, Michele "'o chiazziere", who normally cashed the bribes from the peddlers in the square. On the other side "'o schiavutiello" who looked like a Saracen. In the middle Salvatore, the brother of Marianna (called "the Giovannara", owner of the tavern where the Gotha of the Camorra met), "Tore 'e Criscenzo". Guardians of the underworld, godfathers of the Unification of Italy*"[74].

Thus he does his triumphal entry in Naples and when he passes in front of the forts manned by the Bourbon soldiers, not only they did not open fire ... they present the arms. It is a grotesque and surreal scene. In Naples, as in Marsala, the Bourbon cannons remain silent. A couple of cannon shots would be enough to send Garibaldi with adjoining Camorra flying straight to the sky. Here, as in Marsala, one cannot but comment: an extraordinary courage or an amazing effrontery?

So Garibaldi comments these facts in his *Memorie*: "*And yet the applause, and the imposing demeanor of the great people, managed on September 7, 1860, to keep the Bourbon army quiet, still master of the forts and the main points of the city from where could have destroyed it*".

It was not about the great people but the great corruption. The Bourbon troops left in Naples are under the command of General Cataldo who holds his men closed in the forts. Two days later he delivers the forts to the first Garibaldians that come to town without a shot being fired. The Italian army refuses to take on Cataldo that will be put to rest but ... with his salary.

In the two days that precede the arrival of the Garibaldi's troops Naples is actually in the hands of the Camorra.

According to the pro Bourbon historian De Sivo: "*Now the camorra ministry put camorra generals at the service of Garibaldi; it had the former police officers killed in the streets by its killers; actually it turned the same murderers into police officers; it put camorra intendants to the government of the provinces, to the management, to the administrations, to the courts*".

---

[74] Gilberto Oneto, *L'Iperitaliano* (Rimini: Il Cerchio, 2006), pag.160

According to the Garibaldian chronicler Forbes: *"Anything to equal the masquerade – for it cannot be dignified by the term enthusiasm – of the two days subsequent to Garibaldi's entry, could only be achieved by Neapolitans. Not only was all business sospended, but the entire population roused themselves into a state of frenzy bordering on madness, which offtimes became ridiculous, and at others unfortunately dangerous, numerous assassinations taking place. Night and day the entire population were in the streets; carriages full of "putanas" offered you the alternative of a dagger or the now universal cry of "una", symbolic of a united Italy. Bands of ruffians in red shirts invaded hotels and cafès, and forced, arms in hand, every one to join in their orgies"*[75].

So ends Naples capital of a kingdom, along with London and Paris it had been one of the oldest capitals in Europe. As in Sicily, also in Naples organized crime enters the institutions in the wake of the victory of Garibaldi. So Italy began and so it continued.

On the 9 the first Garibaldian troops arrive and take over the forts from where the Bourbons come out well organized and with their flags. Admiral Mundy is present: *"At sunset the Royal troops marched out of the city towards Capua. I took up a position at the extremity of the Toledo to watch their exit. Every opportnity was given for desertion from their ranks to the army of the Revolution, but few availed themselves of it. Ther was a sullen determination and defiance in the look and bearing of the men, which gave no evidence of sympathy with the cause of the Dictator"*.

Slowly, with the arrival of the Garibaldians the violence of the Camorra subsides, but who will protect Naples from the violence of the Garibaldians? So De Sivo describes their arrival in the city: *"Everything is lawful for them. For them castles, palaces, arsenals, monasteries and houses; everything belongs to them that come out of all parts of the world; followed by Sicilians and Calabrians, hired thugs, robbers already, former convicts, despisers of all rights, blasphemers of all Gods, ignorant of every law. They invade palaces, mansions and towns: they rob every tool, every life they threaten, damage every monument, insult every greatness. Naples, that never saw the Vandals, she saw the Garibaldians!"*.

---

[75] Charles Stuart Forbes, *The campaign of Garibaldi in the Two Sicilies*, (Blackwood and Sons, London 1862, pag.237

To complicate things the first anti Italian riots start; thus Garibaldi informs us in his *Memorie*: "*The first columns of the southern army, just arrived near Naples, were directed towards Avellino and Ariano, to quell some reactionary movements, raised by the priests and the Bourbons. General Turr was in charge, and perfectly fulfilled*". Laconic and brutal.

We must infer that the situation was serious enough if Garibaldi had to divert his troops from Naples. Thus the slaughter of the southern peoples began. It was not the fault of the obtuseness of the Piedmontese if the Kingdom of Italy began immediately after the conquest a war of repression of the anti unitary revolts; this repression began immediately with Garibaldi.

This implacable hatred that the patriots have against the anti Italian reactionaries had already appeared a few days before. In late August, before arriving at Salerno Garibaldi had ordered the elimination of those civilians who had fought against Pisacane when, three years earlier, he had landed near Sapri with 300 criminals to initiate a people's revolt that nobody wanted. In the following days 4 people were murdered in the village of Sanza: two city guards, a pharmacist and a farmer. Probably these were the only people that they had found in town.

Also Abba arrives at Naples: "*Great, immense, to get lost in it and pompous even in the display of misery. I never saw grime carried around like that! I gave a run through the slums; there is something that goes to the brain as when you navigate a marsh. People are teeming, you have to be small to pass, and you come away stunned*". It seems that nothing has changed in these 150 years.

Naples will remain for a few months under the administration of Garibaldi. It's impossible to overstate the disasters that this administration caused to the city and to the kingdom. Just a few examples.[76]

Immediately, on September 7, Garibaldi assignes himself with dictatorial decree a free hand on the public deposits in the Bank of the Two Sicilies, which amount to more than 500 million Euro, and makes them disappear in a few days. Pensions and annuities are granted to all those who can claim to have suffered for the Italian cause, like the daughter of

---

[76] For a detailed list and relative documentation see: Gilberto Oneto, *L'Iperitaliano* (Rimini: Il Cerchio, 2006), pag.160-173

Pisacane or the widow of Agesilao Milano who four years earlier had attempted to assassinate the king. The Rubattino is indemnified for the two steamers used in the enterprise, even if they had already been paid and had also been returned to the company. Mr. Rubattino, however, will complain of not having been adequately rewarded. On October 23 Garibaldi offers all those who had suffered "injustices" by the Bourbons the assets of the Royal House. Also the private properties of the Bourbons are looted. Among the people compensated for the injustices there are the wives of leaders of the Camorra who receive an annuity of 2,000 euros per month. He also makes the Camorra receive a sum of 17 million euros to be distributed to the "people". A special mention goes to Alexandre Dumas who is appointed manager of the excavations of Pompei and Herculaneum for an astronomical compensation.

Exhausted the cash a job is given to all those who claim to have fought for the national cause by filling all public bodies up to capacity, first the Southern Army that will come to have an officer every four soldiers. Bertani is now in Naples and fills his pockets without any restraint. Garibaldi does not notice anything or he pretends. He will declare later: "*If it were not for making a scandal I would take off the coffer to Bertani*". He did not and at the end of the adventure Bertani will be one of the richest men in Italy. The total mass of financial resources destroyed by the Garibaldians has been assessed at 2.000 billion Euro.

So ends the Gold of Naples.

A separate story is that of the Southern Railways. The father of Francesco II had started a major program of railway construction because the kingdom was behind the other European countries. When Garibaldi takes power the project had already been approved, the funds had already been allocated by the "corrupt" Bourbon administration, the contract had already been regularly assigned to a French company and a lot of work had already started. Garibaldi immediately cancels this contract and, having not forgotten his Masonic brothers, gives it to a couple of bankers, Adami and Lemmi that were Masonic brothers as well as in-laws, at a higher cost than already contracted. These bankers had financed his expedition and that of Pisacane, moreover Lemmi had gone to Palermo with a letter by Mazzini to Crispi (Minister of the Interior and Finance in the Government of Garibaldi): "*Brother, the bearer, Adriano Lemmi, has been a very good friend of mine for twenty years and did considerable sacrifices for the cause. He comes to treat an important matter concerning the recent assignment of the railroads to Adami. Hear him, please; he will explain everything. I only tell you that, where others would make his own all the fruit of the enterprise, he aims to found the coffers of our party not his own. Love me well*"[77]. This recommendation is made on the grounds that Lemmi would not act just for his personal interest, but he would also contribute to the coffers of their movement (Republican). This contract will be canceled by Cavour because its provisions guaranteed huge profits to the two bankers and its capital had been destroyed. The two will still manage to finance various Mazzini newspapers including the *Popolo d'Italia*; but this is another story.

In the midst of this orgy of destruction Garibaldi does not seem to notice anything; he has always despised money. He prefers to enjoy another wave of popularity. In London a million copies were sold of his portrait. In Naples he receives groups of English ladies and grants them a kiss and the cutting of a strand of hair while General Turr combs them. His closest associates had put next to him a bodyguard to ward off the too insistent female admirers.

In those days Cavour, Vittorio Emanuele and the European diplomacy were working hard to make sure that this conquest were settled in the best way possible. Cavour manages to convince Napoleon that the best thing for everyone was for the Piedmontese army to go "to the rescue" of Garibaldi, who is still facing the Bourbon army, crossing the State of the Church and annexing the Kingdom of the Two Sicilies. This would stop Garibaldi from attacking Rome or from putting together another state entity independent of Piedmont. In mid-September the Piedmontese army crosses the border of the State of the Church without a declaration of war and defeats a small army that the Pope had sent against it but with the order not to get hurt.

At this point, Garibaldi must move and, if he wants to go to Rome, he must defeat the Bourbon army that is standing in the way before the arrival of the Piedmontese troops. In addition, the popular revolts against him are spreading and the situation could get out of hand.

---

[77] Mario Costa Cardol, *Ingovernabili da Torino* (Milano: Mursia 1989), pag 46

On October 1 the battle takes place along the Volturno river and ends without either of them overpowering the other. Up to the last minute the battle was uncertain, Francesco II can not break through to recover Naples and Garibaldi can not defeat him to complete the conquest and continue towards Rome.

Now the Bourbon army is still intact and, even worse, the troops that Garibaldi had sent under the command of colonel Nullo to Sannio to quell the anti Italian riots had been massacred by the population that is stil fanatically loyal to its king. Five hundred Garibaldians are massacred by the peasants, the worst death toll of the entire expedition. This is what Abba tells us: "*Pettorano, Carpinone, Isernia, you deserve that no more rain nor dew fall on you, until the memory of our fallen will last, deceived and chased and killed on your fields and your woods! They returned the remains of the Nullo column; we do not stand to their stories; they cannot say but dead, dead, dead! They seem to have still around them the orgy of peasants, soldiers, monks who killed to the cry of long live Francesco the second and long live Maria. **Poor Bettoni!** ... He came on the rear wounded on a carriage; they rode at its sides Lavagnolo and Moro, trying to take him to safety in Boiano, and then to rush back where Nullo was fighting, and our men were dying, here, there, in groups, alone, terrified by the wild cries, by the fury of the women, unleashed bitches, rather than by the multitude of the armed men that countless were throwing themselves at them. Poor knights! The next day Lieutenant Candiani found them dead, naked, outraged on the road. Ah! that Sannio!, that Sannio!*"

A dramatic description that renders exactly the hatred that those people felt towards these liberators that no one had called; it is impressive "*the fury of the women, unleashed bitches*". They used various tricks. For example a group of women welcomed the tired soldiers and offered them a drink. They left their guns in a corner and sat down. At this point, the women pulled out their knives, slaugthered them, stripped the bodies and threw them on the road, mutilated. Then they fled. Now Abba knows he is hated and he hates too.

On October 9, the Piedmontese army crosses the border of the Kingdom of the Two Sicilies, without a declaration of war, and marches against the Bourbon army. The European diplomats had protested against this conquest made by stealth, but England intervenes and the

Foreign Minister sends a telegram to the main European chancelleries stating that: "*The Government of His Britannic Majesty does not see sufficient grounds to justify the severe reprimand with which Austria, France, Prussia and Russia have branded the acts of the King of Sardinia*". Which of you gentlemen wants to challenge England?

Garibaldi realized that his Southern Army cannot defeat the Neapolitan army nor can suppress the popular uprisings. It fades away his dream of a triumphal march on Rome and to remain at the head of his army. In mid-October he approves and initiates the plebiscite for the annexation of Southern Italy to the Kingdom of Sardinia. On October 20 the Piedmontese army defeats the Bourbon army and on the 26th Garibaldi goes to meet Vittorio Emanuele en route to Naples: he cedes the Dictatorship and the command of his Southern Army.

Thus ends his adventure.

He must remain in Naples a few more days to hand over his administration to the Piedmontese and to King Vittorio. These days are very sad for him because both the Piedmontese military and the king do not miss a chance to humiliate him. Cavour has appointed Farini, Lieutenant General of Naples, who boasts publicly that he never gave his hand to Garibaldi. The Piedmontese soldiers detest the Garibaldians with an intensity that leaves you amazed. Both the king and the military must show to the Neapolitans and to the foreigners that they do not need Garibaldi and they behave as if they had conquered the Kingdom of the Two Sicilies. In those days the Piedmontese army begins the siege of the fortresses of Capua, Gaeta, Civitella del Tronto and Messina who are in the hands of the Bourbons and refuse to surrender. Except for Capua, Garibaldi and his troops are excluded from these operations.

The embarrassment increases when King Vittorio and Garibaldi move together because the people seek only Garibaldi and to him only makes feast while the king is ignored. Garibaldi tries to step aside so as not to give the impression that the Italians are divided between them. Abba tells us that: "*Yesterday the Dictator did not go to have breakfast at the King's. He said of having already had it ... And this must be the thorn of his great heart he who wanted to give a million rifles to Italy, and Italy gave him just twenty thousand volunteers*".

However, before leaving, Garibaldi gets the king to come to inspect the Southern Army before it is dissolved. On November 6, in front of the Royal Palace of Caserta it's raining and cold. Garibaldi is dressed for the special occasions and the Garibaldians are lined up waiting to be inspected by the king. They remain for hours under the rain until Garibaldi announced that the king will not come, and did not send anyone else to represent him. It is therefore the same Garibaldi that, alone, will inspect the Southern Army. **Abba is present:** "*Ah! The one who rode at the head was not the King: it was him with the Hungarian hat, with the American cloak*". Then the Garibaldians parade in front of Garibaldi: "*So we went towards the Royal Palace, to parade before the Dictator standing there on the great door, like a monument. And you felt that this was the last hour of his command. We had the desire to go and throw ourselves at his feet shouting: General, why do you not lead us all to die? The road to Rome is there, sow it with our bones! ... The General, pale as perhaps he was never seen, looked at us. One guessed that the crying turned backward and flooded his heart*".

On November 9 at dawn Garibaldi leaves Naples with the American ship *Washington* to return to Caprera, Before leaving he calls on admiral Bundy on his ship, the *Hannibal*. The admiral had been instructed to tell Garibaldi that England did not want another war in Italy and had already warned him two months before. Now he makes one last attempt to dissuade Garibaldi from his intentions to attack the French in Rome but this is his reaction: "*He hastily exclaimed, "Before five months have passed I shall again be in the field! In March of next year we must have a million men under arms, and the work of the regeneration of my country must be completed*"[78]. Bundy realizes that it is useless to talk to Garibaldi and resigns himself. Before leaving Bundy asks him to sign the visitor's book of the ship where Garibaldi leaves a warm greeting written in French, then goes on the boat that takes him to the *Washington*.

---

[78]Sir Rodney Mundy, *H.M.S. "Hannibal" at Palermo and Naples*. (London: Murray, 1863), pag.282

The conquest of the South

We must now leave for a moment our hero to examine what has been done and the consequences that it will bring to the new Kingdom of Italy.

As we have seen Garibaldi reached the limit of what he could do with his Garibaldians. Now it's up to the nascent Kingdom of Italy to deliver the coup de grace to the Bourbon regime and to address the problem of the integration into this new state entity of the southern people by destroying the anti unitary revolts. After Garibaldi left the new Piedmontese administration is facing a disastrous situation. Almost everything that Garibaldi did is undone. Dumas loses the management of Pompeii, many of the generous annuities and salaries granted to those who had managed to grab them are revoked, except those given to the Camorra; evidently the new administrators still need it. But the destroyed capital cannot be restored.

The king, for his part, had to take note of the disaster; he is furious.

In the previous years the poor Piedmont spent huge sums for its patriotic-imperialist projects and its financial situation is now close to bankruptcy. They had plundered the finances of the states just annexed, Modena, Parma, Romagna and Tuscany, but it all ended into the pockets of the agents of Cavour and not one cent entered the coffers of poor Piedmont. The Piedmontese government counted on the gold of Naples to settle. Writes Vittorio Emanuele to Cavour: "*As you saw, I quickly dismissed the unpleasant affair Garibaldi, though - be certain - this character is not nearly as docile nor honest as he is painted, and as you yourself believe. His military talent is very modest, as proved by the affair of Capua, and the immense evil that was committed here, such as the infamous theft of all the money of the exchequer, is due entirely to him that surrounded himself by scoundrels, followed their bad advice and plunged this unhappy country into a dire situation ...*". The king goes on to describe the problems that he had to dissolve the Garibaldian army, problems provoked by the hatred that the Piedmontese military leaders nourish against the Garibaldians: "*... If we had not intervened, I and most of the Garibaldian generals, we would have had **an armed uprising*** *and it would have been necessary to spill blood. These unfortunate people who, rightly or wrongly believed that they had done great things, were treated like dogs. Fanti* (lieutenant general of Naples) *treated them with the utmost contempt in public (I saw him beating up the mutilated who were begging) ... be known that I have suffered immensely. ... If you had been among them like me, if you had seen the joy and good will with which they went to fight, if you had seen eighteen hundred of them mutilated, perhaps you would have felt the same feelings and would have praised the value of these unfortunates, that same value that Fanti ridiculed in public*"[79].

While Garibaldi sails toward everlasting fame the king had to take note of the "*immense evil that was committed here*" that "*has fallen this unhappy country into a dire situation*". In Naples, the hatred spreads: between the Piedmontese army and the Garibaldians and between Northern Italians and Neapolitans. An ugly start for this new nation.

To get an idea of why the Piedmontese military hated so much the Garibaldians, we need to stop once again to examine the myth of Garibaldi and to read how Luise Colet, a French writer, describes Naples after the departure of Garibaldi: "*... and when a quarrel burst between them* (the **Garibaldians**) *and the Piedmontese soldiers, the people were always against the latter. All grievances and all discontent fell on the regular government. ... The city was pervaded by a darkly sad atmosphere that struck all observers; the chants, the patriotic shouting, the parades at the torchlight vanished almost instantly. ... The Naples of the King had no more, for me, the charm of the Naples of Garibaldi; They had disappeared that spontaneous agitation, that happy murmur, that visible emotion of an entire people, liberated and happy*"[80]. Therefore, despite the disaster left by Garibaldi now the **Piedmontese** must not only repair it but they must also suffer the resentment of the public opinion while Garibaldi is always hailed as a God: the power of myth. Besides this there is the fact that the Piedmontese army had never won, nor will ever win, any battle of the Risorgimento, therefore it is somewhat humiliating for the army to go to Naples to reap the gains of Garibaldi. There is enough to become furious.

---

[79] Denis Mack Smith, *Garibaldi,* (Milano: Laterza, 1956) pag.235
[80] Denis Mack Smith, *Garibaldi,* (Milano: Laterza, 1956) pag.234

The hatred on the part of Southern people towards the Northern Italians liberators had already exploded with the popular uprisings that we wrote about, now it is exasperated by the plebiscites organized by Garibaldi that are copied from those already done in the other conquered territories. These plebiscites were clearly a farce since Garibaldi had already issued a decree which stated: "*The Two Sicilies, who owe their salvation to the blood of the Italians and who elected me their dictator, are an integral part of Italy, one and indivisible, with its constitutional king Vittorio Emanuele and his descendants*". The matter was therefore to force the southerners to humiliate themselves to accept a fact already established by the weapons and sanctioned by a decree. The voting was done in public with three urns, two contained the cards printed with the YES and the NO from where the voters had to take one card and deposit it into the third urn; this was done on a platform under everybody's eyes but especially of those of the garrison of Garibaldians or other soldiers (taken from the Camorra) who were in charge of the public order. The climate of intimidation was heavy and fraud went beyond the ridiculous. Posters in the streets declared "*Enemy of the Nation*" those who voted NO; the Garibaldians and the Camorra members voted as many times as it was necessary and they were ready to beat or murder those who did not adapt.

This is how Giuseppe Buttà describes the plebiscite: "*In Naples the unanimity was guaranteed by the sticks of the Camorra called by the Liberals to support the new government and later rewarded with the granting of pensions and licenses for the sale of tobacco. Garibaldi and his men amused themselves to vote multiple times and the modality of the vote shocked even the benevolent foreign observers*". Admiral Mundy observed all the unfolding of the plebiscite and felt compelled to go public with his opinion: "*Under regulations such as these ... a plebiscite by universal suffrage cannot be received as a correct representation of the real feeling of a nation*". Without a shadow of embarrassment, the results will be advertised with a triumphant enthusiasm: 99% of YES. The Patriots had no doubt that the Southerners approved of the loss of their independence and the expulsion of a king born in Naples, who spoke in Neapolitan and who had been a southerner for four generations, in favor of the annexation by a king who thought, spoke and wrote in French: now the word is to the arms. Now the real conquest of Southern Italy begins.

The conquest develops in two directions: the annihilation of the Bourbon army and the repression of the popular uprisings against the unification.

First the fortresses of Gaeta, Messina and Civitella must be conquered where the Bourbons were holed up for a resistance as heroic as useless. The Piedmontese have the brand new rifled guns which have a range greater than the smooth guns of the fortresses and so it's just a matter of time and money. Now the Bourbon soldiers give a demonstration of fidelity and self-sacrifice that leaves you amazed. If they were so determined to give their lives for their king, why they did not do it before? Nearly all of them will give their lives rather than to abjure their oath of allegiance and will face torture and death without wavering. Such a loyalty to a lost cause is an outstanding feat in the history of Europe. The king and the queen are in Gaeta and when the port was blocked by the Italian fleet, all officers of the fortress exhorted Francesco II to resist and signed in december a message that ended with these words: "*Wether our destiny is soon decided or a long period of suffering and struggle awaits us, we will face our fate with docility and without fear, with the fair and dignified calm that befits the soldiers; we're going to meet the joys of triumph or the death of the brave, raising the ancient cry of ours: long live the King*".[81]

On February 14, '61 Gaeta surrenders and king and queen go into exile to Rome that it is protected by the French.

On March 13 Messina surrenders. The soldiers cut to pieces the Bourbon flags and hide a piece on themselves not to leave them to the enemy.

---

[81] Giuseppe Ressa, *Il Sud e l'unità d'Italia*, Maggio 2011, pag.129. It can be downloaded from: http://www.ilportaledelsud.org

Withered leaves

In Rome, the Bourbon royal family is hosted by Pius IX in the Quirinale, after they go to live in the Farnese Palace a property of theirs. A Vatican diplomat commented that "*The whole Royal Society seemed to me, in St. Peter, as dry leaves piled up by the wind*". Queen Maria Sofia is determined to avenge the defeat and is busy in fostering the revolt of the southern people while Francesco sinks into his fatalism. Due to a small physical problem and for fear of an operation he had not yet had intercourse with his wife. In Rome Maria Sofia falls in love with Armand, a Belgian nobleman, who was serving in the Papal Zouaves and soon gets pregnant. The family of Maria Sofia is determined to hide the scandal and takes the queen to a convent in Bavaria where she gives birth to twin girls. Armand is not resigned to the loss and tries to enter illegally in Bavaria through the mountains, on foot and in winter but he is hit by a storm; he gets sick contracting tuberculosis of which he will die a few years later. He will manage to see his daughters but not his loved one. The girls become officially daughters, one of Armand and the other of the sister of Maria Sofia, Henriette married to Louis of Bavaria. Maria Sofia decides to remain in the convent and writes two letters, one to Armand begging him to get out of her life and the second to Francesco telling the whole story. He sends her a telegram, "*I'll wait for you*", and finally he finds the courage to have that small operation. Maria Sofia returns to Rome and gives birth to a girl who dies after a few months for the mistreatments by a mad governess: they leave Rome and part. Francesco is in the throes of a manic mysticism that prevents him from having normal relationships with his neighbor. He travels incognito and dies in Arco di Trento in 1894. Only then the inhabitants will know that that modest and gentle man, who every day went to Mass and took communion, was the last king of Naples. Maria Sofia spends the rest of her life plotting with revolutionary anarchists to take revenge of the Kingdom of Italy, she lives in Paris where sometimes hosts the twin girls who go to visit their 'dear aunt'. Only recently the documents have come to light that testify this romantic drama: all the players had kept their secret throughout their lives.

On March 20 Civitella surrenders. The Italian commander (on March17 it was declared the Kingdom of Italy) sends a telegram to Cavour: "*To H.E. Prime Minister Cavour-Turin, our troops entered yesterday at 11 am in the square of Civitella. The garrison at the discretion was translated prisoner to Ascoli, all evildoers are arrested. The damages produced by our artillery are immense, the fort is a heap of ru-*

ins"[82]. And so now the Bourbon soldiers who remained loyal to their country have become "*evildoers*". Some of them, who had distinguished themselves in the resistance, are executed immediately. The commander is sent to prison thanks to the insistence of Napoleon III who had protested for these barbaric acts, but he will be killed the same after a few months.

Now begins the ordeal of the Bourbon soldiers that are prisoners.

It's an ugly story: the annihilation of the Bourbon army must be completed. According to the Italian Minister of War the Bourbon soldiers who refuse to join the Italian army are 80.000, 90% of them. Of these, 40.000 were disbanded during the advance of Garibaldi, they returned to their homes and refused to go back under the arms of a foreign king. Many of them will provide the core of the guerrillas who will fight in the next 10 years against the invader. Thus they are described by the Italian general, Tito Battaglini, who studies the documents of the time to produce a thorough history of the collapse of the Kingdom: "*By now the Neapolitan soldiers, in the majority, had decided within themselves: either with their own king on the Volturno or to return to their homes, where some of them unemployed, persecuted, disoriented, believed to defend their king by means of the political brigandage, a hateful Bourbonic legacy, with so much faith that a colonel of ours who fought them, impressed by their fearless demeanor, exclaimed: If you open their hearts, you will find the image of their king, Francesco II*"[83].

In the five months of military operations that followed the invasion of the Kingdom of the Two Sicilies, the Piedmontese army takes prisoners from 20 to 30 thousand soldiers who are sent to various fortresses of the north to break their resistance with mistreatments and hunger. Only 5% of them will agree to serve in the Italian army and many of these managed to escape to France, Switzerland, Rome or Veneto.

This is the description of his odyssey of the Bourbon soldier Giuseppe Conforti born in Catanzaro in 1836: "*In my exit was the beginning of the war of 1860, after this campaign that for treasons we have lost everything and the rest of us poor soldiers eating grass we had to escape, arrived at the province of Basilicata here came a priest enemy of*

---

[82] Giuseppe Ressa, *Il Sud e l'unità d'Italia*, Maggio 2011, pag.133

[83] Tito Battaglini, *Il crollo militare del Regno delle Due Sicilie* (Società Tipografica Modenese, Modena 1938), pag. 102

God and of the world with a portion of those Jews and he wanted us saying that we deserved to be killed for the fidelity we had to our sovereign. They took us to a Piedmontese executioner telling us because we had taken so long to leave that murderer of Bourbon. I have replied that I could never abandon him because I had sworn allegiance to him and he told me that I had to go back to serve under the flag of Italy. The third day I ran away, reached Girifarchio where I had a priest brother who saw me reduced to that miserable state and saying ill of my king, I answered him that my king had no fault of our sufferings that have been our superiors the traitors; we had an argument and I left. At my village I was arrested, and after seven months of dark prison they took me to Piedmont. On January 15, 1862 they made us take the oath, in that year I was 3 times in the hospital and in prison with bread and water; beginning of 1863 I fled from the army of Vittorio, on the 24 arrived in Rome, on the 30 I went to visit my desired and loved King, Francesco 2 and I told him all my reasons".

It can be estimated at about 20.000 the number of the diehards who will face martyrdom not to betray their oath of loyalty to Francesco II. So they are described by the Piedmontese general La Marmora in a letter to Cavour: "*The Neapolitan prisoners show a bad spirit. Of the 1.600 which are located in Milan they will not reach 100 those who agree to take service. They are all covered in mange and vermin, many suffering from sore eyes and what is more they show aversion to take service by us. Yesterday, to a few who arrogantly claimed the right to go home because they did not want to pay a new oath having sworn loyalty to Francesco II, I highly threw in their face that for their King they had fled and now for our common homeland and for the* chosen *King they refused to serve, they were a bunch of bastards that we would have found a way to put them to the right. In truth I do not know what we can do of these rascals ... the young, maybe we can use them, but the old ones, and they are many, we must get rid of them as soon as possible*". This is what they will do.

We cannot fail to point out that, in the mouth of a soldier, these words are repugnant. He should know the value of an oath.

The Jesuit magazine *Civilta Cattolica* denounces this barbarism: "*To overcome the resistance of the prisoners of war, already carried to Piedmont and Lombardy, they had recourse to an expedient cruel and inhumane, that makes you shudder. Those wretches, barely covered by rags of canvas, exhausted because of hunger, kept on half rations with bad bread and water and a filthy swill, they were taken into the frigid fortress of Fenestrelle and in other places located in the harshest places in the Alps. Men born and raised in an atmosphere so hot and sweet, like that of the Two Sicilies, here they are thrown, worse than you do with the negro slaves, to agonize with hunger and hardship in those iceboxes. This because they are loyal to their military oath and their legitimate King".*

The problem is that the insurgency is raging in the South and these prisoners cannot be sent home. The Kingdom of Italy tries to find them an accommodation abroad, but no one wants them. The only exception was the Confederate States that are preparing for the civil war. About 3.000 prisoners are sent to New Orleans before the unionist fleet blocks the Confederate ports, then this way out closes. They are assigned to the Bourbon Dragoons and, ironically, they will clash with a Garibaldi Guard who fights for the Unionists. The Bourbons will fight to the end for a war that does not concern them; also this lost. A tragic fate. So, in a few years, the Bourbon army is annihilated.

No mention of this drama is done in Gribaldi's *Memorie*, in his writings, letters or other. Nothing at all.

The analysis of the popular revolts and of the resistance to the Italian invasion is more complicated and to understand what happened we have to go back in history where all these problems originated: the French Revolution.

At first it seemed to be the European version of the American Revolution, the establishment of a democratic and capitalist republic inspired by the ideals of the Enlightenment, but when the Jacobins took power the French revolution takes on its own connotations: the first attempt in Europe to build a Totalitarian State. The secular state, separated from religion, becomes a state that persecutes the existing religion that they try to replace with a Pantheon of new deities: the Fatherland, the goddess Reason, the Virtue, the People, etc.. A new dating of the years is established that starts at the beginning of the revolution rather than at the birth of Christ, they change the names to the months and the seasons, they create new symbols and new icons. They start an indoctrination of the people to force them to pay homage to these new gods with an obstinacy that not even the sense of the ridiculous can moderate. The Jacobin Fatherland, nationalism, is by far the most important and, together with the People, will enter the psyche of Europeans becoming an opponent with which Christianity will have to confront itself and to which it will have to yield the field. The Alsatians are obliged to study and speak French; their language from time immemorial, German, is not good they must adapt because the Fatherland can only have one language. So begins the ordeal of the people that live along the borders of the nations who are now determined not to cede not even one inch of the sacred soil of the homeland. Alsace and Lorraine, in particular, will be the subject of a dispute that will drag Europe into two world wars. Within the country paranoia is rampant because the enemies of the revolution are everywhere.

So in addition to the trauma of the dismantling of feudalism, now the people must also undergo the trauma of the uprooting of a culture that they cultivated for centuries. In the regions where the Catholic sentiment is most profound the revolt explodes. In the Vendee, this revolt consolidates and goes on for years with a tremendous bloodshed.

A Vendée commander, Francois de Charette, a few months before being executed in 1795, publishes a manifest that is still the most poetic expression of the rejection of totalitarianism:[84]

"Our homeland is our villages, our altars, our graves, all that our fathers loved before us.
Our homeland is our faith, our land, our king.
But their homeland, what is it? Do you understand it?
They want to destroy the morals, the order, the Tradition.
So, what is this motherland that challenges the past, without fidelity, without love?
This motherland of disorder and irreligion?
It seems that their motherland is just an idea; for us it is a land.
They have it in their brain; we have it under our feet, it is more solid.
It is as old as the devil their world that they call new and want to establish on the absence of God ...

---

[84] Before the execution, they offered him to express a last wish and he asked to give himself the orders to the firing squad

They say that we are the advocates of the old superstitions ... They make laugh!
But against these demons that are born again from century to century, we are the youth, gentlemen!
We are the youth of God.
We are the youth of loyalty."

History has classified under the name of Insurgencies these popular uprisings against the Jacobins and then they have been archived without giving them a great importance, but this is incorrect because these uprisings have been the most authentically popular revolts in the modern European history. They have also been a tremendous bloodshed.[85] They were not closely related to a Catholic culture, but it was in the Catholic countries that the French Empire found the fiercest opposition. In Italy the South had already distinguished itself with an insurgency that had forced the Napoleonic armies to retreat at first and then it made it impossible to consolidate their power. Together with Spain, Southern Italy gave the Empire its bloodiest defeats.

This tragedy repeats itself with the arrival of the Northern Italians. As commander Charette has so elegantly illustrated, Northern Italians had their motherland in their brains addicted to nationalism, the Southerners had their homeland at their feet, for 800 years and without any nationalism because their faith they had already dedicated it to the Holy Roman Church. The Goncourt brothers wrote: "*The mediocre minds, who judge yesterday from what is today, are surprised by the magnitude and the magic of the word King ... they believe it was just servility, but the King was the popular religion of that time as the motherland is the religion of today*".
Southern Italians did not want this new religion and as for a king, they already had their own.
In addition to this profound cultural difference, the rivalry of the south was also exasperated by a greedy taxation as they had never known. Enrico Panirossi, a police officer who participated in the repression, wrote: "*In Basilicata the direct and indirect taxes amount to as many as 15 lira on a poor income of 50 ... But taxes are the same for all Italians! This is*

---

[85] it has been estimated that to crush the revolt in the Vendee 15% of the population of the region was massacred

the extreme injustice, because those taxes, that just graze the fertile plains of Northern Italy, here they exhaust and wear out an area in large part alpine, wooded and uncultivated, non-irrigated and threatened by many elements. Throughout the five years of the Liberation, they even tripled the taxes, but the land did not triple its fruits nor their value grew". The problem was that the Kingdom of Italy was on the brink of bankruptcy and had, at all costs, to make the liberated peoples pay for the cost of their liberation. This seemed more than fair to the patriots, they would have given their lives for the Nation and to the people they were just asking money. But the southerners had never asked to be liberated and to have the bread snatched from their mouth was an intolerable affront. A senior officer of Piedmont, Count of Saint Jorioz, complains that: *"The laws of the register and the stamp duties, the gradual right, the tenth of war, etc. laid waste these people ... he who buys profits of those who need to sell, does not pay the right price and aggravates on the property the tax law. In a few years the property will be counted on the hands of the rich only, of the speculators, of the usurers and manipulators. ... The 1860 found these people well dressed, with economic resources. The farmer had money. He bought and sold animals he corresponded exactly the rents, with little he fed his family, all in their circumstances lived happy of their material condition. Now the opposite".* For the first time in history the peasant had his field seized, the cabin, the mule, the pig, the tools, and not by a violent and ruthless overlord, but by this new Motherland that had liberated him. Having lost everything only revenge was left. Panirossi tells us that *"In only two years, the Unification of Italy has burned in Basilicata over two thousand men"*[86].

We must at this point go into the enemy camp and see how the Northern Italians considered the Southerners.

We can take, as an example, the British ambassador in Turin, Sir James Hudson, when advised Cavour not to annex the South because: *"the Neapolitans are too corrupt, and their entire civil and military administration is so abominable that their union to Northern Italy (where honesty is a rule in the public offices) would only produce a social decomposition, followed by a political putrefaction"*[87]. These statements

---

[86] E.Panirossi, *La Basilicata. Studio amministrativo, politico ed economia pubblica*, (Verona 1868) da C. Alianello, *op.cit.* pag 128

[87] Denis Mack Smith, *Storia d'Italia* (Edizioni Laterza, Bari 1972) pag. 253

were shared by dozens of travelers and European diplomats. To admiral Nelson "*Naples is the only African city without a European quarter*"; for the poet Shelley the people of Naples "*could not be more irritating and shameful*"; for the Piedmontese ambassador in Naples "*the mass is stupid and brutal, basically monarchical; the royalty is still a religion to these brutish people*". Everyone agreed that it was the fault of the Bourbons, although it was patently false, and so the Italian patriots felt compelled to expel the Bourbons to "redeem" the South with a generous impulse of patriotic solidarity. It is with these ideas firmly planted in their heads that Northern Italians invade the Bourbon kingdom to replace its corrupt administration, to redeem the people from a benighted past and to raise them to their civilization in the name of the common homeland. Moreover, the grotesque defeat by Garibaldi could not help you doubt whether the southerners were a kind of inferior race. The slogan is: to italianize.

In November 1860, while King Vittorio entered Naples with Garibaldi, the Piedmontese general Pinelli entered Abruzzo to take it over and published in the towns of the plain of Avezzano the following proclamation:

"*1) anyone who is found with a firearm, knife, stiletto or any other weapon for cutting or for piercing and can not justify having been allowed by our authority he will be executed immediately;*

2) anyone who will be acknowledged to have excited, with words or with money or other means, the peasants to rise up will be shot immediately;

3) same punishment shall be applied to those who with words or acts insult the Savoy crest, the portrait of the King or the Italian flag. Inhabitants of Abruzzo, hear the speaker as a friend. Lay down your arms, go back and relax in your homes, failing which you can be sure that sooner or later you will be destroyed"[88].

So the general urged his men to eradicate the traitors: "*Officers and soldiers! ... A bunch of that seed of robbers still lurks in the mountains, run to dislodge them and be as inexorable as fate. Against such enemies compassion is a crime*". We must consider that a few days before, the Garibaldian column of Nullo had been massacred there. It can be esti-

---

[88] Giuseppe Ressa, *Il Sud e l'unità d'Italia*, Maggio 2011, pag.205

mated on the thousand the civilians executed by General Pinelli; a tough job but he will be awarded with a gold medal for military valor.

Cavour is infuriated by these riots that he does not understand and in December 1860 he wrote to King Vittorio: "*... the purpose is clear; It is not susceptible to discussion. To impose unity to the most corrupt* (who's speaking!) *and weakest part of Italy. On the means there is no doubt: the moral force* (amazing!) *and if this is not enough, the physical*". In another letter to the king he adds: "*Now that the merger of the various parts of the Peninsula is accomplished I would rather let me get killed ten times before letting it be dissolved. But instead of letting me get killed, I would try to kill the others ... do not waste time to take prisoners*"[89].

The massacre begins.

In 1861 the first conscription of a united Italy is called to arms for a duty which lasts five years; in the South only 30% of those called shows up, something that never happened under the Bourbons.

They also have the first elections to Parliament. In the South, only the 0.9% goes to vote; Garibaldi takes 39 votes in Naples.

The members of Parliament are almost all Freemasons and, since only the rich could vote or be elected, the new southern members are the expression of a social class which for years had been hostile to the Bourbons for the problem of the distribution of the land. As in Sicily, although less dramatically, also in the South the dismantling of feudalism had given birth to a class of landowners who wanted to use all means, legitimate or not, to hoard as much land as possible defrauding the peasant people of their most basic rights.

As we have seen when we spoke about the mafia, the Bourbons had been quite successful in the South to take out the lands usurped by the noble landowners during the French occupation returning it to those who had a legitimate title: the peasant people. The class of the "liberal gentlemen" could not wait to get rid of the Bourbons to take revenge. They had seen how Garibaldi had crushed the popular uprisings in Sicily and awaited the arrival of the Kingdom of Italy, who was considered the ideological heir of the Jacobins, to definitively acquire the land taking it

---

[89] Giuseppe Ressa, *Il Sud e l'unità d'Italia*, Maggio 2011, pag.123

away from the people of the villages. These southern parliamentarians will give their full support to the new regime that ruthlessly crushes the peasant people, faithful to the Bourbons, and so a class struggle is triggered that will swerve the Italian Parliament toward the bloodiest reaction. A totally new situation for <u>all the peoples</u> of the peninsula used to the enlightened paternalism of the pre-unification states.

But not all southern MPs were like this. The deputy of Casoria, Francesco Proto Duke of Maddaloni, was a liberal who had participated for the district of Casoria to the Neapolitan parliament of 1848 and then he had to flee into exile. Returned home he is elected again to the Italian Parliament. In November 1861 he presents a parliamentary motion to denounce the senseless monstrosity of this conquest. These are 20 pages of a passionate and dramatic appeal.[90] In no uncertain terms he denounces the corruption, the bad governance and the regime of terror with which the Italians were ravaging the South:

"What did they do instead, the statesmen of Piedmont and their partisans who arose here? They corrupted what was left of the morals, they shattered and squandered the forces and the riches amassed for so long; they have stripped the people of their laws, their bread, their honor, and even from their own God they would want to separate them. ... They have bloodied every corner of the kingdom ... The government of Piedmont removed from the banks the money of the people and the public money is cast among its sycophants; it dissolves the Academies, it cancels the public education; by the most corrupt courts it lets the justice fall into disrepute; to the government of the provinces it puts its partisans, often bloody thieves ... Beautiful is this unification of a country, which is drowned in a sea of blood, which is crucified on a bed of misery ... how under the shadow of a tricolored flag can easily be violated the domicile, the secrecy of the mail and the personal freedom tampered; ... And the accused held prisoners and with no trial for a long time, and put to death without even the procedure of a trial, just for the whim of a corporal, or a suspicion, or for the delation of a scoundrel ...".

He denounces 20.000 civilians killed and 13 villages destroyed in reprisal.

---

[90] This document has escaped oblivion with a publication made in Nice and then reproduced in full in *Le Ragioni del Sud* by Prof. Tiberiis; today you can download it from the Internet.

The President of the Chamber invites the deputy of Casoria to withdraw his motion and prohibits its publication in the Acts of Parliament because it is the expression "*of the most sinister reaction*(!)". In the same session the deputy is prevented from exposing once again the insurrection in the southern provinces as a civil war. The Government does not intend to discuss this matter. The prime minister himself, Ricasoli, intervenes and asks the Chamber "*not to do useless discussions: promoting the matter of the plagues of the southern provinces would be a waste of precious time,it would be a repeat of a painful history of things that, unfortunately, we know*".

A few months earlier, another voice had risen to denounce this criminal policy. This voice is of the Piedmontese Marquis D'Azeglio who had been prime minister and now is a parliamentarian. In an open letter to a Paris newspaper he declares: "*In Naples we also kicked the sovereign to establish a government based on universal consensus. But it takes, and it seems that are not enough, sixty battalions to keep the Kingdom .... But, you will say, and the universal suffrage? I know nothing of suffrage, I know that on this side of the Tronto sixty battalions are not needed and beyond they are. We must therefore have done something wrong; then we must either change our principles or change our acts and find a way to know from the Neapolitans, once and for all, if they want us, yes or not. I understand that the Italians have the right to make war on those who wish to keep the Germans in Italy, but the Italians who, being Italians do not want to join us, we have no right to shoot them*"[91].

These are obvious words that any sane person should have accepted, but it was not.

The Duke of Maddaloni will leave his seat to avoid being an accomplice to this monstrosity, then he leaves the Kingdom of Italy and goes to Rome to keep company to the king whom he had rebelled against 15 years earlier.

The Marquis d'Azeglio dies a few years later.

The South sinks ever deeper into terror and misery.

Here we must note the use of the word 'reaction'. According to the patriots, reactionary is the Duke of Maddaloni who denounces the massacre of the peasants, while progressive is he who, unwillingly of course,

---

[91] Giuseppe Ressa, *Il Sud e l'unità d'Italia*, Maggio 2011, pag.124

is forced by the backwardness of the people to push them, at gun point unfortunately, on the road to Progress. We do not know when the term 'reactionary' entered the Italian or European progressive lexicon, but this is surely a beginning. The reactionaries are those people who react against the progress of the progressives because of their wickedness. They are the personification of evil and should be fought without hesitation and without compromise. A similar phenomenon will repeat itself in Russia when Lenin will be forced, reluctantly of course, to exterminate the kulaks for their stubborn resistance against the Soviet system. The point is that the peasant population is naturally hostile to progressive ideologies while it is stubbornly attached to its religion, Catholic or Orthodox, and from the French Revolution onwards you can always find it on the side of the victims.

Now the war of conquest by the Northern Italians has triggered a civil war in the south between the haves and the peasants because the Kingdom of Italy continued the ultra reactionary policy, initiated by Garibaldi in Sicily, of leaning on the social classes that were sensitive to the charm of nationalism: the agrarians and the intellectuals, the classes that were traditionally hostile to the Bourbons. The landowners had the problem of keeping their control over the usurped land and hired those laborers who had chosen to side with the owners rather than the guerrillas. These "Indian guides" will be crucial to the defeat of the brigands; they knew the area and could guide the Piedmontese to flush out the brigands from their shelters, or they provided the right information that kept up to date the Piedmontese on the moves of the brigands. For the brigands it is the end.

When 60 years later the fascist regime took control of the South it did not have to make any effort, everything was already in place: the people crushed and the agrarians firmly in power.

We cite only one episode to illustrate how casually the southern people could be slaughered.

At Pietrarsa, near Naples, there was the largest metalworking industry in Italy with more than a thousand employees against the 480 of the Ansaldo of Genoa. It produced rails, locomotives, war materials. Here the first Italian locomotive was built and it was from this factory that Piedmont bought six locomotives when it started its program of expansion of the railways. After the annexation, the Kingdom of Italy transfers nearly all production to the north and thus begins the crisis of the company. In August '63 the new director, put on by the Piedmontese, increases the working hours to 11 hours a day, reduces the salary and layoffs a few people. Many workers decide to leave and ask the certificate of testimonial but the director refuses. At this point 600 workers cross their arms and assemble, the director is afraid and runs to call the army "... *to restore the order in Pietrarsa, we do not know how he narrated the incident to the commander. And so a major came with a company of soldiers. Meanwhile a Piedmontese captain, assigned to the factory to direct the works, honest and loved by the workers, kept these quiet waiting for the arrival of some authority, the Police or the National Guard to make their views known. Instead the soldiers came with fixed bayonets. The workers themselves, who were all unarmed, opened the gate and the soldiers rushed in with unspeakable vehemence blindly firing their guns and pulling their bayonets, treating those workers as bandits and not as Italian citizens, which they were those unfortunates! The captain who directed the works, whom we mentioned above, came forward with his hat in hand and shouting in the name of the King put an end to the wrath of the soldiery .... Five workers were killed on the ground, as it is alleged: others who threw themselves into the sea, trying to save themselves by swimming, were shot in the water and two corpses remained floating. The wounded are around twenty ...*"[92].

The Italian Government can no longer ignore the protests that rise both in Italy and in Europe and, after a few tens of thousands of civilians killed, finally it acknowledges that perhaps there is a problem and appoints a parliamentary committee of inquiry to go to the South to examine the situation. In January 1863 the Massari commission embarked for Naples to take contact with the local ruling classes: these are masters that go to ask other masters what's wrong with the people. Obviously there was no attempt at a dialogue with the insurgents since these were reactionaries. The report is read to parliament in a secret session: "... *Misery alone would not have perhaps had so many pernicious effects if it were not combined with other ills that the unfortunate rule of the Bourbons created and has left in the Neapolitan provinces. These evils are the ignorance jealously preserved and expanded, the superstition wide-*

---

[92] Giuseppe Ressa, *Il Sud e l'unità d'Italia*, Maggio 2011, pag.193

spread and accredited, and especially the complete lack of faith in the law and the justice ..."[93].

These words leave you breathless: it was the fault of the Bourbons!

Naturally a wonderful list of great long-term investments follows that would have brought the South up to the rest of Italy resolving definitively the problem but, for the moment, it was necessary to face the uprising with the arms. The final verdict was the result that could be expected by an ultra reactionary parliament: brigands!

The state of siege **was declared** in the South and in September 1863 the Pica law was passed, a deputy from the south (of course). All constitutional guarantees were abolished, eight military courts where set up where the defense team was made up of military only and the judgments were without appeal. A new crime, banditry, was defined that involved the death penalty, and it was defined in a way so generic that the officers in charge could execute whoever they wanted. Women and children, if relatives of the brigands, could legally be involved in the reprisals. This law will go down in history because no European parliament has ever passed such a repressive and bloody law. It should be noted that the Bourbons never did such monstrosities.

By the thousands the peasants were forced to take refuge in the mountains to escape this senseless persecution: "*You have taken away our weapons by treachery, and we are the brigands who fight unarmed and openly? Brigands us, fighting at our home, defending the paternal roof, and you are the gentlemen, who came here to plunder the possessions of others? The host is the robber, or rather you who came to plunder the house? ... Without money, without honors, without officers we fight; and also the prisoner dying under your ruthless shootings, falls shouting: - Long live the King! - Between the pangs of death*"[94].

The losses among the southerners have been estimated at up to 250,000, which is 3% of the country's population. It is a huge figure; is it possible that the Italians did such a slaughter? Another thing that surprises are the losses among the Italian soldiers who were estimated to be greater than the losses suffered in all the wars of the Risorgimento combined. The vast majority of these men were recruited among the peoples

---

[93] Denis Mack Smith, *Storia d'Italia* (Edizioni Laterza, Bari 1972) pag. 121

[94] Giacinto De Sivo, *I Napoletani al cospetto delle nazioni civili:* from Alianello *op.cit.*, pag. 164

of north-central Italy that provided most of the soldiers. How was it possible that Tuscans, Emilians, Lombards continued, for years, to provide cannon fodder to this new country without rebelling? How could they not feel repugnance to kill, for years, people they did not know and that had done nothing to them?

With the unification of Italy a phenomenon gets started that is difficult to understand, and it is that the people of Central and Northern Italy accept without protesting the enormous sacrifices that a warmongering monarchy and a bourgeoisie drugged by nationalism were imposing to a poor and backward people. If we compare Italy to the other European powers, it is not exaggerated to say that the Italians were the people the most exploited and the worse served by their leaders, and yet, not only the people of north-central Italy do not rebel, they accept these enormous sacrifices as if they had made theirs the mission that was imposed from above: to make the Italian people.

Just in those years, together with Italy, a new nation was being born in Europe: Germany. The balance of power of the Old Continent was changing radically and all the European nations, small or big, get excited and start to compete with each other in all fields, from colonialism to scientific research, to athletic contests, to industrial growth not to be overwhelmed. Across the border there is the enemy that is increasingly threatening, the armies swell, military spending grows. Paranoia penetrates all social classes and, to save the country, the people are asked more and more sacrifices by the ruling classes who had the right to vote.

The southern people did not want to participate to this race and did not want to support those sacrifices: a further element of contrast from the northerners.

Now that the union had been achieved, the Italian patriots could not tolerate their country to lag behind in this competition and, as Garibaldi had proclaimed, they would have ensured to Italy "*the place that Providence has assigned her among the Nations*". And they would have done this ... at any cost!

This will be the only battle of the Risorgimento won by the Italian army. It was unthinkable that those few illiterate boors could prevent that the designs of the Divine Providence were realized. If you read the reports and the stories of the soldiers involved in the repression, if you look at the photographs that document extensively the ferocity of this war, you cannot but perceive a certain satisfaction, almost a pleasure, in the fury with which the Italian soldiers raged on those unfortunates.

A tragic warning of how easy it is to become a **Nazi**.

"*Either brigand or emigrant*" said the boors. Thus began the mass migration from the South, but it was not a migration, it was an escape.

Thanks to an inexhaustible supply of cannon fodder, the Kingdom of Italy will manage to bend the southerners, and this gives a grotesque aspect to the patriotism of the people of the Center-North. Although all European peoples were lending themselves to the nationalist and imperialist adventures of their ruling classes, the people of central and northern Italy stand out not only for the extent of these sacrifices; the problem was that these sacrifices, they were made in the name of a nation that <u>did not exist</u>!

Ten years after the adventure of Garibaldi the revolt runs out. A broken people will remain, unsure of their identity and with a devastated economy. A disaster from which they will never recover. The southern people will eventually be converted to the national cause after World War II, and this will be done by the INPS (the Italian pension system) and by "the job". From Trieste to Trapani all government "jobs" will be taken by Southerners, a situation that does not exist in any other country in the world. This is how the people of the South have been turned into a nation of "terroni".

In Garibaldi's *Memorie* there is no hint, no mention of this drama. He was the main responsible of the union and one would expect a critical review of what he had done. Absolutely nothing. We have a brief reference to this disaster in a letter that Garibaldi wrote to Adelaide Cairoli in 1868: "*The indignities suffered by the southern populations are immeasurable. I am convinced that I had not been wrong, nevertheless, I would not take today the way of southern Italy, for fear of being stoned, having been caused there only misery and aroused only hatred*".

He was still convinced he did the right thing and the fault was with someone else that is not mentioned.

Delirium

On November 9, 1860, Garibaldi lands in Caprera from the American ship *Washington*. He is 54 years old, has a wife from whom he is separated, three children by Anita (the two men follow him in his adventures while his daughter lives in Nice) and a daughter by a maidservant, delivered the year before, which is returned home with her mother.

Before leaving Naples he had met Admiral Persano and had complained that "M*en are treated like oranges: after squeezing their juice to the last drop, they are thrown away*". This observation is not right, he was not squeezed. He had certainly been the most important element of success, but not the only one. England, Freemasonry, Cavour, were decisive elements and it was thanks to them that he won. Yet now he plays the victim; it seems that it was Cavour's fault if he could not continue to the conquest of Rome. This is patently false because it is obvious that his Southern Army could not make it anymore. He had failed to defeat the Neapolitan army and, as for the repression of the popular anti Italian uprising, he had no chance of succeeding. We must consider that in the following years the Italian army will employ up to 120,000 men against the brigands.

Bandi remained in Naples at the head of a unit of Garibaldians to collaborate with the Piedmontese army to the siege of Capua. He tells us in his memoirs that he had serious discipline problems with his men. Several times he had to request the intervention of senior officers to be obeyed. The idealist and romantic Italians have returned home, those who remained are not a fighting force on which you can rely. After Capua, Garibaldians and Piedmontese had come to blows, and some blood had been shed; the Piedmontese will not want to have the Garibaldians with them and Cavour will try to dissolve the Southern Army as fast as possible.

Garibaldi nurtures a violent resentment against the Italian government which, in the eyes of the public opinion was justified by the contemptuous way he had been treated but the public did not know the disaster committed by Garibaldi in the conquered territories; a disaster which Garibaldi himself did not even notice. The reality is that he hates the government for having taken away his town, Nice, and for having impeded him (according to him) to advance to Rome and finally realize the dream of his life. Now he plays the part of the victim, which is a great gimmick to win over the public opinion. But perhaps he was not acting, perhaps now he is deluding himself and he really believes that he alone had conquered the South and that he could have continued to Rome and defeated the French army that garrisoned it. His cleavage from reality, that we have already noted, takes over and his mind seems to move towards a delusion of omnipotence. The world public opinion is taken over by his attitude, it is in tune with him and pushes him irrevocably towards delirium.

After having ceded the Dictatorship, the king wanted to reward him with a mountain of gifts provided he had given up his army: a peerage, a promotion to general of the army, a castle, a ship, an estate for his son Menotti, a dowry for his daughter Teresita, the appointment of his son Ricciotti to adjutant of the king. He refuses everything because he does not want gifts. His asceticism never succumbs because he is the High Priest of the Nation and he despises gifts. He wants his toy, the Southern Army, to fight his wars of liberation.

When it becomes known that the conqueror of a kingdom refused all gifts and goes back to farming, the world public opinion goes into a frenzy: Cincinnatus and Washington are the benchmarks. While Garibaldi was sailing to Caprera, the *Punch* of London writes that while Vittorio Emanuele was riding toward the throne, Garibaldi "*alone took possession of a higher throne and a more noble crown*". Almost a God.

The day before leaving Naples he had taken leave from the Neapolitans with this proclamation: "*I will return among you in a few months; you will see me again, but at that time I will need a proof of your love ... Follow me when we will assembe again to free our brothers in Rome and Venice ... Goodbye, we will embrace at the end of March*". To which Neapolitans that proclamation was aimed? The only Neapolitans who had collaborated with him were the Camorra and they did not do it for love of country. The revolt of the southern peoples against the unification had already begun and, moreover, to suppose that the Neapolitans would have marched with him to oust the Pope was clearly absurd.

His cleavage from reality is getting worse ever more to the limits of delirium.

As soon as he lands in Caprera he immediately gives vent to his resentment against the Italian army and government by donating his uniform of general to a laborer who worked for him and afterwards he resumes his bucolic-revolutionary lifestyle that drives the world public opinion crazy. In the tax filings he declares himself a farmer, a job to which he dedicates with commitment and, while his myth spreads worldwide, he starts filling again his Agricultural Notebooks, he does the spading, weeding, planting, pruning and gathering. The Minister Plenipotentiary of the United States wrote to his Government that: *"while he is no more than a lone individual and private, at the moment he is in and of himself one of the great powers of the world"*[95].

Every week a crowd of visitors come to the island and an avalanche of letters with the postal boat. Many of these letters are not stamped and he will have to publish in the newspapers an appeal to the public not to send letters without postage because he cannot afford to pay the relative fine. Caprera becomes one of the most visited pilgrimage sites in Europe. Here come old friends, comrades, Russian socialist, British noblewomen, American abolitionists, patriotic deputations, politicians, revolutionaries, secret emissaries of Mazzini, secret agents of the king and many Italians who had left the territories not yet "redeemed" and called upon him to go and liberate them. To everybody he replied: *"At springtime!"* Caprera is literally buried under a mountain of gifts from his admirers that range from British homemade sauces, to merino sheep, to trees to be planted. In Brighton, England, seventeen thousand people offer a penny each to give him a gift. Always from England they send him a famous gardener to advise him to cultivate Caprera. From Melbourne, Australia, they sent him the umpteenth sword of honor.

Lady Shaftesbury begs him to send her a lock of hair and he answers that so many were cut that it was necessary to wait. *"It was a repulsive form of hero worship, that of the foreign aristocratic ladies who ambushed him for a kiss or went in search of his room to collect nail clippings and hairs from the comb"*[96]. There comes a delegation of Garibaldians who had managed to find a good post in the army or in the Italian parliament: Bixio, Medici, Turr, Cairoli and others. They bring him a

[95] Denis Mack Smith, *Garibaldi,* (Milano: Laterza, 1956) pag.110
[96] Denis Mack Smith, *Garibaldi,* (Milano: Laterza, 1956) pag.111

gift, a diamond star with written on it: "*The Mille of the first expedition to their Duce*".

The third Duke of Sutherland arrives in January 1861 on his luxurious yacht; he is the richest and most powerful British aristocrat. His Grace was an enthusiastic supporter of worthy causes that were aiming at the freedom of the oppressed. He came to study with Garibaldi one of his projects, to attack both the Austrian and the Ottoman empires, to free all people from Venice to Constantinople. In those days the Balkans were in the sights: "*The radical revolutionaries did not know it, but in the last years of his life Cavour had smuggled large batches of weapons in the Balkans for a future war against Austria; and when the weapons were captured before reaching their destination, he had protested indignantly his innocence, accusing Garibaldi*"[97]. In March 1861 he was elected to Parliament in the Action Party with a non well defined program of concord and national unity in which the main objective was to complete the country's unity with Rome and Venice: "*I do not care wether the minister is called Cavour or Cattaneo ... what I wish ... is that on the first of March, 1861, Vittorio Emanuele is at the head of five hundred thousand soldiers*".

His public statements of hatred and contempt for the Parliament and Cavour increase the split between parliamentary politics and the Italian public opinion because, while Cavour knew how to manipulate Parliament, Garibaldi knew how to excite the crowd by inflaming it with rhetorical questions that caused answers burning with patriotic passion. According to Charles Suart Forbes: "*There is a sort of intimate communion of mind between Garibaldi and the masses which is perfectly electrifying. They look up to him as a sort of link between themseves and the Deity – as a sort of father who would pardon their most venial crimes – and who yet, though one of themselves, is immeasurably above them all*"[98]. The problem is that the masses feel in tune with his contempt for the institutions. According to him, Parliament is a "*clique of thieves and windbags*" and its policy is "*dirty and foxy*". The more he denounces and insults Parliament the greater his popularity becomes even among that part of the people who, shortly before, had been hostile to him. A disastrous

---

[97] Denis Mack Smith, *Garibaldi*, (Milano: Laterza, 1956) pag.119
[98] Charles Stuart Forbes, *The campaign of Garibaldi in the Two Sicilies*, (Blackwood and Sons, London 1862), pag.118

liability for the democratic development of this new country. According to him the government of Cavour was composed of "*cowards*" and the House was "*an assembly of lackeys*". Yet in April he had to go to Turin in the Parliament to ask for a job for his Garibaldians that Cavour was dismissing.

He comes in red shirt, poncho and sombrero: an unnecessary insult to the rigid etiquette of the House. When the president gives him the word he begins to speak quietly to plead the cause of his Garibaldians, but soon he loses his memory, hesitates, and looks in vain in the sheets he had for the thread of his speech in spite two friends, who were next to him, try to help by showing on the sheets the steps he had missed. At this point he throws the sheets away and starts a virulent attack against Cavour for having given his Nice to France, insulting the whole government. The House is in turmoil, the session is suspended and then, with difficulty, the president manages to resume the debate. Eventually Garibaldi denounces the dissolution of his Garibaldian army and ends his speech by sitting down on the far left. Cavour easily observes that it was patently absurd to maintain two different armies: the House voted 194 to 79 against Garibaldi.

The cleavage of Garibaldi from reality becomes more and more worrying, how can you ask the government to maintain two armies, one of which would have been faithful to him?

Back in Caprera he remains in contact with Cavour and in his letters he still insists on the establishment of a nation-in-arms and to make the king asume the dictatorship that is indispensable, according to him, to the unification and to the government of the country. Yet he is now the reference point of the Italian democrats who, evidently, have very confused ideas but, as a matter of fact, Garibaldi alone has the prestige to tie all democratic currents in a single project. From now on, whatever he says or does, he will remain the point of reference of the democrats in Italy and vicinity.

In this period Garibaldi begins his contacts with international socialism and receives in Caprera the German socialist Lassalle, presented by Karl Marx. Ferdinand Lassalle, the son of a wealthy jew, was initially a follower of Marx but then he joined the project of the unification of Germany asking for a universal male suffrage so that the workers could participate in the political life of the new country and then take control through Parliament, without any revolution. All businesses were to be workers' cooperatives founded with government capital. In 1863 he had founded the *General Association of German workers*, the starting core of the German Social Democratic Party. Marx opposes forcefully to this initiative, of course, and breaks off relations with him hence Lassalle passes to the nationalists seeking an agreement with Bismarck to insert his workers' association into the forces that were building Germany. He will die in 1864 in a duel provoked by a love story. Lassalle arrives at Caprera accompanied by a friend, the rich Countess Hatzfeld. He wants to propose a plan for the invasion of the Austrian Empire with revolutions spread out over all cities; Garibaldi was supposed to march on Venice.

Nothing will be done, Garibaldi has his own ideas about the participation of the working class to the political life of his new country. In those days he was a chairman of an action committee for Rome and Venice, a patriotic workers' association, to which he had already expressed his opinion: "*The workers should not meddle into politics*". In December 1861 the association meets in Genoa to debate this issue and states that the workers not only had an interest in politics, but they had to become a force in the development of the country. Garibaldi, furious, resignes.

Cavour died in June in Turin and now there is no more his cunning and his authority to remedy the reckless and unrealistic actions of the king and Garibaldi. The new prime minister, Ricasoli, a man of order asked him to form a committee to organize the National Guard and the National Target Shooting hoping to keep him busy and distract him from his warlike projects to which he does not want to pander. Garibaldi agrees: these activities are congenial to him. He has always insisted on every possible occasion that the people must be trained at the use of weapons. So he writes in his *Memorie*: "*And this should help to stimulate the Italian youth to practice; and let them be convinced that valor is not enough on the battle fields of today, you have to be expert in the handling of weapons, a lot*". These are the activities to which the people must dedicate their time, not politics, damn it!

Ricasoli knew he had a new country to build and did not want military adventures, but he does not know with whom he's dealing. The king, finally free of the "brake" of Cavour, was plotting his absurd enterprises with anyone who would listen without informing the government as he was used to do. Ricasoli, when he learned that there were secret agreements between the king and Napoleon protested and the king, simply, dismissed him. At this point the king was looking for a prime minister suitable to him and finds him in Rattazzi who had distinguished himself when he relieved the king from a nuisance with one of his mistresses by marrying her himself, at the express request of the king. In March 1862 the king appoints Rattazzi prime minister with the support of Garibaldi and finally he feels free to give vent to his geopolitical ambitions. What will happen in the following months is what you can expect from a government influenced by the king and led his procurer. The events that follow are so rambling that are hard to tell.

In March Garibaldi goes to Turin where he meets the king and Rattazzi who, it seems, asked him to take the command of two battalions of volunteers to attack the Austrian Empire starting in Dalmatia or in Greece in the direction of Hungary to deal a fatal blow to the empire. They would have supplied him with good weapons and funded with one million lire. It was a stupid and foolish initiative; it seems that the king was in agreement with Napoleon, but it probably was not true. Garibaldi has had enough of staying inert and, perhaps, he thought that they were repeating the policy of deceit who had made possible the Mille expedition. The government provides him with special trains to travel from Genoa through Lombardy to promote, officially it seems, the training of the people to the arms. At each stop he is overwhelmed by a delirious crowd, in Milan it takes him an hour to get from the station to the hotel, the crowd shouts "*Rome and Venice*" and he answers: "*Yes, Rome and Venice are ours and if we are strong we will have them*". "*Wherever he went, mayors and prefects offered him official banquets with pompous and patriotic speeches. All this went to his head; this incandescent atmosphere gave him the illusion of feeling the pulse of the nation when in fact all the speeches and the applause for Venice and Rome, were nothing more than sound and fury, that meant nothing*"[99].

Garibaldi, excited by this enthusiasm, cannot make do with speeches and popular acclaims; he is a man of action. He is accompanied by his sons and by Garibaldian officers while many volunteers beat arond Lombardy to collect clothing and subscriptions for who knows what, but everyody think they were preparing another adventure. When he stops at Trescore he holds a secret meeting with his Garibaldians and illustrates

---

[99] Denis Mack Smith, *Garibaldi,* (Milano: Laterza, 1956) pag.122

them a project for the conquest of Venice, which should start with a landing in Dalmatia. Most of his are opposed, fearing a trap set by the king and by Napoleon to get rid of him by sending him into the fray. One hundred volunteers had already been enrolled under the command of Nullo and were in Sarnico, close to the Austrian border of Trentino, when the scandal broke out.

A few days before, in Genoa, a few robbers had broken into the Parodi bank and had fled on board of a boat that had been secretly chartered by Colonel Catabene on behalf of Garibaldi. The police captures the boat and between the papers finds a plan prepared by Garibaldi for an attack on Trentino that should have started after a few days. The Italian army intervenes on May 14, they stop Nullo with his volunteers and take them to prison in Brescia. Garibaldi runs to the prefecture of Bergamo to send a telegram to Turin to free them. The crowd stands by Garibaldi, they do not believe the government and everyone suspect that he has been betrayed. It seems he is trying to trigger a revolt, but his officers manage to stop him. Meanwhile in Brescia the crowd besieges the prison to free the prisoners and the soldiers open fire: three dead and one wounded remain on the ground. Italy is in turmoil and the public is with him against the government. After a few days Garibaldi is in Turin and Rattazzi manages to make him write a letter in which he gives an explanation of the facts that discharges the government from its responsibilities and explains that everything was due to a misunderstanding. It is a ridiculous explanation, the Parliament rises against the prime minister but Garibaldi supports him and Rattazzi regains the confidence. After a few days Nullo and his men are free.

There is no mention of these facts in his *Memorie* and no one ever found out what really happened. It remains the suspicion that Garibaldi had decided to finance himself not having yet received the promised million lire and, not trusting in the proposed invasion of Dalmatia, had decided to attack Austria alone in Trentino to put the government in front a fait accompli to force it to join him. If this is the truth, it is an insanity: you cannot finance a war by robbing banks and the Austrian army is not the one of Naples.

Garibaldi gets quiet for a few days but the popular excitement is uncontainable. "*While speaking about the dead in the church of San Fermo in Como he saw the crowd crying and yelling: Rome and Venice! He himself, crumpling his hat, let himself be overwhelmed by the emotion and could not continue*"[100].

It is not possible to remain passive in the face of so much popular enthusiasm therefore, after another encounter and clash with the king and Rattazzi, Garibaldi returns to Caprera and at the end of June departs towards Palermo with his most faithfuls on a Rubattino ship (again!). None of his men knows the reason of this travel and to those who ask for an explanation he replies: "*We are sailing into the unknown. Then, what will be will be*". To those who accompany him he seems sure of what he does, but this time there are neither Cavour, nor England nor Freemasonry: this time he is really alone. In Sicily the situation is disastrous. The public opinion is strongly disappointed by the Italian Government which is more centralizing than the Bourbons' and some people even call for their return. The Italian army must preside over the island that is on the brink of anarchy. In spite of the fact that he had been the cause of all this, even in Sicily Garibaldi is considered the champion of the weak and the oppressed and his arrival triggers a popular hysteria even wilder than in Lombardy: the myth of Garibaldi never ceases to amaze.

In Palermo there is a parade in his honor and he goes wild with an arsonist speech against the Pope and Napoleon. In Turin the Parliament begins to protest and Rattazzi dismisses the prefect of Palermo, a friend of Garibaldi, but leaves him alone. He launches himself into a kind of pilgrimage through the "holy places" where he had fought two years before. At Marsala he harangues the crowd urging the people to follow him to Rome and from the crowd a cry raises: "*Rome or death!*". These manifestations are difficult to understand if you consider that when he landed there two years before all the people locked themselves in their homes and shunned him. Now Garibaldi travels across Sicily and every speech ends with: "*Rome or death!*". Back in Palermo, he finds 3000 "volunteers" assembled to receive him, thay are shouting "*Bread, bread!*", But he harangues them with "*labors, hardships, dangers, are the usual promises of mine*". He seems determined to get started for another adventure with these new "volunteers". The government in Torino does not give instructions and the authorities in Sicily do not know what to do, the army could have stopped him but it does not move: there are no or-

---

[100] Denis Mack Smith, *Garibaldi,* (Milano: Laterza, 1956) pag.123

ders. Everybody is convinced that they are all secretly agreed as in 1860 and the volunteers start coming. Even the soldiers start to desert to join him to the conquest of Rome. *"The mission was holy, the conditions were the same, and the generous Sicily ... responded with its usual enthusiasm at the cry of: "Rome or death". Corrao and other egregious, procured the weapons. Bagnasco, Capello, and other illustrious patriots formed a committee for the provisioning ... soon new Mille were in the field, determined as the first ones to face the priestly tyranny certainly much more harmful than the one of the Bourbons"*.

The king issues a proclamation condemning the initiative and invites everyone to go home, but no one believes it.

The public opinion refuses to believe that Garibaldi, the blond hero, is raving. Everyone is sure that they are secretly agreed, but his aides know the situation and gather around him to make him desist from this madness. He is adamant and continues in his delusion: *"We had the veto from the monarchy in 1860 and the we had it again in 1862. ... And in 1862 the same red shirts wanted to bring down the papacy ... the most fierce and relentless enemy of Italy and to acquire our natural capital with no other goal, no other ambition, than to do the good of the country"*. Now a rumor is circulating that Garibaldi has a talisman: a paper written by the king that Garibaldi keeps in a little metal case tied by a thread of white silk. No one had ever seen it nor read about it and Garibaldi never had the need to show it.

In Catania there were a few units of the Navy and the Admiral received from the government the following instructions: *"Act depending on the occasion, but always keep in mind the good of your king and country"*. An officer said he had seen the talisman and so the Navy remained inert while Garibaldi and his men were attacking a couple of cargo ships at anchor in the bay with rowboats stolen in the port. One of these was Italian but the other was French. That admiral will have to resign from the Navy.

Both the king and Rattazzi were afraid to intervene and probably knew they were a little responsible for this madness for not having made their intentions clear to Garibaldi after the accident at Sarnico; but when Napoleon decided to take a stand and declared himself determined to defend the papacy, then Rattazzi found the courage to order General

Cialdini to stop Garibaldi. Cialdini and his men could not believe they could fire on Garibaldi at last: they obeyed with enthusiasm.

The next day, about 2.000 volunteers land on the Calabrian coast and begin to march on Rome but now the Italian army goes to meet them and it shoots. Garibaldi refuses to shed Italian blood and flees to the mountains but he has no supplies, it rains and they are reduced to eat raw potatoes picked up from the ground. Now he has a few hundred men left and on August 29 they are intercepted by 3.000 riflemen. He orders not to fire, he puts himself in front of his men with his red shirt and his American poncho; it is impossible not to see him. He thinks they will not dare to shoot to him. He was wrong, they fire and he is hit in the leg and foot. The Garibaldians respond to the fire but then they give up after twelve dead and thirty wounded. Six Italian soldiers who had deserted to follow Garibaldi are executed on the spot while about 2.000 of his volunteers are interned in the mountain fortresses to keep company with the surviving Bourbon soldiers. Seventy-six Italian soldiers will be decorated for this small battle that did not have anything heroic.

Garibaldi is under arrest and taken to the fortress of Varignano near La Spezia, where 23 of the most famous surgeons in the world rush to visit him to extract the bullet which had remained in his malleolus. The whole world was trembling for him. The English Daily News wrote: "*If Napoleon is tired to reign and to live, he should just touch a hair of Garibaldi*"[101]. Rivers of cigars and letters were flowing from the whole world and his blood-stained bandages were a relic that could be sold at a high price. "*He was a public figure perhaps, in that moment, the living person best known and most loved in the world*".[102] The public opinion of the world is with him, and condemns the cowardly treachery of the wicked Italian government. In October 100.000 people gather in London for a rally to support our hero.

The Italian government initially wanted to prosecute him but then it realized that it would have exposed to the public the recklessness of the king and the rascality of the prime minister for the way they had conducted the affair and eventually Garibaldi was amnestied. The result was that Garibaldi was convinced of being above the law and that he could

---

[101] Montanelli-Nozza, *Garibaldi* (Milano, Rizzoli Editore, 1962) pag.473

[102] Denis Mack Smith, *Garibaldi,* (Milano: Laterza, 1956) pag.130

do anything without incurring the wrath of the Italian justice. A disastrous element for his sanity.

In December 1862 he is back at home in Caprera in convalescence. Throughout 1863 he remains there waiting to recover the full use of his foot. He is always a point of reference for all the deranged revolutionaries of Europe. Now he plots against Russia for the liberation of Poland, then against Turkey for the liberation of the Balkan countries. Since he moves with difficulty he passes the time writing proclamations: to the Poles who had rebelled against the Russians, to the Russians to make them desert, to the French workers to rebel against Napoleon, etc. He receives in Caprera Polish patriots for an expedition from Constantinople to Galicia and for this he sent, no one knows for what, his son Menotti to Constantinople with a few weapons he had at Caprera. There comes a lady on behalf of Mazzini from London to propose an assassination attempt against Napoleon; they would have given him thirty thousand francs. He refuses.

In 1864 he accepts the invitations from various British Garibaldians committees to visit England. The British prime minister was against it, he was afraid that some worker or democratic organization could exploit Garibaldi to demonstrate against the government, but eventually he accepted. The Italian government was terrified, what could he have done far from their control?

It was a triumph never seen. He arrives on April 13 and immediately he receives delegations from aristocrats, revolutionaries, workers and artists. At Portsmouth the English fleet had a live exercise just for him. He arrived in London with a special train. Half a million people were waiting for him, they had been waiting all morning. His coach took six hours from the station to the home of the Duke of Sutherland where he was staying, so great was the crowd. The cream of the British aristocracy was in line behind him with their coaches, while along the way all the components of the English proletariat were represented that continually blocked his coach to touch him, shake his hand, kiss him. The queen did not like it, she said she was "*almost ashamed to govern a nation capable of such a folly*".

Karl Marx was present and judged it "*a miserable spectacle of stupidity*". Bad thing envy. No crowd of proletarians will ever give him such a reception. The socialist left, intellectual and doctrinal, hated Garibaldi as much as he hated them.

More human and realistic Lord Clarendon. He judged the show great *"because the exclusive work of the working classes, that looked at Garibaldi as a hero because he had raised himself from their own condition and because he was poor"*. But there had to be something more because English people of any social class went crazy for him. The fact is that no person in the world had impersonated in his life, as Garibaldi did, the romantic ideal of the hero. Pure as a child, selfless as a medieval knight, a freedom fighter in exotic countries like Brazil, Uruguay, Italy, a winner! The romantic and Victorian England had found its hero.

The modesty of Garibaldi is such that this triumph is not even mentioned in his *Memorie*.

For two weeks, the aristocracy tried to monopolize him in order not to give him the opportunity to meet proletarian organizations where he could have done a mess and put the government in a quandary. But he behaved well and was a great host: *"unusually gentle and insightful, he was at once the hero by a sincere heart and the courteous gentleman, with the right balance between modesty and dignity"*[103]. He loved England.

Even when the Russian revolutionary writer, Herzen, invited him to lunch making him meet the cream of the European revolutionary refugees in London, to which Marx refused to take part, he refrained from any incendiary statement. Even in London he had to hear projects of plots and invasions because, even in England, the king had sent an envoy after him to probe his willingness to invade Galicia; Garibaldi declared himself interested but they would have talked about it back in Italy. He managed at one point to break free from the suffocating embrace of the aristocracy, he went to a famous brewery in London and toasted to the workers of the world. He also went to meet some of the top trade union leaders and *"in a speech he declared his desire to meet ordinary workers: 'the class to which I have the honor to belong because I like being called brother by the workers in every part of the world"*[104]. He also called on Louis Blanc, a French revolutionary, dangerously irritating

---

[103] Denis Mack Smith, *Garibaldi,* (Milano: Laterza, 1956) pag.137
[104] Denis Mack Smith, *Garibaldi,* (Milano: Laterza, 1956) pag.138

Napoleon. At this point the entire diplomatic corps refused to meet him except the American and the Turkish ones while the Italian and the Austrian ambassadors manifested their disapproval. When the British government began to be embarrassed by such a popularity, that never ceased to manifest itself, and it learned that Garibaldi had accepted fifty invitations from various English cities, it made him understand it was time to go home.

Garibaldi obeyed and when he left London on April 22 a huge crowd tried to stop him crying: "*Do not leave general, do not leave*". But the yacht of the Duke of Sutherland was waiting to take him to Caprera where it remained a few months at his disposal. Before leaving he had made his declaration of love to England which was a bit quirky because after he had praised the law, the order, the freedom and the sense of security of the country, he praised its army to be "*still clean of that leprosy of modern times that has the sad name of militarism*". If you consider that the sun never set on the English empire this statement seems a little strange and, moreover, said by one who was still trying to put together a million rifles to arm a *Nation in Arms* what did it mean? At Caprera he receives as gifts from England a yacht and a sum of money to buy the other half of the island.

We need to add a few details to highlight the charm of Garibaldi. He had remained two weeks a guest of the Duke of Sutherland and after his return he received several letters from the Dowager Duchess, 58: "*How would I want you here! ... My every thought all my ideas fly to Caprera!*". And also by the duchess, the wife, 26: "*I love you with a love that will last forever and then more*". Ms. Seely who organized the journey, she wrote him: "*I went to see again your little bed full of emotion. I was contemplating it sadly when I noticed that next to the bedside was the handkerchief that you have used .... Oh, tell me you donate it to me*"[105]. Consider that Garibaldi was 58 years old, he was tormented by arthritis and spoke a terrible English.

Also, before we continue the story, we have to make another observation. You cannot help but notice that, with the opportunity of having Garibaldi there in London, all these enlightened noblemen and all these revolutionary socialists could also have said a word to him to intercede

---

[105] Montanelli-Nozza, *Garibaldi* (Milano: Rizzoli Editore, 1962) pag.505

on behalf of the southern populations that at that time were suffering the most impact of the Pica law which had entered into force a year before. The British were well aware of the situation in the South. The year before Lord Lennox had gone to Naples and had visited some prisons where those unfortunates were held in inhumane conditions and had reported the House of Commons: "*I need to protest against this system. What is called Italian unification mainly owes its existence to the moral protection and assistance of England ... and therefore in the name of England, I denounce these barbaric atrocities ... the description of the conditions of the tortured in Dante's Inferno would give the most perfect idea of the scene that presented itself in that prison*"[106]. That same year the deputy McGuire had declared in Parliament: "*You can rather hope to unite the various nations of Europe into one nation than unite Italy, the South and the North, than make the Neapolitans content to live under the yoke of a people they despise as barbarous and hate as oppressor. ... Meanwhile, what is the result? In place of peace, prosperity, general contentment who were promised and proclaimed as a sure consequence of the Italian unification there is nothing more than a gagged press, stuffed jails, crushed nationalities and a dream marriage that in reality is a mockery, a joke, a sham*"[107]. The problem was that the Southern brigands were despised because they were faithful to the Bourbons and therefore enemies of progress and this mental attitude was shared both by the enlightened aristocrats and by the socialist revolutionaries therefore: no mercy for the reactionaries.

As soon as Garibaldi arrives at Caprera King Vittorio starts immediately, always unbeknownst to the government, his absurd projects to attack the Austrian Empire in Galicia so as to take the empire from behind. "*For an irresponsible guy like Vittorio Emanuele, to have an obedient servant who took the beatings and passed the gains was too tempting*"[108]. Galicia is a region of the Austrian Empire between Poland and Ukraine, and the king is insisting so much because he is looking for a job as king for his son. If Garibaldi had pulled Galicia out of the Austrian empire the Galicians would have asked king Vittorio to give them one

---

[106] Gilberto Oneto, *La strana unità* (Rimini: Il Cerchio, 2010), pag. 159

[107] Carlo Alianello, *La conquista del Sud,* (Milano: Rusconi Editore, 1972), pag. 204

[108] Denis Mack Smith, *Garibaldi,* (Milano: Laterza, 1956) pag.144

of his sons as their king; this was the hope of King Vittorio. Still it seems strange to us that Garibaldi could have accepted, considering that he was a staunch Republican and here the matter was not the liberation of Italy. Problem is that to plan and make wars is a temptation that Garibaldi cannot resist. Despite what had happened two years before he continues to heed the king through more or less secret emissaries. His problem was that after the disasters of Sarnico and Aspromonte he had become an outcast in the national political arena. The Italian Army hates him, the government is terrified of any of his initiatives because it knows it cannot control him while any of his disasters would still have compromised the government provoking its fall. Only that irresponsible of King Vittorio was still interested in using the services of Garibaldi. It is for these reasons that, despite his relentless republicanism, Garibaldi agrees to consider the project: only the king can offer him a war and without a war his life is meaningless.

He now lives in Caprera surrounded by aristocratic admirers and field labourers. He hosts everyone and all eat together as if they were a happy brigade. Here comes the Duke of Sutherland (without his wife), the princess of Oppen Schilden with her maid, the Polish count Manke and many others. There was always a place for all at his table.

There are three information services that control him without his knowledge: Mazzini controls him through a Garibaldian loyal to him to try to win him back to the Republican cause and to involve him in his conspiracies, the king controls him with an envoy that shuttles between Turin and Caprera and finally the Italian government has its own spy. This is his most faithful Garibaldian, Canzio, who married his daughter Teresita and therefore he is his son in law. Canzio is paid handsomely for this service and sets up a secret code to communicate with the prefect of Genoa via the telegraph of Maddalena without arousing the suspicions of the operators. Canzio was instructed to monitor especially the emissary of the king who in May had gone four times to Caprera. In fact the project of Galicia goes on. The king offers him one million lire (again!) and all the weapons he wants for this venture that should start from Constantinople. Garibaldi must consult with his more loyal aides and convenes a meeting at Ischia to take a decision on this project. Ischia is chosen because in the island there is a treatment for his arthritis, that does not give him peace and the yacht of the Duke of Sutherland is still at his disposal. The government quickly rents an apartment in the building where Garibaldi stays and fills it with spies. At this point the confusion of Garibaldi's projects is such that we cannot describe them: we can say that, with regard to Galicia, his men are absolutely against it and one of them leaks it to the press. A scandal breaks out and the king must desist from the project and must leave Garibaldi alone, after his emissary and a Garibaldian had a duel for the insults they had exchanged. After this scandal Garibaldi returns to Caprera and must find other outlets to his exuberance.

Several months of idlesness follow; now he is the owner of a luxury yacht in teakwood and could have some fun with it but his health does not allow it and he will have to sell it after a few years. This inactivity haunts him and he looks around for beautiful and noble causes to fight for: he could go to Mexico to fight for its independence alongside of Benito Juarez. Nothing will be done. Then he asks the king to be appointed dictator of the southern provinces where he would have put all things right with his charisma. The king drops the proposal.

In April 1865 Francesca Armosino comes to Caprera. Garibaldi had asked a friend in Piedmont to send him a servant but she had to be ugly because there were too many men in Caprera with few women and a beautiful woman would have created problems. This Armosino had been made pregnant by a policeman who later refused to marry her and, after having abandoned her son, she made a living doing the servant in a small pension. She was ugly and illiterate but shrewd and determined and … Garibaldi cannot say no. After a few months she is pregnant: she will become his third wife and will give him three children.

Finally in 1866 Prussia and Austria enter into conflict for the hegemony over the Germanic world. It's War! Austria knows that Prussia is a formidable enemy and tries to keep Italy out of the war by offering her the Veneto immediately if she remained neutral. The Italian Government refuses with indignation, they would have never let themselves to be bought. *"In several posters addressed to the Italians in 1864 and in 1865 Garibaldi had urged them "to the harmony of sacrifice and duty" waiting for "the day desired for the battles" and concluded: "It is once again the Roman fascio that asks it to the Italians; may their hearts un-*

derstand the sanctity of my intentions".[109] If Venice had to join the Motherland it could not be with a gift, the honor demanded that the "redemption" were made with blood. In those five years of existence, the Kingdom of Italy had spent huge amounts of moneis for the war by snatching, literally, the bread out of the mouths of the people with an exorbitant taxation. Its navy was strong of 12 battleships and the army was armed to the best: the time had come to use them. In April, the government led by General La Marmora concludes an alliance with Prussia but, due to the anarchy reigning in the Italian government and to the outright contempt of the Prussians towards the Italians, they could not coordinate their strategies and so Italy heads towards a disaster. A small foretaste of what will happen 80 years later.

The king made it known to Garibaldi that there will be something to do for his Garibaldians too, but ordered him to stay in Caprera, La Marmora does not want him in the way. At first they think of using Garibaldi for a landing in Dalmatia to raise the Croats and kick off a revolution within the empire but La Marmora does not want revolutions and does not want to give free rein to Garibaldi, he wants to keep him close. Garibaldi was excited about the project: "*What a beautiful horizon presented itself to the Orient for us! On the Dalmatian coast, with thirty thousand men, there was enough to upset the Austrian monarchy; how many sympathetic elements and friends we would have found in that part of Eastern Europe, from Greece to Hungary! ... To penetrate in the heart of Austria and throw the firebrand of the Risorgimento at ten diverse nationalities that make up that monstrous body*". He keeps dreaming popular uprisings. Not being satisfied with what happened in the South he is convinced, actually it is assumed, that also Dalmatians and Croats are waiting for him to be freed.

Eventually the government decides to give Garibaldi the left wing of the front for an offensive to conquer Tyrol. They were to attack through the mountains in the direction of Trento, a difficult and bloody operation not suitable for a volunteer army. Garibaldi accepts without objections and a river of volunteers comes to be enlisted, many more than La Marmora was willing to arm for him. In spite of all that happened the charm of Garibaldi is intact.

---

[109] Mario Costa Cardol *Ingovernabili da Torino* (Milano, Mursia editore 1989) pag.319

The government allows him to leave Caprera to join his volunteers only ten days before the beginning of the operations because they fear his initiatives. On arrival he finds a disastrous situation. They showed up in 30.000 but the government had not given them enough weapons and equipment and, worse, it does not want to give him his former officers who are now Italian Generals because it does not trust him. Still in a few days he manages to put together a fighting force, it seems, of 10,000 men. Some were wearing their own clothes, the weapons are museum exhibits, they are not supervised by experienced officers and yet they follow him immediately to attack the formidable Austrian positions. In front of them there are the Kaiserjaeger that are half as many as the Garibaldians but are well armed and determined to defend their land. They are on the defensive because the fortunes of the war are decided in Bavaria and it is there that Austria commits the bulk of its troops; in Italy they just defend their territory.

On June 24, while Garibaldi has already begun to attack, the Italian army, while being twice as large than the Austrian one, is defeated at Custoza, they panic and flee leaving behind large amounts of material even if nobody was chasing them, turning a small defeat into a disaster.

La Marmora sends a telegram to Garibaldi: "*irreparable defeat, we retreat beyond the Oglio river, save the heroic Brescia and the upper Lombardy*"[110]. So the butcher of the southern peoples gives us a demonstration of his military capabilities. That little defeat was not irreparable and there was nothing to be saved because the Austrians have no intention of attacking, of course, they prefer to keep their positions that are protected by the forts of the Quadrangle: they are still half as much as the Italians. Now he asks for help to the Garibaldians that he despises so much and Garibaldi must leave Tyrol to return to Lombardy to save Brescia: a useless maneuver. When the Italian general clears his mind Garibaldi is sent back to Tyrol where he resumes to attack.

On July 3, the Austrians suffer a disastrous defeat by the Prussians at Sadowa and must start negotiations for an armistice: the war is lost for them. In Tyrol Garibaldi needs to compensate for the shame of Custoza and attacks relentlessly the Austrian army that now seeks only to limit the damage and keep the Italians in check until the armistice. Garibaldi

---

[110] Montanelli-Nozza, *Garibaldi* (Milano, Rizzoli Editore, 1962) pag.515

exposes himself to the forefront and is injured, he can no longer ride but he's not discouraged and has him carried on a carriage on the battlefield: he hopes to get to Trento before the end of the hostilities. His tenacity is staggering: he is 59 years old, he is wounded, he is eaten by arthritis but he never stops.

On July 20 there is another defeat for Italy this time on the sea, at Lissa. The Italian fleet, despite having twelve battleships, is defeated by the seven battleships of the Austro-Venetian navy. In fact the battle of Lissa is the last triumph of the Venetian navy. The official name of the fleet is Austro-Venetian because the crews are almost entirely Venetian, the commander, although an Austrian, had to speak Venetian because the orders were given in Venetian. At the command of the Italian fleet there is admiral Persano who made a career as we know, not exactly for military merits. He will be tried, demoted, expelled from the Navy and deprived of the pension: the revenge of the Bourbons.

When on August 10 the terms of the armistice between the Austrians and the Prussians arrive, Garibaldi has reached the small village of Bezzecca, he only did 20 miles in enemy territory and at a high price: his losses are 10 times higher than those of the Austrians who fought well. The dedication of the Garibaldians to the redemption of the motherland is amazing. They are not equipped for the mountain weather and their weapons are absolutely inadequate in comparison of the enemy, they must attack difficult positions manned by determined and disciplined soldiers and yet they never hesitated to jump forward and get slaughtered. They have a blind faith in Garibaldi that still manages to be obeyed up to the Supreme Sacrifice. The terms of the armistice stipulate that Tyrol remains to Austria so that sacrifice was completely useless.

Austria delivers Veneto to France with the clause to have a plebiscite and to deliver it to Italy if approved. But France does not want to get bogged down in the Italian issues and delivers Veneto immediately. The plebiscite will be done by the Italians resulting in a 99% in favor. Garibaldi's volunteers are dismissed with a severance pay of six months' salary. He returns to Caprera, where he becomes a father for the sixth time at sixty.

Also during this campaign Garibaldi must take note that nobody from Tyrol went to fight for him and, as usual, for the umpteenth time they have occasionally sided with Austria. "*Not a single farmer had volunteered to fight. Evidently the most vigorous and working Italian class, who was by far also the most numerous, considered itself neutral or on the enemy's side*"[111]. The thing hurt him but, of course, did not cause him any reflection about the real popularity of his initiatives because, as we have already noted, his obtuseness is invincible.

He had to acknowledge that not even the Veneto was won by a popular movement, but rather by means of a successful alliance. It was now clear that the unification of Italy was the result of a series of more or less fortuitous circumstances related to the concert of European politics and it was not the conquest of a people determined to build their homeland as it happened, instead, in Germany . This fact will produce a grotesque inferiority complex in the Italians towards the Germans which will have dramatic effects in the following century.

The reason for this situation is clear to him. It is the fault of the Church who has poisoned the minds of the people making them hostile to the faith in the Motherland which for him is the only true faith. It is imperative to do something to win the hearts and minds of the people: "*The day that the peasants are educated to the Truth, the tyrants and the slaves will be impossible on the earth*". Hence the need to indoctrinate the masses so that they too might know the Truth, that is: they too must be possessed by <u>his faith</u>. Now his asceticism takes a step forward and he decides to face the Church on its own ground: faith.

A year prior to the war, the capital of Italy had been taken to Florence following an agreement with France which withdrew its troops from Rome against a commitment from Italy not to attack it. Now the city is garrisoned by Catholic volunteers from various European countries, mainly from France, which he describes as: "*a few thousand mercenaries, scum of all European sewers, they should keep off a great nation and prevent it from using its most sacred rights*". This seems the right time to Garibaldi to deal the final blow to the temporal power of the popes. In early 1867 there are new elections and Garibaldi decides to work hard to make the left win, the party of the revolution, against a right too timid, cautious and submissive to the diplomacy to face the Pope. It is essential that this time the thrust for the liberation of Rome

---

[111] Denis Mack Smith, *Garibaldi,* (Milano: Laterza, 1956) pag.151

comes from the people and therefore it is necessary that he takes the field for a work of political proselytism which, in his simple mind, takes the form of an attack on the Church by covering it with insults.

He starts traveling around Italy and in his speeches he rages against the Church which he defines: "*the denial of God*" or "*a pestilential institution*" or "*a nursery of vipers*". However this is not enough, to undermine the Catholic superstition from the minds of the people he begins to mix his speeches with "*strange sentences about a new revelation and a natural religion of Christ which can do without priests, altars and doctrines. It seems that even in this initiative he finds a good audience. The cheers gave him the illusion of being the promoter of a religious revival with himself as a prophet*"[112]. He explains it to us: "*The aim is to enlighten the people on the parliamentary elections, not only, but also to sow the seed of the emancipation of the consciences so as to lead Italy to a new record, a new initiative that will lead humanity to the destruction of that tabernacle of idolatry and imposture called Papacy, by guiding them on the path of the religion of Truth*"[113]. Although he is a simple and modest person, Garibaldi took always himself very seriously, and when some parents brought their children to be baptized in the name of this religion, he baptized them with the utmost seriousness and none of those present laughed.

As usual it was only a show in which nobody believed but himself: the Right won the elections, none of the candidates that he recommended was elected, only him, because he was the show. The Prime Minister is Rattazzi again. The thing wounded him deeply: "*And Venice! Like Rome, like the other Italic sisters she has degenerated! My appearance in that city preaching the holy principles of freedom and truth brought little fruit. Wild cries were heard there as I passed, but little or nothing in the facts corresponded to the cries. At the place of the good deputies that I recommended, almost all serfs were elected. The priests that I painted as they were, with their vile evil, are walking insolent and revered as before*"[114].

---

[112] Denis Mack Smith, *Garibaldi*, (Milano: Laterza, 1956) pag.154

[113] Giuseppe Garibaldi, *Clelia*, (Roma: Bariletti Editori, 1990) pag.175

[114] Giuseppe Garibaldi, *Clelia*, (Roma: Bariletti Editori, 1990) pag.230

174

His bitterness and contempt for the people the, real one, increase but he is not discouraged and engages in a frenetic activity to organize the conquest of Rome. The Rattazzi government is, as always, uncertain and he is more obtuse than ever. The misunderstandings start again, his staff tries to stop him by highlighting the ambiguity and the bad faith of the government but, of course, it is useless: Garibaldi does not listen to anyone. The excitement of the patriots is such that in June 1867 a band of a hundred volunteers gets started, without him, but it is stopped by both the papal and Italian armies. He sets the date for his invasion at September 15 when an hypothetical popular uprising (again!) would have provided the pretext for the intervention.

On September 17 he is in Florence to begin the operations but there is no revolt in Rome (again!) and his men ask him to desist because the government already declared, officially, his opposition to this undertaking: he does not give up. On the 23rd he leaves to begin the invasion but he is arrested and sent to the fortress of Alexandria with a special train. The soldiers of the fort welcome him to the cry "*Roma, Roma!*"; Italy is in revolt and the government could fall. They offer him the freedom if he agrees to withdraw to Caprera, he refuses; therefore he is sent under escort to Caprera where he is guarded by nine warships that should prevent him from returning to the continent. They will not suffice.

Garibaldi was so sure that Rome was on the brink of revolt and was just waiting for a little encouragement from the outside, that he had managed to convince both his men and the government: incredible but true. The Garibaldians begin the operation on October 7, without him, secretly armed by the government who was playing a double game hoping to deceive France by provoking a "spontaneous uprising" in Rome. In fact the agreement with France stipulated that Italy would not attack militarily the State of the Church but it did not exclude the possibility that the Roman people could liberate themselves with a spontaneous uprising: it is a rogue and ridiculous politicy. The Garibaldians are under the command of his son Menotti and had entered the State of the Church without any resistance from the army of the Pope. Unfortunately, in Rome there was no revolt (again!) and the government cannot bring itself to continue an illegitimate invasion but, at this point, it realized that it did not have the power to turn back the Garibaldians while, in France, the Catholics invoke the intervention. So far this whole thing is a farce, but now enters Garibaldi.

He had managed to hide a small boat near home and on the night of October 14, taking advantage of the help of some friends, he takes the boat alone, he passes in the midst of the Italian warships in silence rowing with one oar, he lands at La Maddalena by escaping the sentries that guarded it and finally hides in the house of an English friend. The next day he passes to Sardinia and then, after various adventures, Canzio arrives that takes him to Tuscany with his boat. On the 20th he is in Florence and harangues a delirious crowd in Piazza Santa Maria Novella while the government, a few steps from the square, had received a telegram from the commander of the squadron at Caprera: "*Nothing new, the general is sulking at home*". Rattazzi resigns. In his *Memorie* this escape is told in detail and it is a wonderful story of adventures: it is not for nothing that Garibaldi is a myth (he just turned 60!).

The Italian government is paralyzed, and he is free to do whatever he wants: on the 23rd he is at the head of his 8.000 Garibaldians and advances towards Roma sure that at his appearance the Roman people will drive out the hated Pontiff from the capital of Italy. These Garibaldians are not the Mille. There is no faithful Bandi nor the noble Abba and there are no romantic Europeans. Probably the tricks and hypocrisies of the last years have turned away from him the sincere patriots who were the protagonists of his first adventures; now they are a gang of criminals and misfits. "*Some were the same boors and unemployed good for nothing that at other historical moments helped to swell the ranks of the militias, the fascists and in some cases even of the partisans. Garibaldi publicly acknowledged this factor and the shameful acts they committed*"[115]. France, in the face of such a bad faith loses patience, all of Europe was watching, and sends an expeditionary force to aid the Pope. King Vittorio is uncertain whether to go against France or against Garibaldi but, after a while, he condemns the invasion of Garibaldi, as he always had done, and sends the army on the border to block any reinforcements that were not coming anyway. Later the army crosses the border to "restore order" but without daring to intercept Garibaldi.

---

[115] Denis Mack Smith, *Garibaldi,* (Milano: Laterza, 1956) pag.161

While his army of liberation advances towards Rome, four teams of Garibaldians try some surprise attacks within the city hoping to catch the papal forces by surprise and provoke the revolt of the population. One tried to take over the Capitol but was rejected, one tried to introduce a load of weapons but was captured, one blew up a police station but had poor results, the last and most consistent, seventy-five elements, was intercepted at Villa Glori and repulsed with heavy losses . No inhabitants of Rome raised a finger to help these liberators. None at all.

Garibaldi knows that he can not attack the city of Rome because his forces are not enough. Rome is not Palermo: there is no English fleet, there are no Americans, there is no Freemasonry and there is no one to bribe. The Romans have no intention of being liberated, the city is defended by the Swiss guards, by the regular papal soldiers and by the Catholic volunteers who are not a great fighting force but they cannot be bought and are determined to fight. In addition, the French are coming. He needs a base of operations near Roma and attacks by surprise the small fortified town of Monterotondo but is rejected. The surprise fails because all the inhabitants of the area, not only refuse to cooperate, but also keep informed the papal soldiers of his moves. *"It 's amazing the state of cretinism and fear in which the priest has reduced these descendants of the ancient legions of Mario and Scipione! I already had experienced it in my retreat from Rome in '49, when with gold in hand it was not possible to find a guide. And so it happened in '67. When you think: in an Italian city such as Monterotondo ... not being there a single person capable of giving us report on what existed inside, while we were Italians by God! fighting for the liberation of the motherland"*.

The poor peasants of the Roman countryside did not know it yet, but they had become the heirs of the legions of Mario and Scipione and from now on they will be expected to live up to it. They will notice it immediately because two days later, having conquered the town, the Garibaldians will punish the population for its lack of Italian spirit. *"It happened in Monterotondo what happened in a city under siege, and that had deserved little sympathy for the silence and indifference, almost aversion, manifested towards us. And I must confess that there were violences"*. There is something terrible in this sentence. Garibaldi seems to justify the violence to civilians because, not considering themselves Italians, they did not cooperate with him.

Headquartered in Monterotondo, Garibaldi awaits the insurrection of the Roman people to attack the city, he comes close to its walls, clashes with a few papal soldiers but there is no insurgency inside (again!) and therefore he must return to Monterotondo. Despite this, he writes in his *Memorie*: "*The Roman people, oppressed, massacred in their attempts at insurrection, cried revenge, and was getting ready with new spirit ... to cooperate with their liberators from the outside, to do away with priests and mercenaries . Everything promised, finally, the fall of the priest, the enemy of the human race*". This he writes shortly after telling us how the Roman villagers were hostile to him and having just experienced that in Rome there was no uprising. His delirium is out of control, two pages follow filled with insults against the Pope, Napoleon, France, the Italian government, the Italian army but mainly against Mazzini who was responsible, according to him, of the defections of his volunteers. In fact, his volunteers have realized that they cannot make it and, as it always happened, half of them throw their arms away and go home. Mazzini had nothing to do wih this, it is his mind that is raving. According to him, the kingdom of Italy could have entered the field by his side and faced a war with France to annex Rome: a suicide.

Now he finds himself caught between the city of Rome and the Italian army stationed at the frontier that prevents him from receiving supplies. The French just landed at Civitavecchia, thay are coming and he, as usual, does not give up. He decides to continue his campaign and face the French: maybe he hopes that Italy would have awakened and have rushed to his aid? He collects the forces that were left and moves toward Tivoli to have the mountains behind, where he can escape in case of defeat. Along the way, on November 3, he is intercepted by the papal soldiers near Mentana, the papal soldiers fight fiercely and are backed by some French units. The sight of the French and the noise of their repeating rifles discourage the Garibaldians that begin to flee. According to him, it is due to the defeatist propaganda of Mazzini and of the priests if he cannot stop the fugitives and attack: "*Human wickedness! I exclaim. And how many bad people there are to be purged in this Italian society, so corrupted by the priests, and by the friends of the priests!*". As we know, he never gives up, he is on horseback and tries to gather his men: "*Come and die with me! Are you afraid to come to die with me?*". His son in law Canzio is close to him, he grabs the reins and stops him: "*For whom do you want to get killed, General? For whom?*". The Garibaldians have left 150 dead on the field against 20 papal soldiers and two French. So ends this adventure.

Two days later he is on a train towards Florence to return to Caprera but at the station of Figline the police arrests him. He refuses to follow them, they lift him and load him on another train that takes him to the fortress of Varignano. In late November he can return to Caprera where he is awaited by his daughter, Clelia, born a few months before.

A solitary man

While he was in full swing to organize the expedition to Rome, suddenly, on September 9 he had left to his son Menotti the direction of this "popular uprising" with relative invasion of encouragement, and had gone to Geneva at the congress of the *International League for Peace and Freedom* where there will be the cream of European progressivism. He is determined to keep the spotlight on himself to present himself to the world public opinion as the Prophet of a better world. He wants to overcome his character of the legendary warrior because he knows he has ideas and wants to publicize them to foster the betterment of humanity. This Congress was an exceptional event which was attended by 6.000 people and should have established the *League for Peace and Freedom*. The organizers called him to assume the honorary presidency with the motivation: "*This name is the clearest of all programs. It means heroism and humanity, patriotism, brotherhood of peoples, peace and freedom*"[116]. Still it was of public knowledge that, just at that moment, Garibaldi was organizing a military expedition to conquer Rome. The irrationality and bad faith of pacifists never ceases to amaze.

He arrives in Geneva with a triumphal welcome. At the Congress he is among the firsts to take the floor to present his 12 articles that should be included in the program of the League: it is stated that all nations are sisters, the war is banned that should be made impossible by republican institutions, the disputes between nations will be judged by a body elected through a democratic process, the papacy is condemned, and: "*7) The religion of God is adopted by Congress and each of its members agrees to propagate it. 8) To replace the priesthood of the revelations and of the ignorance with the priesthood of science and intelligence. 9) Propagation of the religion of God, through training, education and virtue*", at the end there is the article that justifies the war that he is about to start:"*12) The slave only has the right to make war on the tyrant*". And so he would be justified because, in his sick mind, he is the one who decides who is and who is not a slave. As we have seen, the inhabitants of Monterotondo are "idiots" because they do not want to be freed by him

---

[116] Alfonso Scirocco, *Garibaldi*, (Bari: Laterza, 2001), pag.359.

and therefore, in this case, he has already made it known that "*sometimes the same freedom should be forced on the people for their future good*". So, with this psychotic mental mechanism he will always be "the Just".

The audience is divided: someone called him "*a man of truth*", someone said that his features "*recall the figure of Christ*", Bakunin hugs him while the crowd applauds. He leaves the Congress the following day and does not participate to the debate on his proposals because he must run to Florence to begin his war to the Pope. His dictatorial nature makes impossible to him to argue with others about his ideas, he launches his ideas and leaves. In fact he proves arrogant and obtuse but who cares, he's Garibaldi and the others are nobodies. Many delegates did not like it, a few days after Auguste Blanqui writes: "*As for the congress of peace, a complete fiasco and thunderous. A ridiculous mortification. Garibaldi made a huge mistake. He's a grown up kid ... It happened that the poor speakers left faster than they came and Garibaldi gave the signal of the heeling. The Congress of peace was a crazy idea*"[117].

Not surprisingly, from now on, Garibaldi will feel very lonely.

His ideological solitude is enhanced by his ideas about religion. The three articles on religion that he presented in Geneva are taken from the Jacobin ideology when, during the Terror, Robespierre spoke of the goddess Reason and of the practice of the Virtues. It's a rationalist attitude that was very fashionable in those days but it would have excluded him from socialism to which he wanted to belong. From his speeches and his writings emerges a violently anti-Catholic religiosity and so rationalist that its mysticism must feed itself exclusively from the mysticism of nationalism and from the cult of his personality.

The Garibaldinism was born with its grotesque manifestations. His used red shirts, his tools, his hair and his trimmed nails are selling fast and are bought to be preserved as relics. His daughter Clelia tells us with how much religiosity all these relics were collected and preserved by his mother Francesca, before being sold.

He called his religion: the religion of Truth.

He was not an atheist, he disliked the "*miserable materialism*". God exists because "*... a factory announces an architect; a machine in mo-*

---

[117] Gilberto Oneto, *L'Iperitaliano* (Rimini: Il Cerchio, 2006), pag.216

tion announces a mechanic. The motion and the harmony of the worlds announce a regulator". According to him the "*true ministers of God*" were Galileo, Kepler, Newton. His could be defined a natural religiosity. So he describes the way of life that was held in Caprera: "*the lack of priests is the greatest blessing of the island. God is worshiped as it should, with the cult of the soul, without pomp, in the great temple of nature that has the sky as roof and the stars for lighting*". He had a great admiration for the man Jesus: "*and here I see Christ as the virtuous man and legislator, not that Christ made God by the priests who use him to cover the obscenity and the fallacy of their existence*".

In 1869, in concomitance with the Second Vatican Council, the Italian anticlericals organize an Anti-council in Naples. Not being able to go in person, Garibaldi sent a letter of greetings: "*Here in the contaminated former capital of the world, they will dispute on the virginity of Mary, who gave birth to a beautiful male 18 centuries ago ... on the Eucharist, that is, how to swallow the ruler of the worlds and then deposit him in whatever Closet. A sacrilege which proves the stupidity of men who do not offer a handful of mud to the priest, who so brazenly mocks them. Finally about the infallibility of that cubic meter of manure called Pius IX. There, in the ancient Partenope, the apostles of Truth will gather, the pupils of Newton, Kepler, Voltaire, Franklin, the exterminators of tortures and pyres, the superb columns of human dignity! What a contrast!*".

As his hatred for the Church grows, he identifies himself more and more in the role of a prophet of this new religion and devotes time and energy to gather converts. From a speech in Frascati: "*And we will get this amazing result by replacing all revealed or mendacious religions with the religion of Truth, a religion without priests based on reason and science. The religion of Truth, you may wonder, explain it to us and I will do it in a few words. Going down to the bottom of your consciousness you will easily distinguish truth from falsehood. For example, who can truly believe the infallibility of the Pope? ... Instead it is true the greatness of the ancient Rome whose vestiges are found everywhere ... Then there are the many mathematical truths: two and two make four, who can deny that?*". It is not a comprehensive argumentation. It must be noted that in his mind the ancient Rome assumed a stature to be offset against the miserable superstition of the Papacy as though the cult of the ancient Rome could provide a religious inspiration.

As Garibaldi took himself seriously, so did his fans. Someone wrote a kind of prayer: "*In the barracks and on the battlefields Thy will be done. Give us our daily ammunition. Lead us not into temptation to count the number of the enemies. But deliver us from the Austrians and the priests*".

Someone wrote a kind of catechism:
Q. How Garibaldi compensates those who love Italy?
A. With victory.
Q. What do you get by winning?
A. The sight of Garibaldi in person and every kind of pleasure without pain.
Q. Who are the three distinct persons of Garibaldi?
*A. Father of the nation, **son** of the people and spirit of freedom.*
Q. How did he become man?
A. He took a body and a soul just like the rest of us, in the blessed womb of a woman of the people.
Q. Why did he become man?
A. To save Italy.

There was also a Decalogue:
"Thou shalt not kill, if not the enemies of Italy.
Do not fornicate, if not to the detriment of the enemies of Italy.
Do not covet the national territory of others.
Honor the motherland, so that you can live there forever."[118].

The second line might seem an incitement to rape the women of the enemy.

Garibaldi never belied these grotesque manifestations of idiocy. Indeed, he seemed to favour them. This problem was compounded by the fact that he was totally devoid of humor. Those who knew him said they never saw him laughing and that he could not understand jokes. Eventually he came to accept his own legend because he believed too easily in what his admirers claimed to believe. Although spontaneous and unprovoked by a propaganda machine, a cult of the personality was born to which he adapted perfectly.

---

[118] Denis Mack Smith, *Garibaldi,* (Milano: Laterza, 1956) pag.169

In the years thet follow the Roman adventure he lives confined in Caprera always controlled by the Italian fleet and fills his days by writing because arthritis prevents him from working the land. Francesca Armosino created a vacuum around him; the house and its outbuildings are occupied by her family that came from Piedmont. These newcomers turned away that river of visitors who constantly kept company to him and filled his days with merriment. This further increases his solitude but gives him something that he has not yet had: a family. It's something that he badly needs because arthritis advances and is crippling him; he spends his days in bed and, although with some difficulty, he spends his time writing. In 1869 a daughter, Rosita, was born who will die two years later while in 1873 at 66 a son, Manlio, was born, the eighth and last child: a remarkable performance.

In July 1870 France suffered a disastrous defeat at the hands of Prussia and abandons the Pope to his fate. The Kingdom of Italy took the opportunity to occupy Rome without inviting Garibaldi to participate. Perhaps this is why in his *Memorie* there is no mention of this fact which however was the culmination of the project to which he had devoted his whole life. On this occasion too there was no popular uprising and his contempt for the Italian people, the real one, keeps growing.

In France the Empire has fallen and they are trying to set up a republic. He cannot resist the lure of war and, although 64 years old, he runs to help the republic by escaping the control of the Italian fleet and lands at Marseille on October 7, 1870. Nobody invited him officially, he does all on his own. In those days the situation in France was desperate. Almost all the French army that had started the war fell prisoner of the Prussians, the north east of France is in their hands, Paris is besieged and cut off from the rest of the country. The city is defended by a citizen militia, the National Guard, that elects its own officers many of which have been won over by the ideas of socialism and anarchy while the republic, which is based in Tours and later in Bordeaux, has garnered the votes of the province and is dominated by conservatives, in particular Catholic royalists. The republic is putting together another army but does not have well-trained officers and its equipment is not up to the Prussian's. These lay siege to Paris since early September and are determined to take it by starvation or, if necessary, by bombings: they know that the city has food for 2 or 3 months only. While the French army tries to break through the encirclement from the south, failing it, the Prussians press southward to ward off the French from Paris.

Garibaldi is received very badly by the Republican government and even worse by the military. At first they did not want him and then they entrust him a body of 4.000 volunteers who must operate in the area of Dijon. He installs his command at Autun where he organizes his Army of the Vosges with volunteers who are criminal gangs of all races and all nations. So a magistrate of the city describes them: "*a gang of vandals, bandits, robbers, wretches, hyenas looking for corpses that paralyze the defense of Autun, they only look for chevrons, in a month they cost 1.250.000 francs and lead a sweet life by participating in shady dealings on the borders*"[119]. The French province, conservative, hates Garibaldi and feels deeply offended for having to accept the help of a foreign free-booter that even declared himself a socialist. The prefect of the Depart-ment writes to the Republican government: "*The Italians, who have been roaming in Lyon for six weeks under the pretext of forming the army of Garibaldi, indulge in every kind of excesses. They just killed two men in one night ... It is imperative that Lyon is cleansed of this scum*". The French army is even more hostile and when Garibaldi sentences to death a French colonel for insubordination, the army intervenes and frees him. Although these volunteers are not reliable, Garibaldi manages to keep them together and to engage a number of Prussian troops; sometimes he wins, sometimes he loses and at the time of the armistice the positions are unchanged.

On January 18, 1871, the Prussians are one step from victory and proclaim the German empire in the palace of Versailles.

One can not but observe that it did not make sense that the unity of the German people were celebrated in the palace of the kings of France. They did not do it to pay tribute to the greatness of France, it was done only to humiliate the French. Also in this context, the terms of the armi-stice of the following month state that the German army will not enter Paris if not to celebrate his victory with a parade on the Champs Elyseé: the Germans will have their triumph but they will do it on a deserted

---

[119] Montanelli-Nozza, *Garibaldi* (Milano, Rizzoli Editore, 1962) pag.558

street. Thus began a senseless chain of vendettas that will take Europe to two world wars.

In late January, the city of Paris has remained without food, they ate the animals of the zoo, all dogs, cats and rats that were able to catch, and have cut all the trees of the avenues to warm up: they surrender. By the terms of the armistice the area of Dijon is excluded, perhaps to give the Prussians time to kill Garibaldi, but he does not give in and manages to hold together his band of unfortunates retreating in good order in French territory without being hooked. In early February he leaves to his son Menotti the command of his small army that now has more than 10.000 men and goes to Bordeaux to introduce himself to the National Assembly where he had been elected in five departments although he had not applied. His person triggers the rivalry between left and right. The conservative newspaper *Le Figaro* asks: "*by which mental flaw the electorate could take seriously this puppet, half brave soldier, half circus juggler*".

Garibaldi had written to the President that he would show up "*with the sole intention of bringing my vote to the unhappy republic*" and in any case presented his resignations. The majority of the Assembly is conservative but there is a strong presence of leftists and it is already evident the cleavage that, in a few days, will bring France to the civil war. It becomes evident when Garibaldi stands up to speak at the end of the first session. The conservatives detest him and he is received by angry protests over his strange clothing and for his refusal to take off his hat.

The president denies him the word because, having resigned, he was no more a member of the assembly. A riot brakes out between those who want him to speak and those who are opposed, the public joins the uproar. He will not speak, he leaves the Assembly, he leaves France, he returs to Caprera.

On March 18, 1871, Paris rises against the national government when the French army enters the city to pick up the guns that the Parisians had not surrendered to the Germans who withdrew a few days before. They are soldiers of a defeated army, humiliated and hostile to their own officers and government; they fraternize with the Parisian National Guard, they rebel against their officers and shoot two generals who had remained loyal to the national government.

The Socialists

The First Socialist International was founded in London in 1864 after a meeting of delegations of British and French workers. It was originally participated by anarchists, revolutionary and utopian socialists, mazzinian republicans and other workers' associations. The two most important characters are Karl Marx and Bakunin. The mazzinians come out soon after and become strong opponents of the International because they are contrary to the class struggle: the social problems had to settled by national solidarity. Within the organization the confrontation continues between the revolutionary, utopian, marxist socialists and the anarchists. At the outbreak of the war Socialism was mainly divided between anarchists and marxists and in Paris both these currents participated at the government of the city. It was after the defeat of the Commune that Socialism had its first serious split and the anarchists were expelled from the International. In particular, in France revolutionary socialism was not led by Marx, who was a German jew transplanted into the English-speaking world, but by the Frenchman Auguste Blanqui. Auguste Blanqui was born to a wealthy family in the French province and joined socialism as a young man. He was considered one of the leaders of utopian socialism, with libertarian and communist tendencies. He was a man of action rather than a theorist. He was convinced that the proletariat could create a society of free and equal men only by an armed insurrection led by a small minority of well-organized and determined proletarians who would have imposed their dictatorship. Blanqui devoted his whole life to this cause, undeterred either from exile or from prison where he was repeatedly condemned. Blanqui was always esteemed and quoted by the revolutionary fascists and by the same Mussolini. The header of *Il Popolo d'Italia*, the newspaper founded by Mussolini, displayed the maxim "*Who has iron has bread*", typical of Blanqui.

Thus begins a small civil war that will last only two months but will go down in history for being the first revolt inspired by Socialism: the Paris Commune.

The national government immediately orders all troops that are still loyal to abandon Paris fearing that they too could pass to the side of the rioters, and retreates to Versailles. The Parisian Central Committee of the National Guard declares: "*The proletarians of Paris, in the midst of the defeats and the betrayals of the ruling classes, realized that has sounded the hour when they must save the situation by taking into their own hands the direction of all public affairs*"[120]. Now the government of the city of Paris is in the hands of the revolutinary Central Committee.

Is not surprising that immediately, on March 24, Garibaldi is acclaimed as commander in chief of the revolutionary army and is called to Paris; there are many things they have in common besides the red color.

It is not possible to expose briefly the ideas that sparked this revolution because the galaxy of socialism was so diverse and confusing that it is difficult to give a precise connotation to its actors. The starting point is the French nationalism humiliated and frustrated by an imperial regime that had led the country to disaster and a bourgeois republic that had accepted a shameful surrender: hence the need to get rid of the ruling classes. This disaster had destroyed the established order, and thus made it possible to the socialist ideas, that were cultivated by a gang of "loonies" kept in jail or at the margins of society, to emerge and take over the government. In its two months of life, the Commune had no time to produce a well-defined social program, all its forces were absorbed by the defense. It can only be said that a particular emphasis was given to a "social republic" that would be different from the "bourgeois" because it would have been "fairer". No Communard had theorized this new society, so there was no element to judge whether it would have been more or less just: it was assumed that a society born of a socialist revolution was by itself more just, obviously!

This is a principle, justice, to which Garibaldi is particularly dedicated and at first he accept the post but a few days later he has second thoughts and sends a letter in which he declines the post for health reasons but warns them from the divisions within advising them to give all

---

[120] Alfonso Scirocco, *Garibaldi*, (Bari: Laterza, 2001), pag.363.

the power to one man and trust him. It was his usual recipe: the dictator. The reason for his refusal can be understood from a letter he sent to his son Ricciotti who had remained in France to liquidate the Army of the Vosges. This letter tells him to be ready to intervene only if the war against the Germans had resumed, *"but if it remains a matter between the French, do not meddle"*. He was totally opposed to civil war because nothing should disrupt the unity of the Motherland. This was a fundamental principle that will make him steadfast in his opposition to revolutionary socialism: the Motherland before everything.

The revolution proceeds without him and without a leader. The socialist leader recognized by the Communards was Auguste Blanqui who had been arrested a few days before by the French Government and taken to safety. To no avail the Municipality tried to exchange Blanqui with the Archbishop of Paris whom they had taken hostage along with others because the government refuses to free Blanqui. When the government troops manage to enter the city a fight house to house begins and the government executes all rebels who resist. The Communards respond by shooting the bishop with a few hostages. At the end of May, the city is all under the control of the government and the shootings and the deportations of the rebels begin. Several tens of thousands of deaths and 7.000 deported to New Caledonia are estimated. It was a small revolution, but it was the advance of what will arrive in Europe half a century later on a vastly larger scale.

This is the last episode of war in which he participates and here Garibaldi closes his *Memorie;* social, political or personal events do not deserve to be recorded, only war. For the last few years of his life our quotes are taken from his letters and his novels.

In 1868 he began writing his first novel, *Clelia or the rule of the priests* and in its preface he tells us that he wrote it to remind Italy of those brave who left their lives on the battlefield, to show the Italian youth *"the turpitudes and treacheries of the governments and the priests"* and finally to *"make a living with the earnings too"*.[121] It was a bad novel, he struggled to find a publisher, he did not earn much from it and the book was then used mainly by his opponents to criticize him. It's

---

[121] Giuseppe Garibaldi, *Clelia ovvero il governo dei preti*, Bariletti Editori, Roma 1990

set in the Rome of those years, still under the government of the Church, and is one of the clearest examples of how nationalism can make itself ridiculous.

Clelia, the heroine, is a beautiful 16 years old girl, the daughter of a sculptor in Trastevere "*who descended from the old Quiriti*". The wicked one is "*Cardinal Procopio, factotum and favorite of His Holiness*" who hatches a plot to kidnap the girl because "*... she alone can ease my boredom and sweeten my stupid existence which I drag alongside that old fool* (the Pope)". Clelia has a boyfriend, the twenty year old Attilio "*... the courageous representative of the Roman youth, not the effeminate youth given to dissipation and bent by servitude, but the one from which one day came the backbone of the legions in front of which the Macedonian phalanx retreated*". Attilio is a conspirator "*... because the despotism of the priests is the most odious of all, the most degrading and shameful*". Along with his fellow conspirators Attilio manages to wrest Clelia from the clutches of Procopio. This uses the services of vile characters: "*the miserable eunuch, that he was, because similar to the Turks those perverse* (the Cardinals) *do not trust their women but to neutered men, mutilated from childhood, under the pretext of making singers out of them*".

The description of Papal Rome is even more colorful. He tells us that when he was in Rome to defend the republic "*... in 1849 ... I have asistedt to searches into the recesses of those pits of hell which are called convents, and in each monastery there were always the instruments of torture and the ossuary of children. What was it that hidden cemetery of newborn or not yet born creatures? A sense of horror upsets every soul, that is not of a priest, in front of that view*". They were the cemeteries of children born to illicit relations of priests and nuns. "*And so born, strangled or slaughtered and buried was a human creature to hide the lust of those who were consecrated to chastity. The land, the rivers, the sea certainly hide by the millions the victims of the wickedness and imposture*". Not only the convents of Rome had their cemeteries for infants they also had dungeons, unknown to the public, where unwanted people were relegated to make them disappear with a horrific death. This is the story of a character of the book, persecuted by the priests: "*I urged the step but, not far from me, God forgive me! What a horror! On the walls of the dungeon where I was walking a mass of hu-*

man beings chained by the neck, by the waist and both arms, they dangled mostly corpses more or less rotten". According to him torture was a common practice in the State of the Church in 1860: "*Yes! Torture! Since in the human family there were men who undressed their human forms to become impostors, ie priests, since there were priests in the world there was torture. ... Yes! In Rome where the vicar of the God of peace sits, the Redeemer of mankind, there is torture as in the time of St. Dominic and Torquemada! And in these days of political convulsions and priestly fears the rope and the pincers were commonplace in the horrible dungeons of Rome*".

The novel is packed with characters of innocent victims of priests dominated by lust and greed of money. The insults towards the priests are repeated with a manic monotony; it is hard to follow the plot of the events because the story has no plot: it's all incredible and rambling.[122]

The only interesting part is when he enters the scene in the third person with the name of "the Solitary". The Solitary lives in the Solitary Island (Caprera) and joins our heroes to help them in their adventures. This text is interesting because here he describes himself and the life he actually lives. Thus he describes the life of the Solitary in Caprera: "*its few inhabitants, who live not beautifully but in abundant comfort with the products of fishing and hunting and a little from agriculture and much from the very generous providence of the friends who from the continent send what is needed*". Thus the Solitary describes himself: "*Cosmopolitan, he passionately loves his country Italy, and Rome with idolatry. He hates the priests as an untruthful and harmful institution*". He vents his anger on everything and everyone, also on the Italian people. When the Solitary learns that Rome is still in the hands of the Pope: "*Oh! Shame of the modern era; he exclaimed the Solitary. Italy! One day store of all glories! Today of all shames! Garden of the world one day, sewer today! Oh! Giulia! A dishonored people is a dead people!*" Despite the poor reception the public gave to Clelia he wrote two more novels which were even worse and had a worse welcome.

Now we must ask ourselves why Garibaldi saw himself as a loner despite being one of the most famous and admired person in the world.

---

[122] We had to read this novel twice

His loneliness was ideological and political because no one fully shared his ideas.

We have already seen that in the elections of 1867 his efforts had no success yet he continued to engage to divulge his social, religious and political theories without being able to dialogue with his audience because he never listened to anyone. His inability to confront the others and his cleavage from reality had isolated him although he was always hailed as the greatest hero of the Risorgimento both at home and abroad: it was his myth that the people were hailing: he was ignored.

His spiritual loneliness is exacerbated by economic problems. He sells the yacht that the British had presented him but he entrusts the proceeds, a substantial sum, to one of his loyal Garibaldian who escapes to America with the money. Moreover his sons Menotti and Ricciotti squandered a capital in reckless businesses and he was forced to borrow from the Bank of Naples with a mortgage on Caprera. Garibaldi will never repay this sum and the Bank will not have the courage to seize the island. In those years also his son in law, Canzio, goes bankrupt. His partner Francesca, on the contrary, without his knowledge put regularly togheter relevant sums with some businesses of hers investing the proceeds in real estate in the Astigiano. In 1874 the government granted him a pension and other benefits that he refused since it was a right-wing government but he accepted it all in 1876 by the new leftist government. Needless to say, friends and admirers did not let him lack anything.

In these last years of his life he devotes all his energies to the dissemination of his ideas by writing countless letters. Now he cannot make war and therefore he writes and travels much more than his doctor advised him: even at such an advanced age and paralyzed by arthritis he never stops.

He does not neglect his Masonic brothers and accumulates a quantity of titles from all lodges that want to give them to him. Even the title of Grand Hierophant of the Egyptian Rite of Memphis-Misraim from the lodge of the National Grand Orient of Egypt. Not content with his not florid situation he embarks on absurd entrepreneurial adventures as the deviation of the River Tiber or the reclamation of the Po delta that were never approved. For these projects and to get the annullment of his marriage with Raimondi he goes to Rome three times, but all went wrong: his plans were rejected and the annullment too. At this point he threatens to leave Italy and go to France where he would have resumed the French citizenship with which he was born and would have obtained the divorce. With this threat he finally he succeeds in obtaining the annulment in 1880 and he can marry Francesca; so he can give his name to the two children by her, and leave them his belongings that are the island of Caprera.

In 1874 he is elected deputy, in 1875 he goes to Rome. At Civitavecchia they must upload him on the wagon and at Rome they must work hard to load him on the coach that takes him to the hotel. Even in Rome the crowd is roaring and his carriage is pulled by the people to the hotel. As usual on these occasions he pronounced a speech to the crowd from a window or from a balcony. This time he delivers the shortest speech of his career as an orator: "*Romans, be serious*". He had not forgiven the Roman people their hostility when, seven years before, they closed the doors of the city on his face and left him alone against the French.

He participates at various sessions of the House to advance his projects and to give us another example of his cleavage when he asks the Italian government to become a promoter of the "*absolute abolition of wars between nation and nation*" and then promotes strong appropriations for the construction of large battleships which he recommends to be made more powerful and faster. Thus he explains how Europe should be organized: "*Let us have a European Union of nations with one representative from each and a statute whose first article sounds: - War is impossible - and the second: - Any dispute between the Nations will be settled by Congress-. Here is how war, plague and human shame, is made impossible. Then, no more standing armies and the children of the people, who are now driven to the slaughter with the pompous words of patriotism and glory, are returned to their families and to the fields ... These are the beliefs of the Solitary, and I confess, mine too*"[123]. These ideas clashed against nationalism that in those years was seizing the hearts and minds of the Europeans and thus they isolated him from the majority of the public opinion but, what is worse, these ideas sounded amazing on the lips of a man who had **dedicated his life** to war and to the triumph of Italian nationalism. When the denounces "*the pompous words of patriotism and glory*" he does not realize that his followers have

---

[123] Giuseppe Garibaldi, *Clelia ovvero il governo dei preti*, (Bariletti Editori, Roma 1990) pag. 139

launched themselves to the attack and gave their lives for just such *"pompous words"*. So he alienated the sympathy of the right without obtaining consents to the left.

In April 1879 he accepts the presidency of the *League of democracy* although his ideal form of government should be met with hostility by the democrats: "*For him* (himself), *the worst enemies of the freedom of the people are the democrat or republican doctrinaires, who preached and preach the revolutions for a living and for their own advancement, and he believes it was they who ruined all the republics, not only, but also discredited the system and the republican name. ... As for himself, he believes that the Republic is the government of honest people ... He does not believe, however, in the duration of a Republican government made up of five hundred individuals* (the parliamentarians). *He is of the opinion that the freedom of a people consists in the right to elect their own government, and this government, according to him, must be dictatorial, that is of one man only. ... He also wants that the dictatorship had a limited time ... In no case he would accord an hereditary power*"[124].

Garibaldi offers us a democracy exercised by a temporary dictator who should hand over his power at the end of the mandate. It's an absurd proposal: dictators do not yield power easily. What did he plan to do if the dictator had not ceded his power? Who should intervene? He claimed that an honest man should be chosen. And if he was not? And if at the proof of facts he proved to be an incompetent? It is not surprising that the "doctrinaires" were hostile to him.

Through this League of Democracy he strives for universal suffrage: "*We must also give warm adherence to universal suffrage. It rises to the dignity of citizens the downtrodden, gives them back their fundamental rights ... the proletariat, so far excluded from the legislative representation, will be able to claim justice*". Inspired words and very right that unfortunately remained unanswered because of the isolation that he had created to himself. Considering the extravagance of his theories, no parliamentarian was willing to listen to him.

---

[124] Giuseppe Garibaldi, *Clelia ovvero il governo dei preti*, (Bariletti Editori, Roma 1990) pag. 138

The most striking example of his cleavage from reality and its inability to dialogue, that is to listen to the other person before answering, is given to us when he deals with socialism. When the term socialism enters the current use he declares himself a socialist without having the faintest idea of what it meant. He wrote to a newspaper: "*my republicanism differs from that of Mazzini, since I am a socialist*". He declared to adhere to the Socialist International even if he did not share their ideas and programs.

The Marquis Pallavicino had written him criticizing his judgments on the International and highlighting the fact that he did not know what he was talking about. So Garibaldi replied: "- *But do you know the International? - This is the first question you made to me. I belong to the International since I was serving the Republic of the Rio Grande and Montevideo, that is, long before that society started in Europe*". That is even before the socialists themselves; the first International Socialist is from 1864. Than he continues by listing the ideas of the International to which he is opposed: "*I can not bear the International, as I do not tolerate the monarchy, their foolish anthropophagous ambitions. And in the same way that I would send to jail those who study the whole life how to extort the existence from the hungry to fatly feed the bishops, I would also send there the archimandrites* (the leaders) *as well of the society in question, if they would persist in the precepts: War to the capital, the property is a theft, the inheritance another theft, and so on*". These were in fact the fundamental principles enshrined by the International Socialist in those years.

It's very effective the adjective "*anthropophagous*", man-eater, with which he calls the monarchies and the leaders of the International. When he was writing these words, no one could have even imagined how many men would be devoured by both nationalism and socialism in the following century. Hence he goes on with a stunning candor: "*I have no interference in the International certainly because they know I do not approve all their program, this is the reason for their leaders to keep me excluded*". Then he explains to the Marquis that if the International would become what he wanted it to be, then: "*I will be with the International*".

In vain his friends protested that the International <u>was not</u> what he wanted to be. In vain they answered that his idea of socialism existed only in his mind. The director of *La Roma del Popolo* notes: "*If you take away from the International the denial of the nationality, of the property, of the family what remains of its own?*". In fact, the founding principles of socialism were the class struggle that was to go beyond the boundaries of nations including all proletarians of the world, the abolition of private property and of the family.

In a letter to his friend Arthur Arnold, he tells us what he wanted the International to be: "*But consider this association with calm; leave apart certain principles, unacceptable, such as these: the property is theft, inheritance is another theft, principles that, in my opinion, do not even deserve of being discussed and that certainly today's generations will not see the fulfillment in practice. The International will, however, have as a basis of its program ...*" and he lists what he wants from the International, namely: universal brotherhood among races and nations, no priests, no standing armies, only popular militias and governments on the type of the Paris Commune.

"*What I want and what also the honest men will want, it is that all governments, without distinction, they themselves take the initiative of doing what there is good in this society and that we have already mentioned, for example: the abolition of war, of standing armies, of priests, of privileges. That cannons, bombs, shells be melted to make plows, picks, machines useful in many ways. And the millions of soldiers who are maintained for the ruin of our countries and to destroy each other, let them be returned to industry and agriculture*".

Rather than persist in wanting to realize an inhuman ideology, the International should "*improve the human society with gradual progress and feasible ... Instead of rocking the masses with such maxims, unrealizable, to guide them on the practical path, without making them lose any time to drag them to a social cataclysm that none of us would want to witness*"[125]. Prophetic words, but the "*social cataclysm*" will arrive on time the following century, and today millions of people could witness it. Garibaldi had enough intelligence and common sense to perceive that element of criminal folly inherent in the socialist ideology; he clearly foresaw the disaster were socialism will lead several countries in the following century.

---

[125] Denis Mack Smith, *Garibaldi,* (Milano: Laterza, 1956) pag.178

Unfortunately, at that time, no one listened to him because socialism is a doctrine and a non doctrinaire socialism will come some time later with the name of Social Democracy: at the time of Garibaldi it did not exist.

His was the socialism of the common sense, full of humanity and genuinely interested in a realistic improvement of the life of the lower classes, but absolutely hostile to the principles of the socialist doctrine. We should note that his mental attitude towards the people had nothing socialist; rather it was very similar to that of the aristocracy and of the enlightened paternalistic Italian states before unification, first of all the Bourbons. How ironic!

"Be glad the International of what is right for it, without touching the property or inheritance of others. And then it can highly tell to the bullies of the earth: I come to partecipate at a banquet to which I am entitled as much as you do. I will not touch your assets, although much fatter than mine; but you do not touch this little, that I exude from my sweat with the odious means that you have used so far, taxes on flour, on salt and many other injustices that aggravate my misery"[126]. Fine words and said in a wonderful way, but why did he not realize that this was the position of the Church that he hated so much?

Could he have been the initiator of a social democratic movement?

No way, his love of war and of weapons put him in a position that would have been unacceptable for the Social Democrats.

He writes to the Director of the *Gazzetta della Capitale*: *"When I mention the transformation of the standing army in the Army of the Nation, do not think that I recommend to disarm. Quite the contrary: while a dozen majestic families keep the world in the state of anarchy in which we see it today, the weaklings can not talk about disarmament. ... On the contrary, I repeat, but disarm while you have at the head of the nations certain corporals who would like to girt about the universe with armours and guns ... to militarize the nation, and make a militiaman of every citizen able to carry the arms. Who, on earth, would dream to invade this Italy strong of two million militiamen ... Every town must have its own guard of militiamen and instead of sending them to the shop of the priest on Sunday, send them to the military camp, to be instructed at military*

---

[126] Alfonso Scirocco, *Garibaldi*, (Bari: Laterza, 2001), pag.369.

*maneuvres, handling of the arms, physical training and literary educa-
tion*". Schooling would have to be accompanied by military training so
that the young people "*having reached the age of the militiaman, will
present themselves in the ranks already instructed ... The day standing
armies are transformed into national armies, the invasions will become
impossible*".

It's a small but influential advance of Mussolini's "Book and musket".

It's impossible that the Social Democrats could have taken him as
their leader.

According to him the Nation-in-arms would have reduced defense
spending but who would have payed for two million soldiers? Or did he
really think that these soldiers could have been used on Sundays only? It
was an absurd idea that brings to mind the balilla of Mussolini with his
eight million bayonets.

In his writings he asks of becoming lions, to frighten the neighbors, a
first-rate power, fear of attacks. No one at that time was threatening Italy; it was rather Italy that threatened the others. His patriotism had
turned into a nationalism where it was becoming increasingly clear a
paranoid component. He speaks more and more of an Italy humiliated by
the foreigners, weakened by its own diplomacy, threatened by foreign
powers, paralyzed by a political class cowardly and Byzantine, impotent
because of a coward people. In short the whole universe was plotting
against his Italy to prevent it from regaining its "*throne from which our
ancestors ruled the world*".

It was inevitable that slowly the idea advanced that only the Man of
Destiny could break these chains. This element of paranoia was not present only in his mind. All European nationalisms were initiating on this
road. Nationalist paranoia was penetrating all layers of the society of all
European countries. In the next century it will explode in two world
wars upsetting Europe and the rest of the world. Considering all these
theories of him, it is natural that the leaders of the International did not
want him around and he felt isolated. It was a shame because Garibaldi
denounced, insistently and with full right, the bad government of the
Kingdom of Italy. In fact, if you were to make a judgment on the Italian
states before the unification and the new kingdom, it is impossible not to
say that this new kingdom was the worst of all.

He wanted an extension of suffrage, fairer taxes, public expenditure dedicated to the reclamation of the marshes rather than to imperialist adventures, and many other measures which would have led this new Italy on the path of progress. Wasted words.

In an attempt to advance these ideas he becomes a founder of the *Fascio dei Lavoratori* (Workers' Bundle) which wanted to gather several workers' associations, free from the follies of the doctrinaires, and to organize them to promote a social policy aimed at improving the living conditions of the new industrial proletariat that was crowding the Italian cities. With this "*robuste et redoutable faisceau*" he will attempt to organize in a single body all the associations, more or less leftist, which had as their end the "*betterment of humanity*", but the left was too anarchic to be organized and the ideas of Garibaldi were too confused, contradictory and impractical to become a rallying point for the forces of the left outside of socialism.

For its part, the International will not stay silent; in 1874 it launches the following proclamation: "*Do not listen to Garibaldi. Socialism as he understands it is a misconception. What he calls Socialists exaggerations are just our basic principles ... He would want the workers' associations to be just mutual aid societies. They would become petty and narrow groupings of which the bourgeoisie would laugh ... Proletarians of Italy, forward!*"[127].

Garibaldi will continue to declare himself a socialist all his life.

Another element that consolidates his solitude is the cult of the ancient Rome.

"Oh! Rome! Motherland of my soul! You are the only! The eternal! Above every human greatness, even today under this degradation! Your resurrection is a catastrophe that will upset the world!"[128]. His cult of the ancient Rome began when he was very young. In 1825, on the occasion of the Holy Year, he accompanied his father to Rome for a transport of wine. While the pious father hopped around churches to accumulate

---

[127] Max Gallo, *Garibaldi*, (Milano, Rusconi Libri, 1982) pag.446

[128] Giuseppe Garibaldi, *Clelia ovvero il governo dei preti*, (Bariletti Editori, Roma 1990) pag. 202

indulgences, he wanders around the ruins of Rome. He remains enslaved.

"Rome! And Rome was not to seem to me if not the capital of a world! ... The capital of a world, from its ruins, sublime, immense, where the piled relics are found of what the past once had the greatest! ... The Rome I could see in my youthful understanding, was the Rome of the future; Rome! of which I never despaired, castaway, dying, relegated to the bottom of the American forests! Rome the regenerating idea of a great people! A dominatrix idea, of what the present and the past could inspire to me, actually of my whole life! Rome is a symbol of Italy, in whatever form you want it".

More: *"How proud I was of being born in Italy! ... where, for many centuries, having fallen from the throne from which our ancestors ruled the world ... we were imposed the black reptile of theocracy, to humble us, to deprave us, to corrupt us ... as if their reign of pygmies were to endure forever, while time, with its cold wings, had swept away even that giant of all human greatness, past, present and future, whose ruins are raised today on the seven hills"*.

This reference to the fatal hills of Rome is not accidental. Garibaldi loved to associate the Italians of his time to the ancient Romans. According to him the Italian people should regenerate themselves having as a model the glories of ancient Rome. His Italians were *"fallen from the throne from which our ancestors ruled the world"* but *"are raised today on the seven hills"*. There is talk of world domination: fanciful, pathetic and criminal!

What is that now rises on the seven hills? But, it's the glory of Italy!

This cult of the ancient Rome could have been accepted by the imperialist right, but he hated it. To the left, to which he wanted to belong, it was a blasphemy.

He was a solitary man because the political movement that had synthesized these ideas was not born, not yet.

Nazional Socialism

Garibaldi dies at Caprera on June 2, 1882.

The last years of his life were sad and resentful because the Italy that was taking shape was not the one he wanted. As it happens to the revolutionaries, reality did not want to conform to his dream and he had come to despise the creature that he had helped create. He writes in 1880: "*A completely different Italy I dreamed in my life, not this miserable and humiliated abroad and in the grip of the worst part of the nation*".

His Political Testament to the Italians is the reflection of this disappointment. At the last point he writes: "*Italy must proclaim the Republic, but not to entrust his fate to five hundred doctors* (the parliamentarians), *who after having deafened her with chatter, will lead her to ruin. Instead, to choose the most honest of the Italians and appoint him temporary dictator, with the same power that the Fabi and the Cincinnati had. The dictatorial system will last as long as the Italian nation is more educated to freedom, and that her existence is no longer threatened by powerful neighbors. Then the dictatorship will give way to a regular republican government*". With this sad recommendation he takes leave from the Italians. After all, the dictatorship was always his favorite recipe, indeed his only recipe.

These sentences contain only the end point of the parable of his political activity and alone they would not suffice to define the positioning of Garibaldi in the European ideological spectrum. What you should notice, instead, is that there is an ideological element that links all stages of his life. As far as you can admire the man, as far as you can be charmed by him, it is impossible not to note that in his thinking, in his life, in his way of doing politics, there are all the elements of that ideology that the world will know, years later, by the name of Fascism.

The love of adventure regardless of the impact that this adventure could have on the lives of ordinary people, with no consideration for the trail of blood, tears and destruction that he was leaving behind. And this adventure will always be undertaken with a total improvisation relying on luck but, above all, on the spirit of sacrifice of his "disciples".

The love of war that is an end in itself because the justifications that he was giving himself were clearly incredible. It is a love lived and fed by a deep sensuality: "*I and my young companions, yearned for the time of the battle, as the man to join the woman that he idolizes*". Or: "*These bodies, so compact, so prosperous, so brilliant, in a short time will be loose, broken, horribly mixed and breathing the lust of destruction! Soon the blood, the broken limbs, the bodies of so many superb youths will sully these beautiful and virgin fields*". Along all his *Memorie* this love is expressed with a childlike innocence and is affirmed along with protests of pacifism. All the time he declares himself a pacifist and without the slightest embarrassment. If he had to spend his life making war it was because "*I found on the path of my life, the Austrians, the priests and despotism*". It was not his fault, but of others!

The contempt for the parliamentary system and the intrigues of politicians without understanding the difficulty of obtaining consent and the need to adapt to the choices that you do not share. This will give the Italians the illusion that other systems, authoritarian, could solve the problem.

The idea that the Italian people were unworthy of freedom and that only a dictator, the Man of Destiny, could resurrect Italy and have it cope with the other nations. This is a real inferiority complex that is inherent in the Italian nationalism because of the way in which Italy was born. The fear of not living up to other European nations adds to the insecurity inherent in the consciousness, repressed, of belonging to a "contrived" nation. This will give the Italians the determination to make any sacrifice in order not to fall behind.

The cult of the ancient Rome without realizing how ridiculous it was to compare the Italian populace, hungry and illiterate, to the Roman legionaries.

A paranoid nationalism lived with the fanaticism and obtuseness of a religious faith. The "*holy cause of Italy*" was his religion and his God to which everything shoul be sacrificed. It was a total passion that knew neither doubt nor uncertainty. Who was with him was a heroic patriot, who was not with him was a coward or a traitor or a poor ignorant, "*creature and food of the priests*". Garibaldi and a good part of the higher social strata of northern Italy lived the Risorgimento as a divine mission to which all the people had to submit, even against their will.

The cult of the Supreme Sacrifice, a drug which will poison generations of Europeans turning them into cannon fodder and instruments of the imperialism because this worship brings with it the vocation to martyrdom. We have seen Abba in Caserta, after Garibaldi had inspected the Garibaldians that are about to leave, who asks Garibaldi to take them to die: "*And you felt that this was the last hour of his command. We had the desire to go and throw ourselves at his feet shouting: General, why do you not lead us all to die? The road to Rome is there, sow it with our bones!*".

A pompous and grandiloquent rhetoric that should have impressed the simple and modest people.

A violent anti-clericalism in words, up to the ridicule, but ready to compromise in practice. This anticlericalism is not an end in itself, it is the prelude to a new "positivist" religiosity that becomes a fundamental element of the Totalitarian State and is expressed with the Cult of the Nation.

The woman as an object. Garibaldi used to declare that the woman "*is the most perfect of all creatures*", but he said it because all women had to adapt to him. Bandi, who spent much time alongside Garibaldi, noted that: "*Garibaldi was most courteous with women and he liked women beyond measure, although he did not use to give women any value beyond the one that they have for the most common of men*". He never had any hesitation to mate with any woman available, after all it is the woman who gets pregnant. If he had a problem with women it was how to send them away: "*Wherever Garibaldi appeared, there the women rushed in flocks, ... under the eyes of that man the women usurped men their courage and often they became daring and terrible ... most happy the one that managed to have a handshake from him or, even better, to kiss him after fending the crowd*". The problem was that Garibaldi considered himself above the law, the rules and the customs. "*Garibaldi, who did not have a right idea of the value of money, of the value of laws, and neither of the weight of certain rules and customs of our society, most respected by other men, did not give to the intimacy with a woman and not even to marriage the importance that the majority of men is used to give both*".

The People. Garibaldi always claimed to fight for the people. Yet it is clear that when he spoke of the emancipation of the peoples he did not refer to the real people. The people for which he was fighting was rather the projection of his romantic dream. But it would be more realistic to say of his hallucinations. For this reason his judgments on the Italians always oscillate between exaltation and contempt. A classic manifestation of a paranoid nationalism frustrated by the inadequacy of the real people in front of his dreams.

The Cult of the Personality that brings with it an attitude of blind obedience to the leader who becomes for his disciples the Man of Destiny who is above the laws which are made only for the people because they are the people who have the Duty.

Most important of all it is the ideological element. He was the first who realized in his thought the synthesis of nationalism and socialism and lived this synthesis dedicating to it all his life even though this was completely irrational and isolated him from the socialist community. He hated the socialist leaders and was deeply opposed to their ideas, an ideological rivalry that will deeply mark Western Civilization.

Garibaldi was the first prominent Italian politician who expressed in a clearly defined way in his whole life, both in his actions and in his thought, the elements of this ideology: **Fascism**.

Now we have to travel the years following the death of Garibaldi to trace the thread that will lead Italy and Europe to implement this new ideology. This thread runs through the history of socialism.

As we have seen Garibaldi declared himself a socialist and defended this new movement against all his friends, even though the leaders of the International had disavowed him. But what was socialism for Garibaldi? It is difficult to answer this question, but here is the key to understand. It was clear that he was absolutely opposed to the principles of the socialist doctrine as they were enunciated by the first International that had made its the theories of Marx. These theories, in short, proposed a completely different society from the one that homo sapiens had developed over thousands of years of evolution. Abolition of the family and the private property, everything is owned by the community represented by the Totalitarian State which would provide for all in accordance with their "needs". Here it is necessary to use the conditional because Marx never elaborated his principles to define how it would be organized, in reality, this new society; his vision was essentially anarchic because it did not propose anything concrete. This new society was to be born from a traumatic event, a revolution, and could not arise with democratic methods. It would have been the proletarians of the world that, allying with each other by means of the socialist movement, would have destroyed the nations creating a single global society governed by the Dictatorship of the Proletariat. Nationalism and religion were a fraud with which the bourgeoisie framed the people to enslave them and distract them from their goal which was in fact the world revolution. This revolution could have been successful only if led by a single party using violent means and without the limitations of democratic structures. In time, after this transition, it would have been the Dictatorship of the Proletariat that would have led us towards a genuine democracy!

The great majority of the public opinion, including the Socialists, agreed with Garibaldi that all that was a folly, yet socialism continued to grow. It grew because many adherents, like Garibaldi, adhered to socialism while ignoring, more or less unconsciously, its doctrine and by "transferring" into socialism their "desires". The why and how all these people had such a desperate need of socialism to "remove" its theories, established by the leaders of the movement, to graft on this "idea" their "desires" it is a very complex problem that should be studied by examining the evolution of Christianity in its 2.000 years of life. This study is not part of our essay, for now we take note of the fact that Garibaldi, along with many other people and in a completely unconscious way, called themselves socialist still maintain their faith in the nation although this was clearly absurd if you consider that the core of the socialist faith was the annihilation of the fragmentation of humanity into nations. Not surprisingly the life of this new faith, socialism, will be very troubled.

The first clash within the movement occurs between anarchists and marxists after the defeat of the Parisian Commune and the anarchists are expelled from the International: the anarchists did not agree on the single party and on the dictatorial methods within the movement. The nationalists remain in the party togther with the other socialists; since it is all a delirium these definitions are necessarily approximate.

After the death of Garibaldi, towards the end of the century, a social democratic current begins to develop.

What happened was that the theories of Marx on the accumulation of capital were proving unrealistic because the new market oriented societies of northern Europe were producing a myriad of businesses, of all sizes, fragmenting the global capital and moreover the property of large industries had changed its consistency through the pulverization of the capital in shares traded in the world stock markets and the real control of the business was no longer in the hands of the capitalists but of a new class of professionals: the **managers**. Perhaps the most important element has been America. Millions of Europeans were able to escape from poverty or oppression simply by emigrating. This, together with a drastic reduction in the birth rate, took away from under the feet of socialism the hard core of the desperadoes available to any adventure. It grew more and more the number of socialists who looked with apprehension at the prospect of a violent event like a revolution to move towards a dark goal like the proletarian dictatorship.

It was plain for everyone the fact that society was evolving and therefore the objectives of the abolition of family and property could be implemented with reforms obtained through democratic methods allowed by universal suffrage which gave the workers too a chance to change society peacefully. The institution of the family could be emptied by divorce and by the empowerment of women. Women gain power through work and, thanks to abortion and contraceptives, they can control their fertility and hence their dependence on man. Private property can be castrated with taxes and regulations. Given that these objectives could be achieved (may be partially) in peace and comfort, many socialists refused to be dragged, as Garibaldi told us, towards *"a social cataclysm that none of us would want to witness"*.

This situation changed over the years and the publication in 1899 by Eduard Bernstein of *The preconditions of socialism and the tasks of Social-Democracy* started a thorough review of the Marxist thought and the abandonment of the necessity of a revolutionary new way. Despite their differences the reformist and the revolutionary socialists remained united until the outbreak of World War I. Also the nationalists, like Garibaldi, remained in the movement and, to remain in Italy, we have a couple of famous examples with Edmondo De Amicis and Giovanni Pascoli.

Edmondo De Amicis at the beginning of his adult life was a patriot and joined the army as a career soldier, afterwards he devoted himself to journalism and published his book *Heart* which is an ode to the most grotesque nationalism. Ten years later, in 1896 he joined the Socialist

Party but without repudiating his past and without even trying to produce a synthesis of the ideas that had shaped his life.

Giovanni Pascoli signs up in the International at age 22 and becomes an anarcho-socialist activist but ends up in prison in 1879 and then abandons politics. Some of his works are imbued with a poignant patriotic passion, others with an intense compassion for the suffering of the poor people. He gave us an interesting definition of his personal socialism because he claimed to be *"profoundly socialist, but socialist of all of humanity, not of a class"*. In 1911 on the occasion of the war in Libya he delivers a speech that will go down in history: *The Great Proletarian has moved*. It overflows with nationalism, sometimes pathetic, sometimes grotesque and sometimes moving. It hails the glory of Rome and exalts the work of the humbles, a combination that seems a bit odd but it will become fashionable twenty years later. The inferiority complex of the Italians pervades the whole speach and produces a deep resentment against the other European nations as if it were their fault if the Italian army had not won any battle of the Risorgimento or if the Italian people were starved by an economic system parasitic and corrupt: also this will become fashionable twenty years later.

This speech will remain in history because, for the first time, the term 'proletarian' is attributed to a nation rather than to a class of people. Pascoli moves substantially the terms of the Marxist analysis from the power relations between social classes to the struggle between nations. And since Italy is the proletarian among the peoples, the poor nation that has always enriched the others, she deserves a redemption by means of colonial conquests that will finally give justice to the *"people more labourer, industrious and frugal in the world"* and will put an end to the miseries of emigration.

As we have seen, for reasons that are difficult to analyze because it is completely irrational, the socialist movement was from the beginning strongly participated by nationalist elements in all countries of Europe even if nationalism was clearly condemned by the socialist doctrine. Until the outbreak of the Great War the Socialist Party retains all its souls: socialists, revolutionaries, nationalists and social democrats in a precarious balance but without more schisms after the anarchists.

The Great War explodes in May 1914 and all of Europe is overwhelmed by a nationalist psychosis.

Nationalism triumphs and blows away all other faiths, religions, ideologies or social ideals. The religion, Catholic or Protestant or Orthodox, must bend itself and give up its vocation for love of neighbor resigning itself to give its blessing to the arms of both parties. The internationalism of the market oriented parties disappears from the scene and they too must, reluctantly, take part in the orgy of destruction. The socialist movement must face its contradictions and in the face of such a cataclysm its several souls split up.

The Communists denounce the "bourgeois" war and sniff the opportunity they were waiting for to kick off their revolution. They start a work of proselytism and infiltrate the armed forces of all sides as well as the workers in the factories. They do not care if the bourgeosie consider them traitors; long before they have delivered their loyalty to the Party.

The Socialists denounce the "bourgeois" war but forgo both the passive resistance of pacifism and the actions of Marxist propaganda that could be considered as a betrayal of their country.

The Social Democrats declare their loyalty to the matherland and are in favor of the war in all European countries. The reformist socialists chose, in fact, to support their national governments on taking up war which meant to the revolutionary socialists a real betrayal of the proletariat because they betrayed the principle that the proletarians of all countries were to be united in their struggle against capitalism by refusing to take part in the conflicts between the capitalist governments: this provoked violent clashes between the two sides. This new development and the subsequent Russian Revolution of 1917 led to a split in the socialist movement between the Social Democrats, who abandoned the revolutionary methods, and the Marxist Socialist revolutionaries who took the name of Communists.

The nationalists seize the opportunity and leave the Socialist Party to start a new political movement and a new culture. The record for this novelty belongs to Italy with Benito Mussolini.

Before continuing we want to offer, as food for thought, a description of Garibaldi given by Edward Dicey, president of the Cambridge Union, which in our opinion fits neatly in Mussolini too: "*missing of any political education, without knowledge of government principles, deprived of that rough intelligence that often helps ignorant people to conceal their hatred. Not having the capability to evaluate characters, nor to resist adulation, he was deceived by all those that an elementary prudence would have advised to distrust. The fact that his thought was limited and his mind could not grasp more than one side of a problem at a time, gave him that concentration of will and that intensity of faith that are necessary to form a popular leader*"[129].

Benito Mussolini was 17 when in 1900 he joined the Italian Socialist Party. Two years later he flees to Switzerland not to do his military service, he joins the bricklayers' union of which he becomes the secretary and distinguishes himself by his activism and his extreme position in favor of revolutionary socialism. In 1904 he returns to Italy to take advantage of an amnesty and serves his time in the army. His violent temper and arrogance, his contempt for the laws and his activism for revolutionary socialism put him often in trouble with the law and he is arrested several times. He has a talent for oratory and writing. He contributes to several socialist publications standing out for his violent intransigence against moderate socialism. In 1910 he is the secretary of the Socialist Party of Forlì where he directs the weekly *Lotta di Classe* (Class struggle) and participates at violent demonstrations against the conquest of Libya which he calls "*an act of international banditry*" while the flag is "*a rag to be planted on a dunghill*". He ends in prison again but is released. At a conference of the Italian Socialist Party in 1912 he is the organizer of a motion for the expulsion from the party of some moderate socialists, who are expelled. He becomes a leader of the party up to being appointed director of its official journal the *Avanti!,* he was 29 years only. In the two years of his leadership the newspaper doubles its sales.

At the outbreak of the war Mussolini keeps on the *Avanti!* the official position of the party, against the intervention in the war, with his usual imperious and violent style, "*not a man, not a penny*". But in the following months a surprising "conversion" occurs for which on October 18, 1914, he publishes on the *Avanti!* an article, *From an absolute neutrality to an operating and active neutrality*, where it is declared that the socialists should be in favor of the intervention because the war would have created the necessary conditions for the proletariat to begin the revolution against the bourgeois society. The day after Mussolini, noting that he was the only one among the leaders of the party to have changed his mind, resignes and so, in one fell swoop, he loses everything he had

---

[129] Gilberto Oneto, *L'Iperitaliano* (Rimini: Il Cerchio, 2006), pag.268

achieved when he became one of the youngest leaders of the Socialist Party: he finds himself alone and penniless. This is the power of faith, a faith that now possesses him and will never leave him anymore.

Some industry groups intervene immediately and give him the funds to open his own newspaper, *Il Popolo d'Italia*, in November 1914. In the subtitle of *Il Popolo d'Italia* it is written "*a Socialist newspaper*" and then two quotes: "*The revolution is an idea which has found bayonets*" by Napoleon and "W*ho has iron has bread*" by Blanqui, a revolutionary socialist the spiritual leader of the Parisian Commune.

It must be clear to the whole world that he, Mussolini, always has been and always will be a revolutionary socialist.

From his newspaper Mussolini attacks the socialist party which a month later expels him; the revolutionary left intervenes to his aid.

Antonio Gramsci, a revolutionary socialist, made his debut as a journalist a few days later on *Il Grido del Popolo* (The Cry of the People) with an article, *An operating and active neutrality,* supporting the thesis of Mussolini.

Pietro Nenni, had been in prison together with Mussolini following their opposition to the war in Libya and a few months before, in June 1914, he had fought by his side in the "red week" when the Italian revolutionaries thought that the time had come to overthrow the monarchy and the bourgeoisie. It was a rebellion, anti militarist, anti bourgeois and anti monarchist which had no effect, it died after violent clashes and without having minimally affected the institutional framework. Nenni now works with him at the newspaper, but this time in favor of the war!

Il Popolo d'Italia does not go well and soon funds are needed from the allied secret services which are in desperate need of an intervention of Italy against the Central Empires.

Now we must pause to reflect on what has happened because this "conversion" of Mussolini seems astonishing to us. In fact in his socialist past there is no element which could make us suspect him of nationalist sympathies, far from it, it was clear that he was positioned at the far left of a unionism most vulgar and violent and if we were due to make a prediction we would have seen him participating to the communist movement. We have already seen in these pages the faithful Garibaldian Crispi to switch from the revolutionary and republican left to a monarchist nationalism and also the German socialist Lassalle, a friend of Garibaldi, to perform a similar turnaround. Both cases could be considered phenomena of opportunism as they passed by the ruling class. In the case of Mussolini there was nothing opportunistic because he threw away an important position in a fast and unpredictable move. Evidently an historic event as the Great War has provoked a reworking of his ideas and led him to a new ideological base, a new idea that will shape the rest of his life.

We can only take note of what happened and bring out that socialism and nationalism, evidently, have a common root in the depths of the human psyche that we are unable to analyze.

Let's go back to Mussolini that after leaving the Socialist Party helps to found, at year end, the *Fasci di azione rivoluzionaria* (Fasci of revolutionary action) and gives us another definition of this new culture by defining his political thought of that time: *National Unionism.*

With a stunning rapidity now Mussolini rages with his usual violence against those who oppose the war: "*These deputies threatening pronouncements in the style of little South American republics, these deputies who spread - with the most improbable exaggerations - panic among the faithful electoral herd; these deputies pusillanimous, charlatans ... these deputies should be handed over to the courts of war! Discipline should start at the top if you want it to be respected at the bottom. As for me, I am more and more firmly convinced that for the health of Italy they should be shot, I say shot in the back, a few dozen deputies, and at least a couple of former ministers sent to life imprisonment. Not only that, but I believe with ever deeper faith, that the Italian Parliament is a pestiferous bubo. We must eradicate it*". He will succeed.

The interventionist push has the better of the Catholic-liberal-socialist pacifism despite this represents the majority of the Italians and Italy enters the war in May 1915. Mussolini volunteered.

As Mussolini, Gramsci and Nenni (besides Lenin) had predicted, the trauma of war excites the masses who now have a certain familiarity with the weapons and in Russia in 1917 Communism sweeps away the Social Democrats and imposes the Soviet regime. In Italy and Germany, for very different reasons, one has won the other lost, the anger explodes of the masses and the Communists try to seize power while the other parties fail to keep control.

In Italy Mussolini founds the *Fasci Italiani di Combattimento* (Italian Fasci of combat) in March 1919 with the declared aim of stopping the advance of the Communists. Most of the participants were veterans who had faced the difficult return to civilian life and that before the war had served in leftist formations (socialists, republicans, unionists, etc.). The manifesto of the Fasci is published in June:

"This is the program of a healthily national Italian movement.
Revolutionary, because against dogma and demagoguery; highly inno-
vative because against prejudices.
We place the valorization of the Revolutionary War above everyone and
everything
The other problems: bureaucracy, administrative, legal, educational, co-
lonial, etc.. we will draw them when we create the ruling class".

It's a strongly leftist program where it is asked, among other things, universal suffrage with vote to women, working day of 8 hours, minimum wage, employees' management of public enterprises of services and the establishment of a People's Militia, the dream of Garibaldi. This program also called for: *"A strong extraordinary tax on capital and progressive, that has the form of a real partial expropriation of all riches"*. Still many believed it!

In January of 1921 the Communists, with Antonio Gramsci, leave the Socialist Party and found the Communist Party of Italy (the Social Democrats will leave a year later founding the Socialist Unity Party). Gramsci is arrested by Mussolini and will die of illness 15 years later always remaining faithful to the Communist Party

Pietro Nenni enters, a few years later, the Socialist Party and becomes the director of the *Avanti!*. He must flee to France to avoid being arrested by Mussolini but he is caught by the Gestapo during the war and handed over to Mussolini that sends him into internal exile in the island of Ustica. After the war he becomes secretary of the Socialist Party.

Mussolini will be killed by the communists 20 years later.

Here we can see how these hallucinations, nationalism and socialism, combine in unpredictable ways in the human mind and produce opposite results in different people unleashing the ideological hatred which puts one against the other even people who had fought together before, because no hate can equal the hate between brothers who consider the other the traitor of the faith.

Finally, in November 1921 the Italian Fasci of combat are merged into the **National Fascist Party** and a few years later the first National Socialist regime in history is established. This term 'fascist' is not in itself indicative of the orientation of the party, it is simply a tribute to the nostalgia for the greatness of Rome and to the inferiority complex of the Italians; the name that properly expresses the nature of this new movement will be given to us by Adolf Hitler.

Hitler in Germany is closely following the progress of Mussolini.
"At that time - I admit it openly - I conceived a profound admiration for the great man beyond the Alps, whose ardent love for his people inspired him not to bargain with Italy's internal enemies but to use all possible ways and means in an effort to wipe them out. What places Mussolini in the ranks of the world's great men is his decision not to share Italy with the Marxists but to redeem his country from Marxism by destroying internationalism. What miserable pigmies our sham statesmen in Germany appear by comparison with him. And how nauseating it is to witness the conceit and effrontery of these nonentities in criticizing a man who is a thousand times greater than them"[130].

After the war he joins a tiny left-wing nationalist party the DAP (German Workers' Party) and in February 1920 he takes its leadship and transforms it into the National Socialist German Workers Party (Deutsche Nationalsozialistische Arbeiterpartei, shortened in Nazi Party), putting together a few small parties of socialist orientation, statists, anti-capitalists and nationalists.

Nazism expresses a conception of the state that is totalitarian and nationalist with workerist aims (völkisch) opposed to the internationalist Marxist socialism, and it materialized as a reaction to the humiliation of the defeat and the subsequent economic disaster. As for Fascism, also in the Nazism of the origins there is an ideological component of a socialistic and collectivist mold, that managed to attract support also from militants of the communist parties. In its program the principles of 'Blut und Boden' (Blood and Land) and 'Arbeit und Brot' (Bread and Work) that saw in the state the ultimate guarantor of the economic prosperity of the nation, of the job security of the citizens, of the abolition of wage dispar-

---

[130] Adolf Hitler, *Mein Kampf* (London: Hurst and Blackett, 1939) pag. 519

ities, of the maintenance of the social peace and of a just profit for the capitalists with an iron control of banks and finance.

So this new political, social, cultural movement has found its name: **National Socialism**.

National Socialism (both Italian and German) changes the Marxist logic by placing at the center of history the conflicts between nations instead of the conflicts between classes. There are exploited nations and exploiting nations: this is the source of Evil. The exploited nations must redeem themselves with a traumatic event: War. To do this, all its social components must be solid, therefore the main enemy of the nation is Marxism that wants to break it up with the class struggle. It's therefore essential that all social conflicts are resolved by the Totalitarian State which decides the fair wages and the right profits: no strikes, no bargaining, no free market, it is a command economy and statist where monopolies triumph. Before the state all citizens are equal, regardless of their social class and wealth, because they are all children of the nation. Private property and family are protected just in that they can participate to the growth of the nation, however it is up to the Totalitarian State the final decision on everything and both private property and family suffer restrictions on individual freedom that are considered intolerable in the capitalist countries. In the country you live in an atmosphere of state of siege, because the synthesis of socialism and nationalism produces a dramatic effect.

National Socialism adds to the class hatred of Marxism the ethnic hatred of nationalism producing the **Apotheosis of Hate**.

Paranoia reaches paroxysmal levels giving the regime the control of the mind of the individual thus making possible follies otherwise unimaginable. The state is in competition with religion with its Cult of the Nation and paranoia allows it to do so for a nation of secure consistency as the German one, for a nation of dubious consistency as the Italian one and for a completely invented nation as the Aryan Nation. The persecution complex produces enemies that exist but are not present, as the Perfidious Albion, and also totally invented enemies like the Zionist Conspiracy.

This hatred infects Europe at first and then spreads to the other continents because now the Socialist family is split in two.

The Nazis hate the Communists for betraying the Motherland shattering it with the class struggle and the Revolution, weakening it and making it vulnerable to the attacks from other nations.

The Communists hate the Nazis because they betray Socialism and the proletariat and block the advance of humanity towards a New World and a true democracy which can be achieved only by the Dictatorship of the Proletariat.

It's a hatred between brothers that feeds itself from their own hallucinations and will provide the ideological impetus to the great criminals of the twentieth century.

The Great War throws on the stage of history the masses forcing them to participate in a holocaust that has been something more than a war: it was the collective suicide of a civilization.

It provides Socialism with the catalyst that gives birth to two monsters, Communism and National Socialism, that in human history will give Europe (and beyond) several firsts in the field of criminal folly.

Bibliografy

Abba, Giuseppe Cesare. *Storia dei Mille.* Firenze: Bemporad, 1928

Abba, Giuseppe Cesare. *Noterelle di uno dei Mille.* Milano: Garzanti, 1991

Agrati, Carlo. *I Mille nella storia e nella leggenda.* Milano: Mondadori, 1933

Alianello, Carlo. *La conquista del Sud.* Milano: Rusconi Editore, 1972

Bandi, Giuseppe. *Da Genova a Capua.* Milano: BUR, 1960

Battaglini, Tito. *Il crollo militare del Regno delle Due Sicilie.* Modena: Società Tipografica Modenese, 1938

Bracalini, Romano. *Non rivedrò più Calatafimi.* Milano: Rizzoli, 1989

Buttà, Giuseppe. *Un viaggio da Boccadifalco a Gaeta.* Milano: Bompiani, 1989

Carrano, Francesco. *I Cacciatori delle Alpi comandati dal generale Giuseppe Garibaldi.* Torino: Unione Tipografica Editrice, 1860

Costa Cardol, Mario. *Ingovernabili da Torino.* Milano: Mursia, 1989

Costa Cardol, Mario. *Venga a Napoli Signor Conte.* Milano: Mursia, 1986

De Sivo, Giacinto. *I Napoletani al cospetto delle Nazioni civili.* Roma: Borzi, 1967

Gallo, Max. *Garibaldi.* Milano: Rusconi Libri, 1982

Garibaldi, Giuseppe. *Memorie.* Milano: Rizzoli, 1982

Garibaldi, Giuseppe. *Clelia.* Roma: Bariletti Editori, 1990

Hitler, Adolf. *Mein Kampf.* London: Hurst and Blackett, 1939

Mack Smith, Denis. *Garibaldi.* Milano: Laterza, 1956

Mack Smith, Denis. *Storia d'Italia.* Bari: Laterza, 1972

Mack Smith, Denis. *Storia della Sicilia medievale e moderna.* Bari: Editori Laterza, 1973

Martucci, Roberto. *L'invenzione dell'Italia unita.* Milano: Sansoni, 1999

Montanelli-Nozza. *Garibaldi.* Milano: Rizzoli Editore, 1962

Mundy, Sir Rodney. *H.M.S. "Hannibal" at Palermo and Naples*. London: Murray, 1863. Google Books.

Nievo, Ippolito. *Diario della spedizione dei Mille*. Milano: Ugo Mursia Editore, 2010

Oneto, Gilberto. *L'Iperitaliano*. Rimini: Il Cerchio, 2006

Oneto, Gilberto. *La strana unità*. Rimini:Il Cerchio, 2010

Pellicciari, Angela. *L'altro Risorgimento*. Ares

Petacco, Arrigo. *La Regina del Sud*. Milano: Mondadori, 1992

Radice, Benedetto. *Memorie storiche di Bronte*. da: http://www.bronteinsieme.it/2st/mo_601.html

Ressa, Giuseppe. *Il Sud e l'unità d'Italia*. Maggio 2011. da: http://www.ilportaledelsud.org

Scirocco, Alfonso. *Garibaldi*. Bari:Laterza, 2001

Stuart Forbes, Charles. *The campaign of Garibaldi in the Two Sicilies*. London: Blackwood and Sons, 1862. Google Books